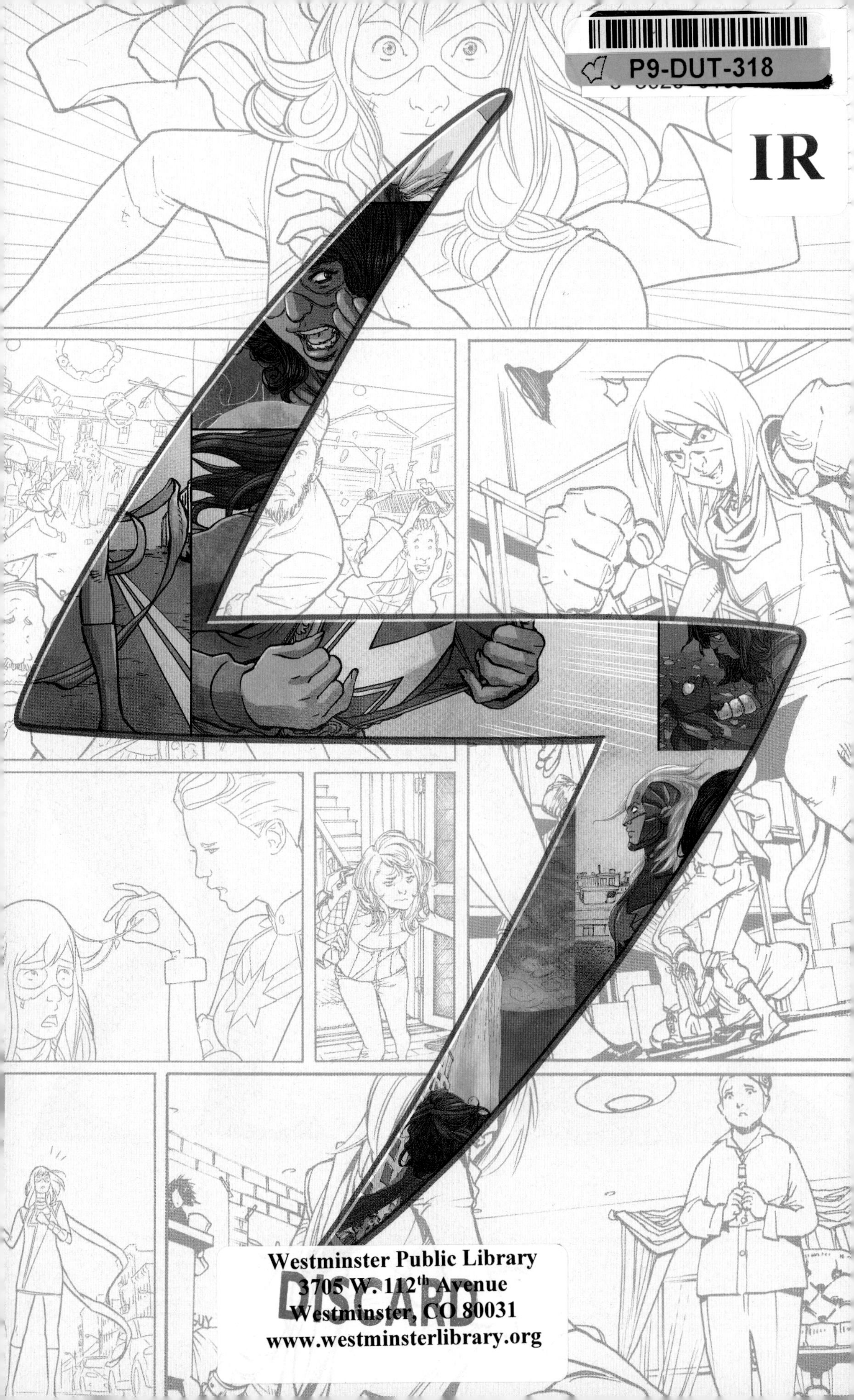

PREVIOUSLY

AFTER A STRANGE TERRIGEN MIST DESCENDED UPON JERSEY CITY,
KAMALA KHAN WAS IMBUED WITH POLYMORPH POWERS. USING HER
NEW ABILITIES TO FIGHT EVIL AND PROTECT JERSEY CITY, SHE BECAME
THE ALL-NEW MS. MARVEL!

MS. MARVEL VOL. 5: SUPER FAMOUS. Contains material originally published in magazine form as MS. MARVEL #1-6. First printing 2016. ISBN# 978-0-7851-9611-2. Published by MARVEL WORLDWIDE, INC., a subsidiary of MARVEL ENTERTAINMENT, LLC. OFFICE OF PUBLICATION: 135 West 50th Street, New York, NY 10020. Copyright © 2016 MARVEL No similarity between any of the names, characters, persons, and/or institutions in this magazine with those of any living or dead person or institution is intended, and any such similarity which may exist is purely coincidental. **Printed in the U.S.A.** ALAN FINE, President, Marvel Entertainment; DAN BUCKLEY, President, TV, Publishing & Brand Management; JOE QUESADA, Chief Creative Officer; TOM BREVOORT, SVP of Publishing; DAVID BOGART, SVP of Business Affairs & Operations, Publishing & Partnership; C.B. CEBULSKI, VP of Brand Management & Development, Asia; DAVID GABRIEL, SVP of Sales & Marketing, Publishing; JEFF YOUNGQUIST, VP of Production & Special Projects; DAN CARR, Executive Director of Publishing Technology; ALEX MORALES, Director of Publishing Operations; SUSAN CRESPI, Production Manager; STAN LEE, Chairman Emeritus. For information regarding advertising in Marvel Comics or on Marvel.com, please contact Vit DeBellis, Integrated Sales Manager, at vdebellis@marvel.com. For Marvel subscription inquiries, please call 888-511-5480. **Manufactured between 4/29/2016 and 6/6/2016 by HESS PRINT SOLUTIONS, A DIVISION OF BANG PRINTING, BRIMFIELD, OH, USA.**

10 9 8 7 6 5 4 3 2 1

MS. MARVEL

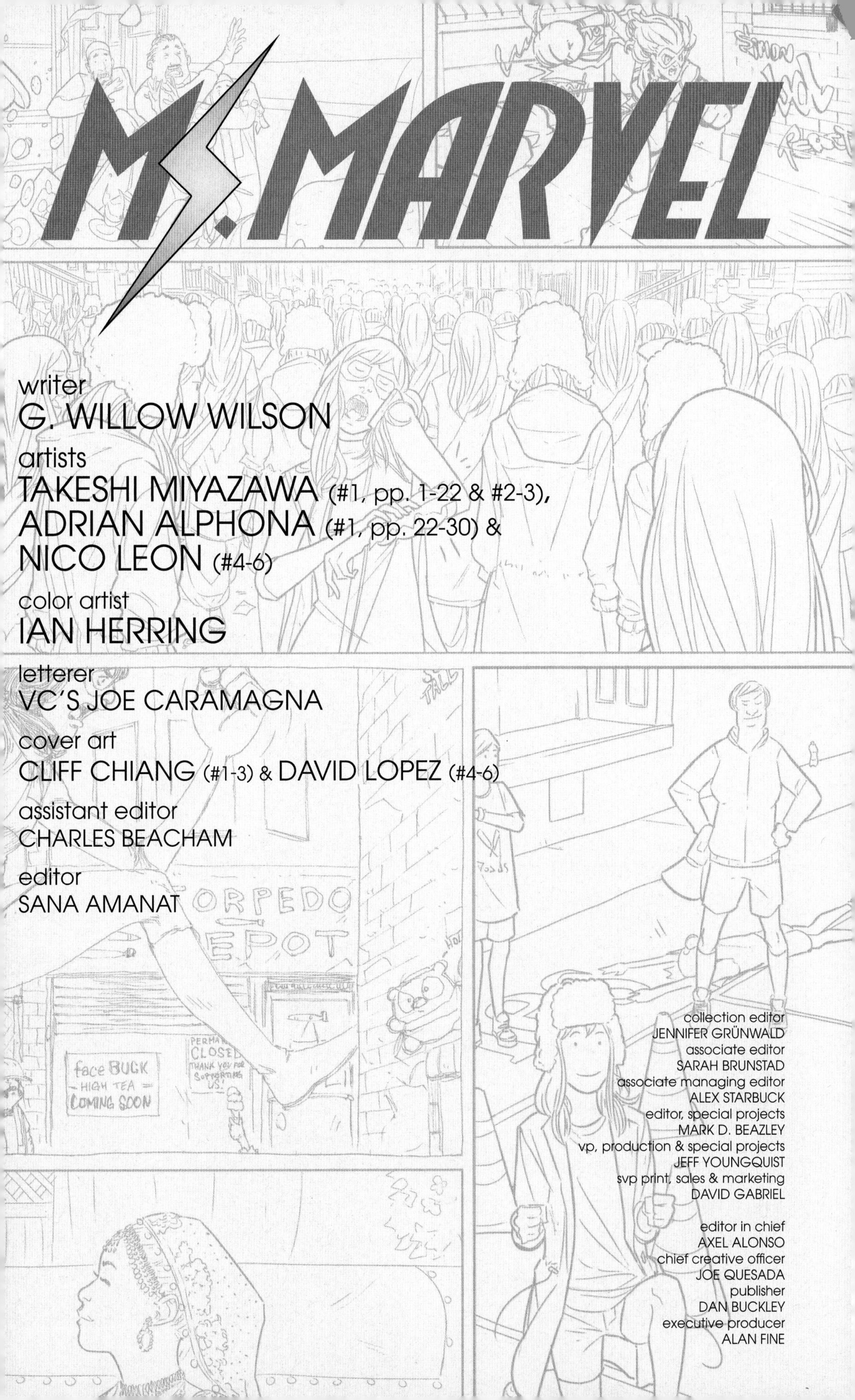

face BUCK
HIGH TEA
COMING SOON
THANK YOU FOR SUPPORTING US!

writer
G. WILLOW WILSON

artists
TAKESHI MIYAZAWA (#1, pp. 1-22 & #2-3),
ADRIAN ALPHONA (#1, pp. 22-30) &
NICO LEON (#4-6)

color artist
IAN HERRING

letterer
VC'S JOE CARAMAGNA

cover art
CLIFF CHIANG (#1-3) & DAVID LOPEZ (#4-6)

assistant editor
CHARLES BEACHAM

editor
SANA AMANAT

collection editor
JENNIFER GRÜNWALD
associate editor
SARAH BRUNSTAD
associate managing editor
ALEX STARBUCK
editor, special projects
MARK D. BEAZLEY
vp, production & special projects
JEFF YOUNGQUIST
svp print, sales & marketing
DAVID GABRIEL

editor in chief
AXEL ALONSO
chief creative officer
JOE QUESADA
publisher
DAN BUCKLEY
executive producer
ALAN FINE

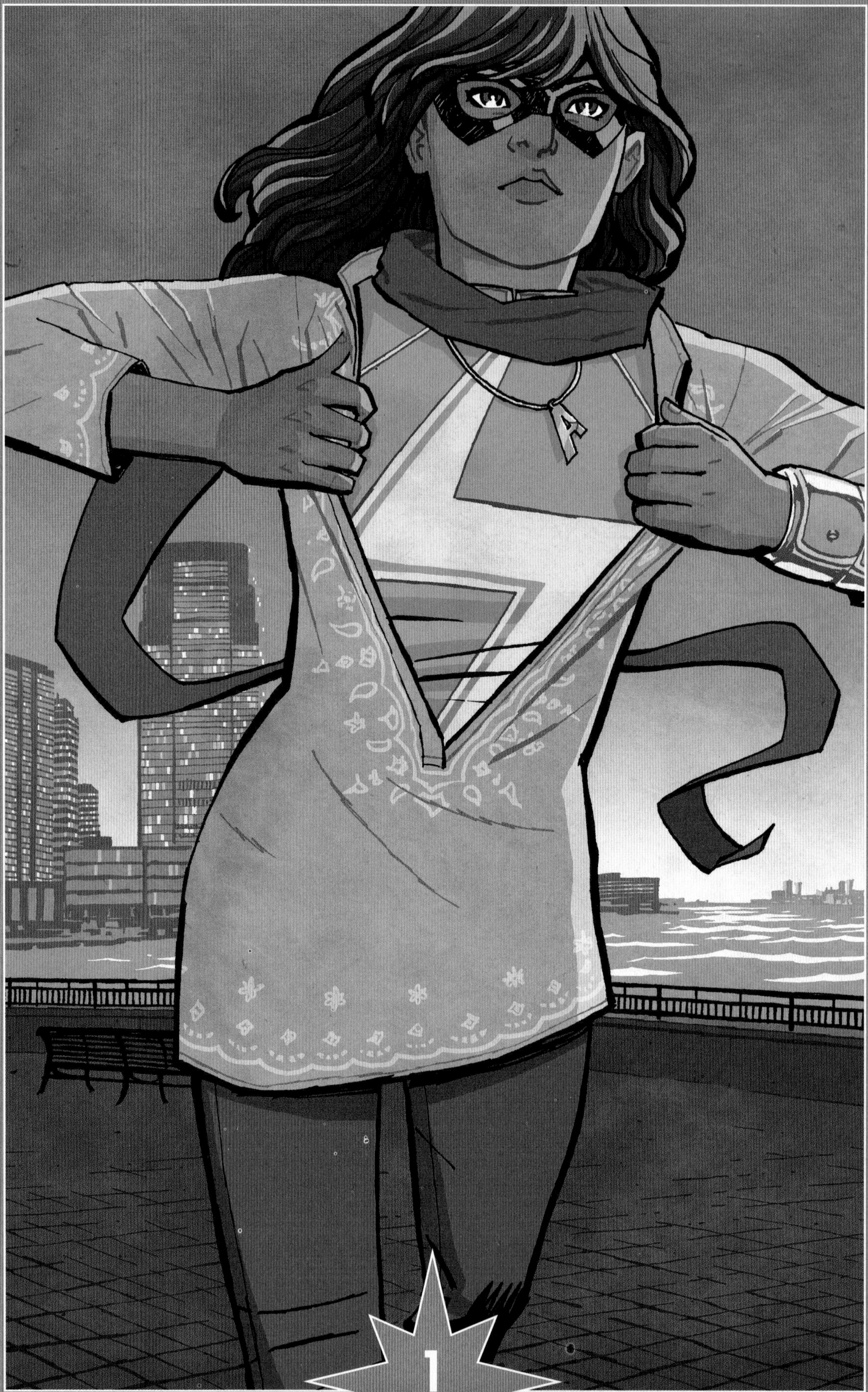
1

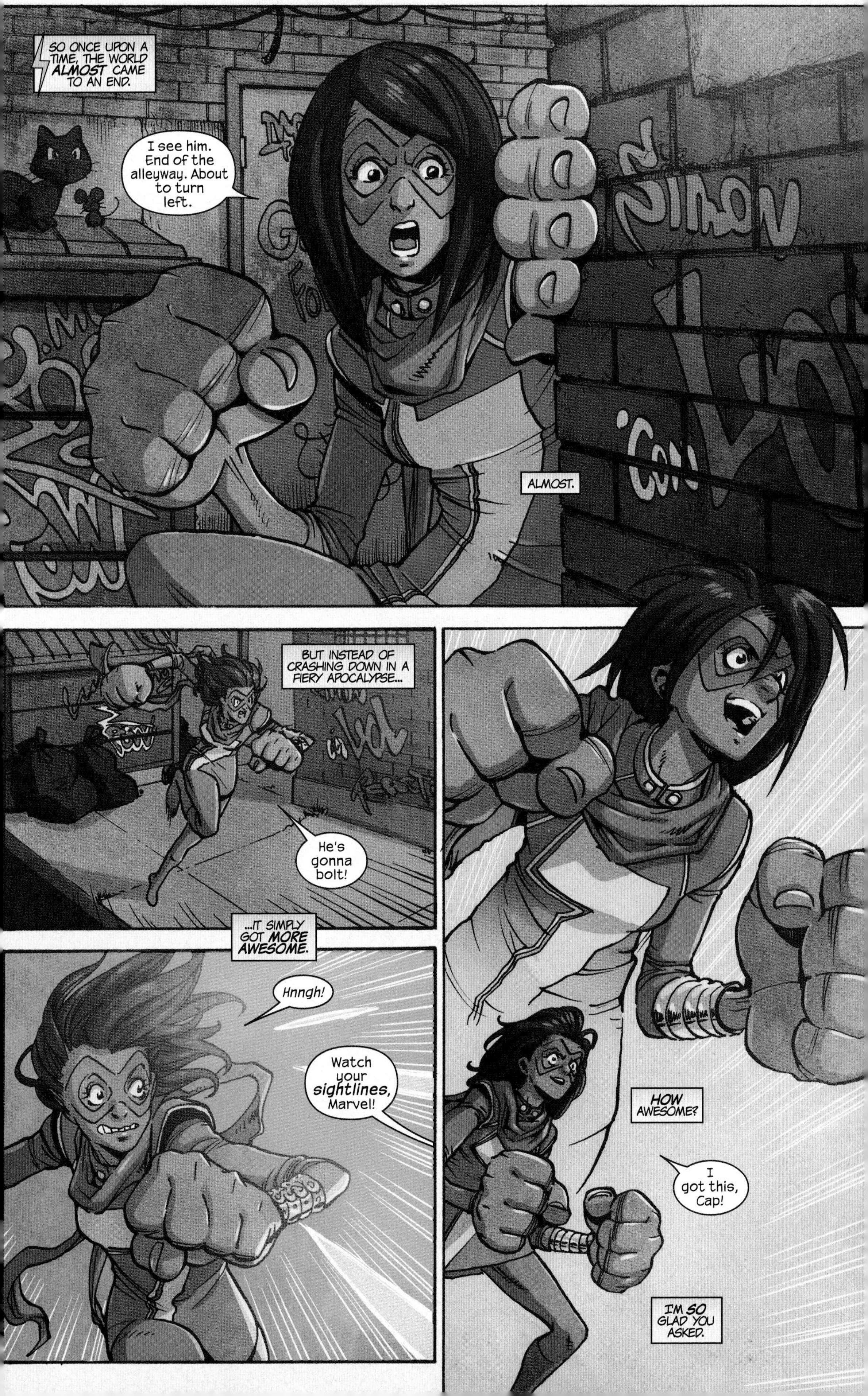
SO ONCE UPON A TIME, THE WORLD ALMOST CAME TO AN END.
I see him. End of the alleyway. About to turn left.
ALMOST.
BUT INSTEAD OF CRASHING DOWN IN A FIERY APOCALYPSE...
He's gonna bolt!
...IT SIMPLY GOT MORE AWESOME.
Hnngh!
Watch your sightlines, Marvel!
HOW AWESOME?
I got this, Cap!
I'M SO GLAD YOU ASKED.

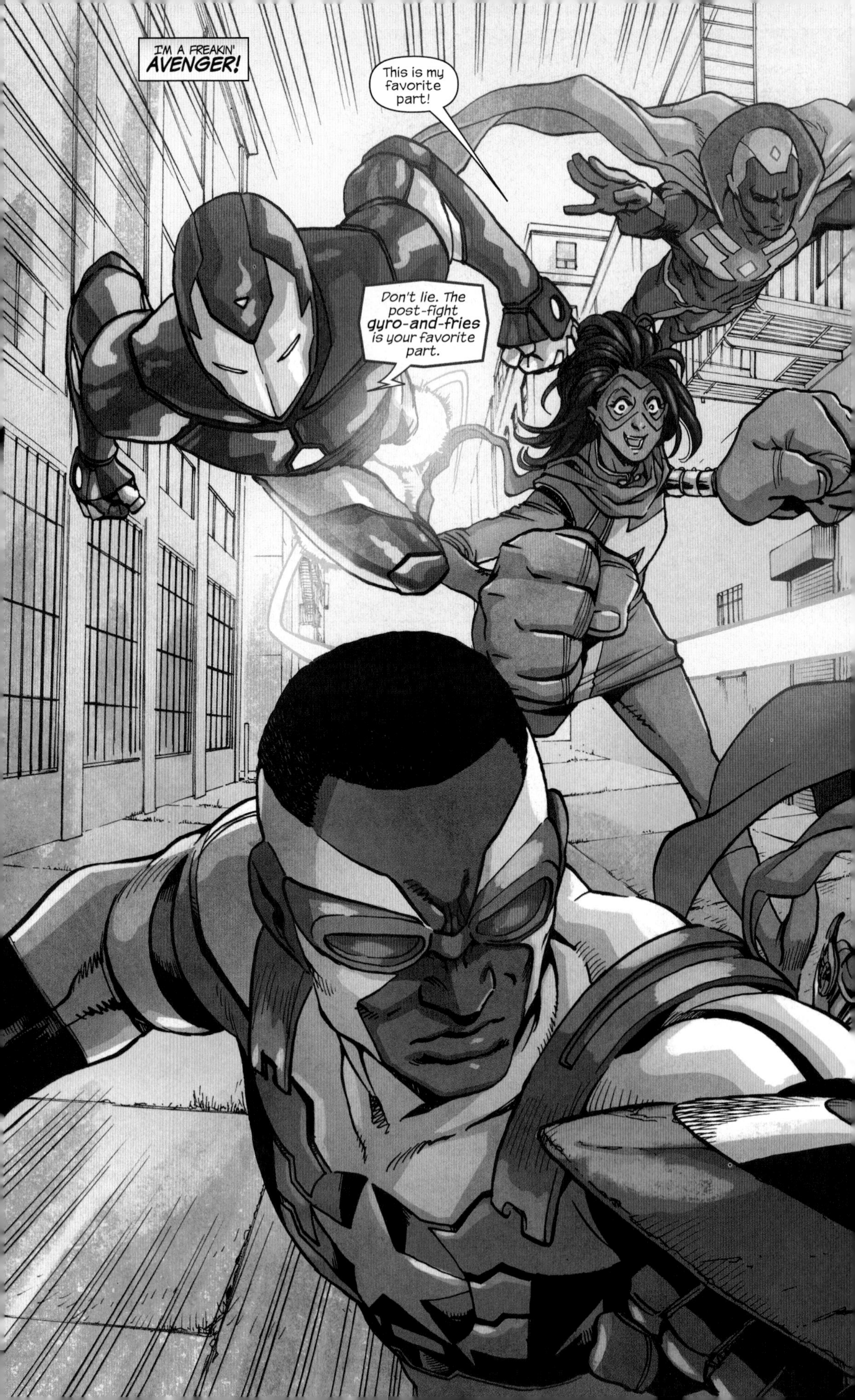
I'M A FREAKIN' AVENGER!
This is my favorite part!
Don't lie. The post-fight gyro-and-fries is your favorite part.

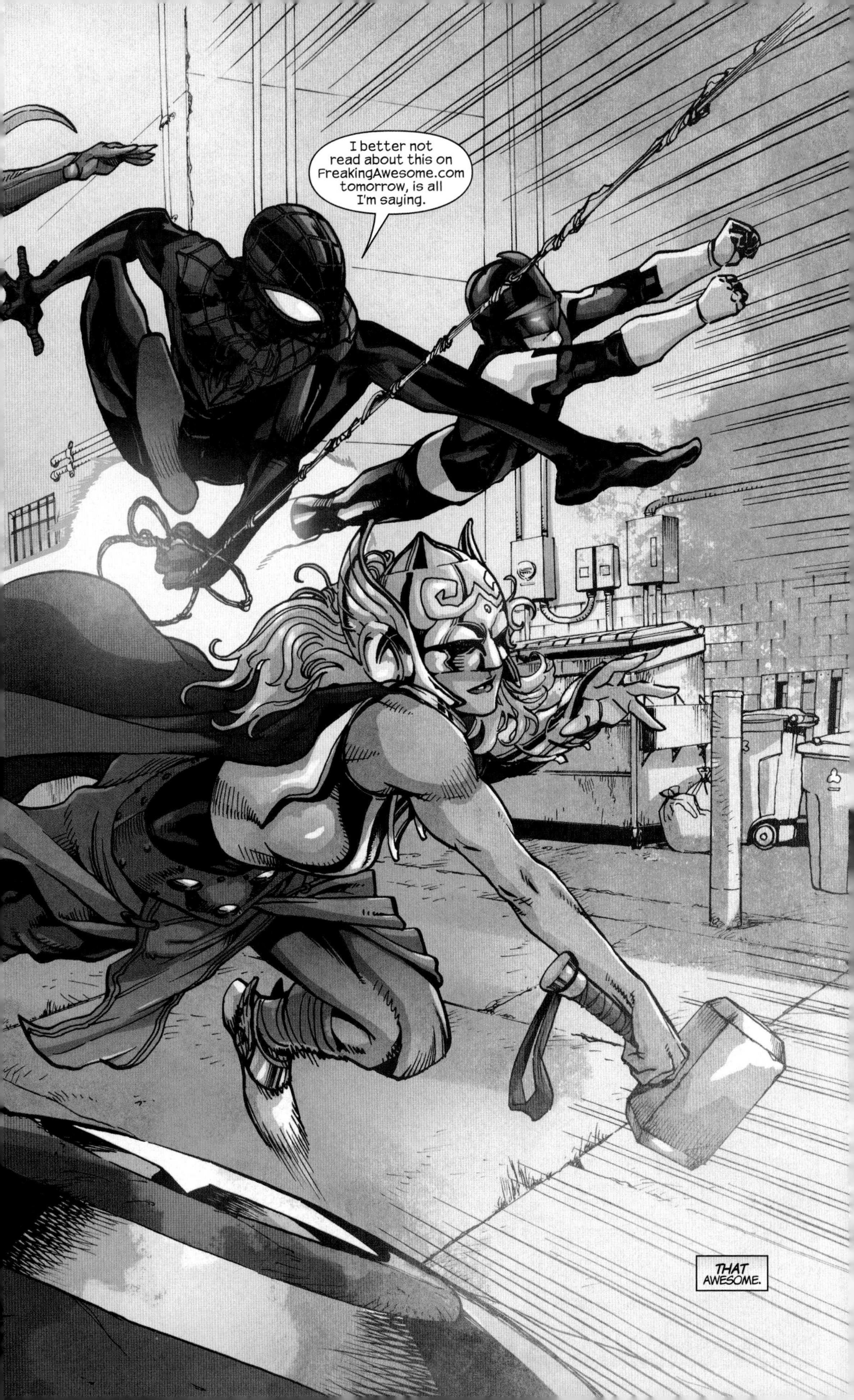
I better not read about this on FreakingAwesome.com tomorrow, is all I'm saying.
THAT AWESOME.

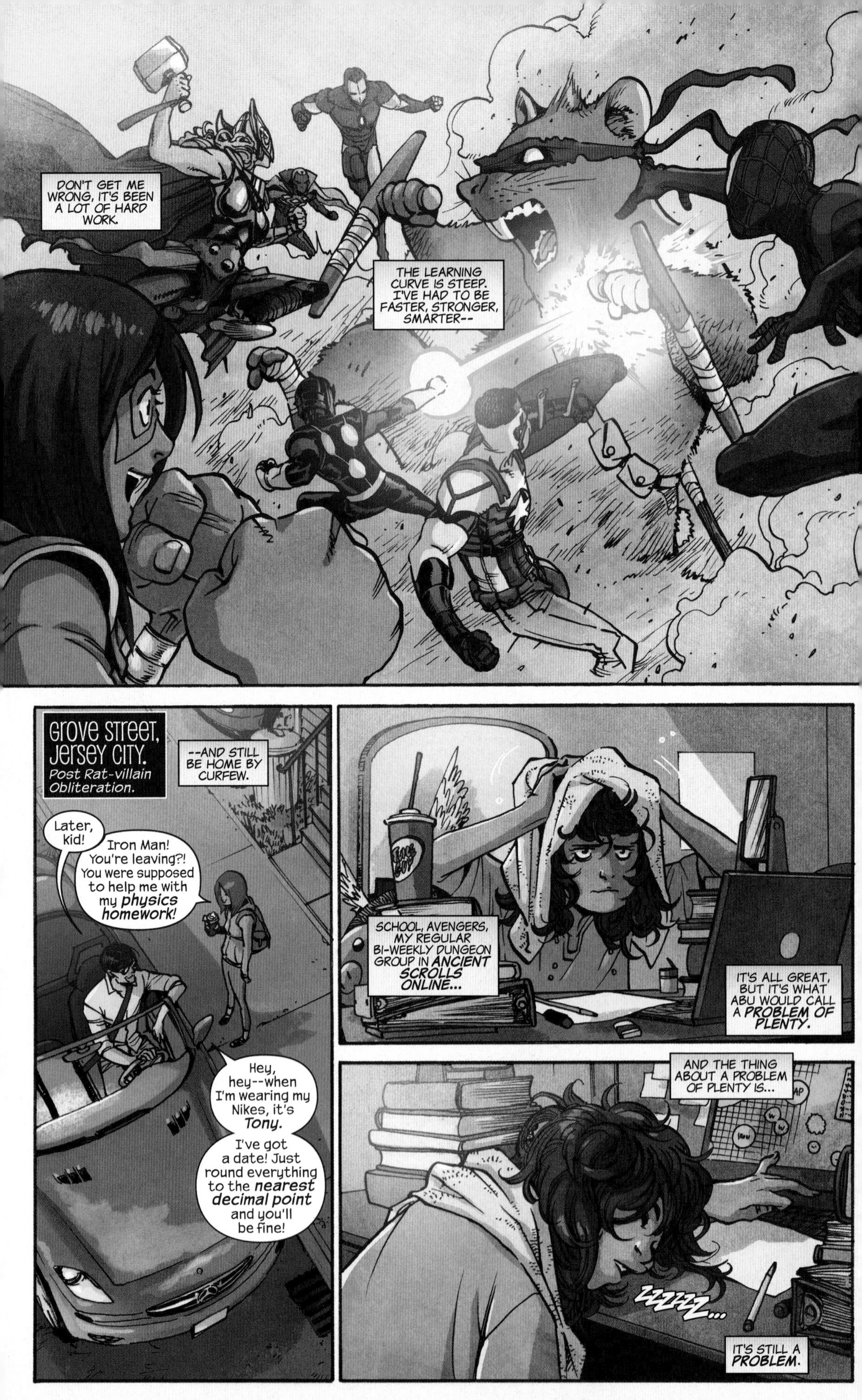
DON'T GET ME WRONG, IT'S BEEN A LOT OF HARD WORK.
THE LEARNING CURVE IS STEEP. I'VE HAD TO BE FASTER, STRONGER, SMARTER--
Grove Street, Jersey City.
Post Rat-villain Obliteration.
--AND STILL BE HOME BY CURFEW.
Later, kid!
Iron Man! You're leaving?! You were supposed to help me with my physics homework!
Hey, hey--when I'm wearing my Nikes, it's Tony.
I've got a date! Just round everything to the nearest decimal point and you'll be fine!
SCHOOL, AVENGERS, MY REGULAR BI-WEEKLY DUNGEON GROUP IN ANCIENT SCROLLS ONLINE...
IT'S ALL GREAT, BUT IT'S WHAT ABU WOULD CALL A PROBLEM OF PLENTY.
AND THE THING ABOUT A PROBLEM OF PLENTY IS...
ZZZZZZ...
IT'S STILL A PROBLEM.

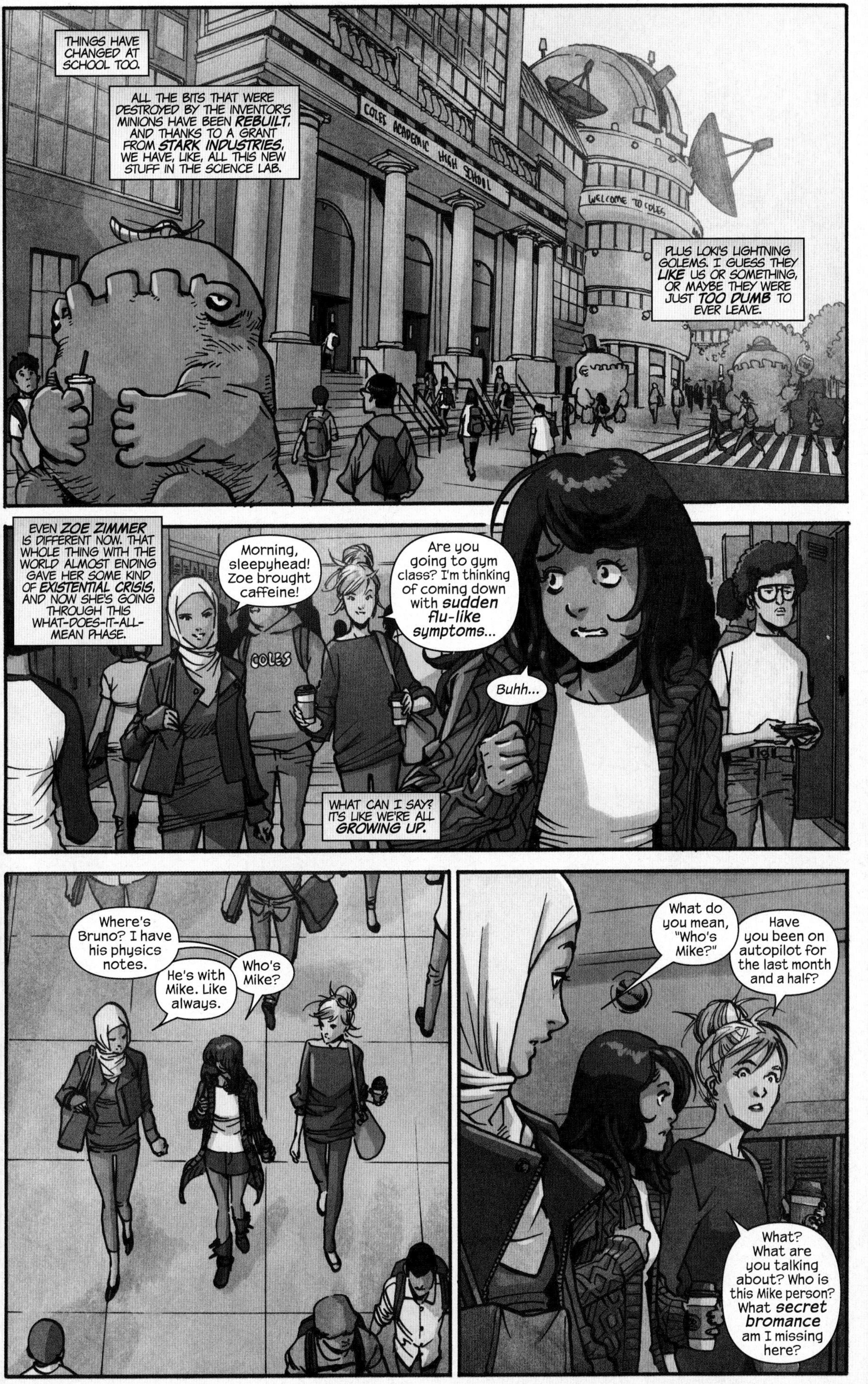
THINGS HAVE CHANGED AT SCHOOL TOO.
ALL THE BITS THAT WERE DESTROYED BY THE INVENTOR'S MINIONS HAVE BEEN REBUILT, AND THANKS TO A GRANT FROM STARK INDUSTRIES, WE HAVE, LIKE, ALL THIS NEW STUFF IN THE SCIENCE LAB.
COLES ACADEMIC HIGH SCHOOL
WELCOME TO COLES
PLUS LOKI'S LIGHTNING GOLEMS. I GUESS THEY LIKE US OR SOMETHING, OR MAYBE THEY WERE JUST TOO DUMB TO EVER LEAVE.
EVEN ZOE ZIMMER IS DIFFERENT NOW. THAT WHOLE THING WITH THE WORLD ALMOST ENDING GAVE HER SOME KIND OF EXISTENTIAL CRISIS, AND NOW SHE'S GOING THROUGH THIS WHAT-DOES-IT-ALL-MEAN PHASE.
Morning, sleepyhead! Zoe brought caffeine!
Are you going to gym class? I'm thinking of coming down with sudden flu-like symptoms...
COLES
Buhh...
WHAT CAN I SAY? IT'S LIKE WE'RE ALL GROWING UP.
Where's Bruno? I have his physics notes.
He's with Mike. Like always.
Who's Mike?
What do you mean, "Who's Mike?"
Have you been on autopilot for the last month and a half?
What? What are you talking about? Who is this Mike person? What secret bromance am I missing here?

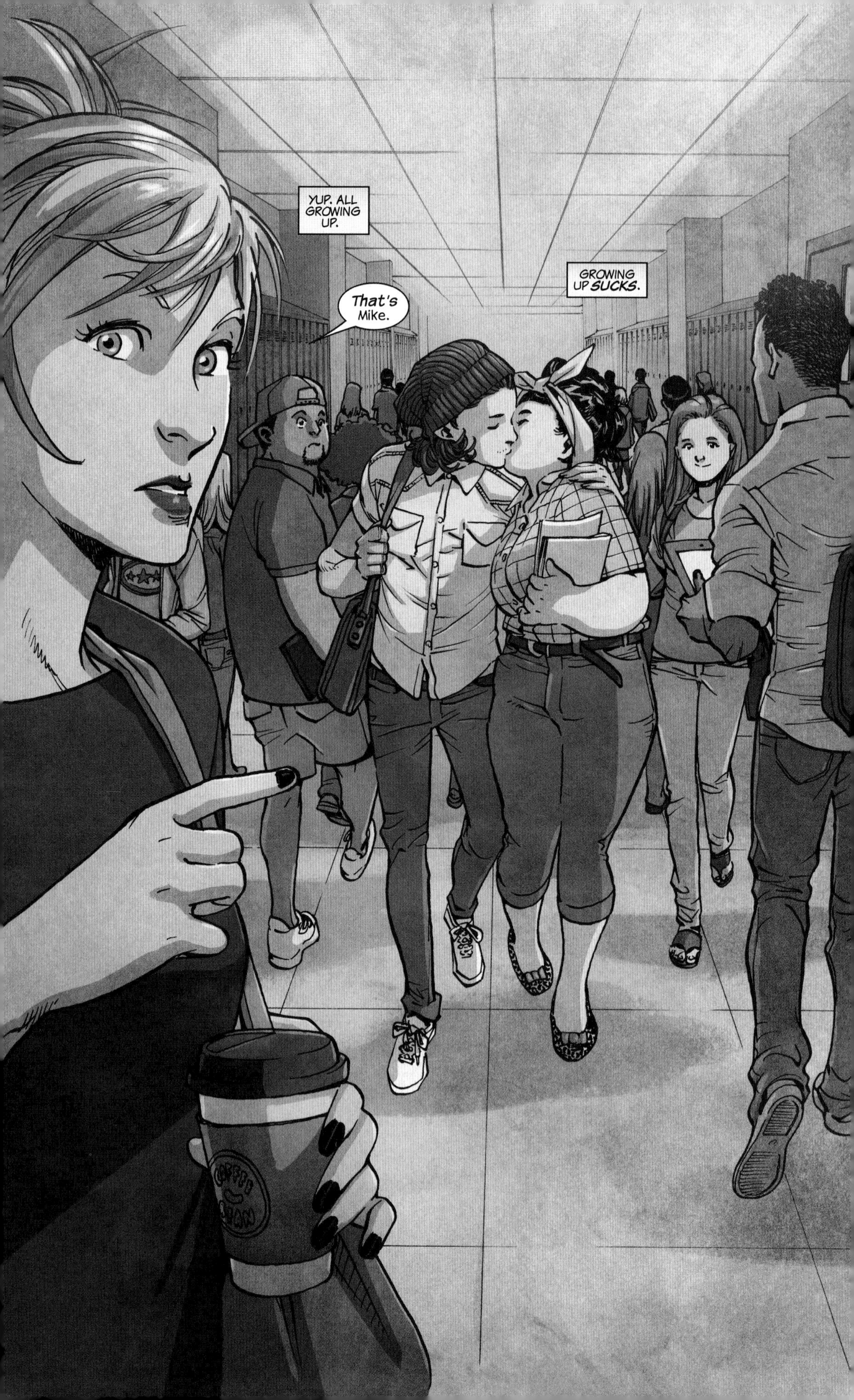
YUP. ALL GROWING UP.
That's Mike.
GROWING UP SUCKS.

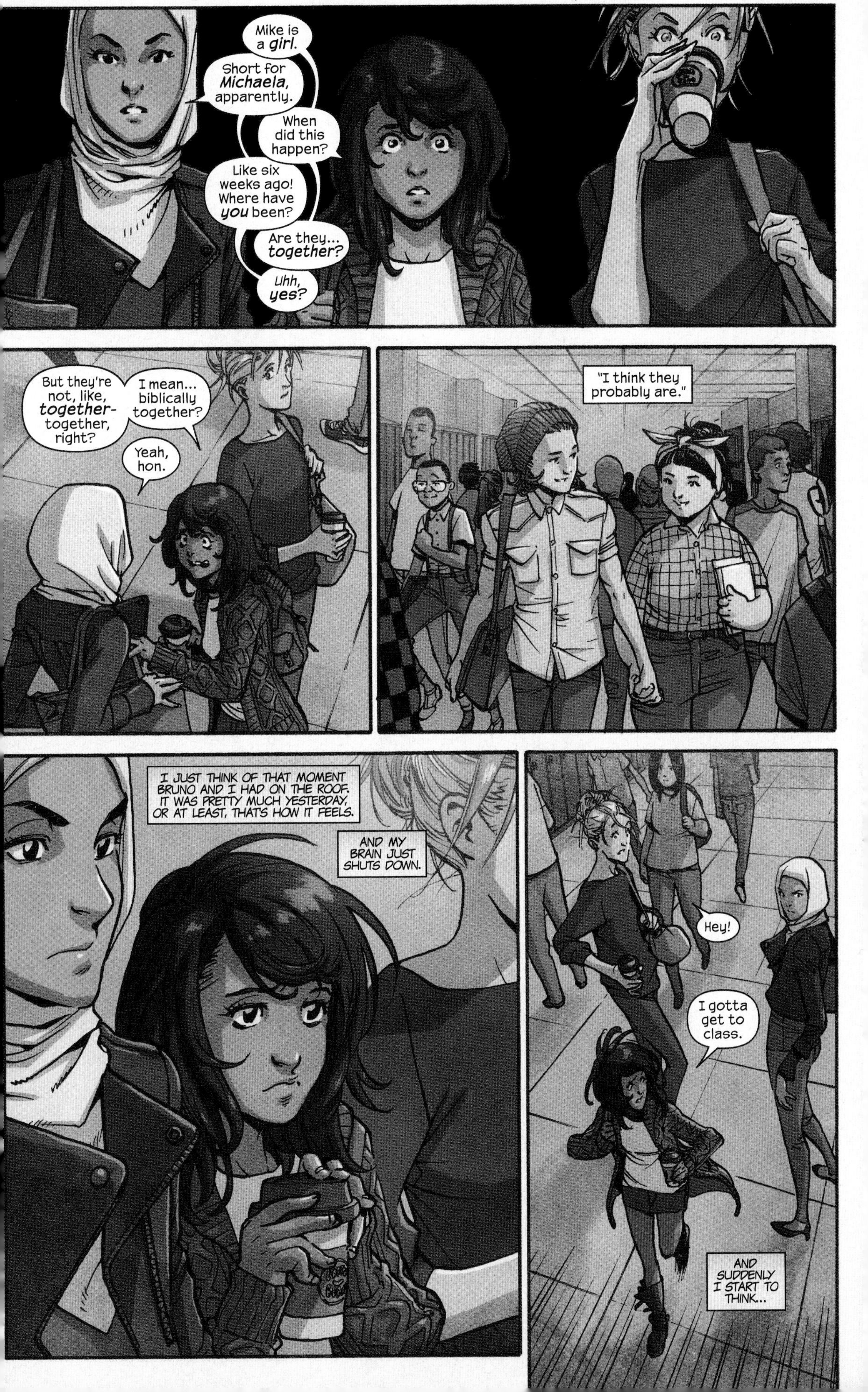
Mike is a *girl*.
Short for *Michaela*, apparently.
When did this happen?
Like six weeks ago! Where have *you* been?
Are they... *together*?
Uhh, *yes*?
But they're not, like, *together*-together, right?
I mean... biblically together?
Yeah, hon.
"I think they probably are."
I JUST THINK OF THAT MOMENT BRUNO AND I HAD ON THE ROOF. IT WAS PRETTY MUCH YESTERDAY, OR AT LEAST, THAT'S HOW IT FEELS.
AND MY BRAIN JUST SHUTS DOWN.
Hey!
I gotta get to class.
AND SUDDENLY I START TO THINK...

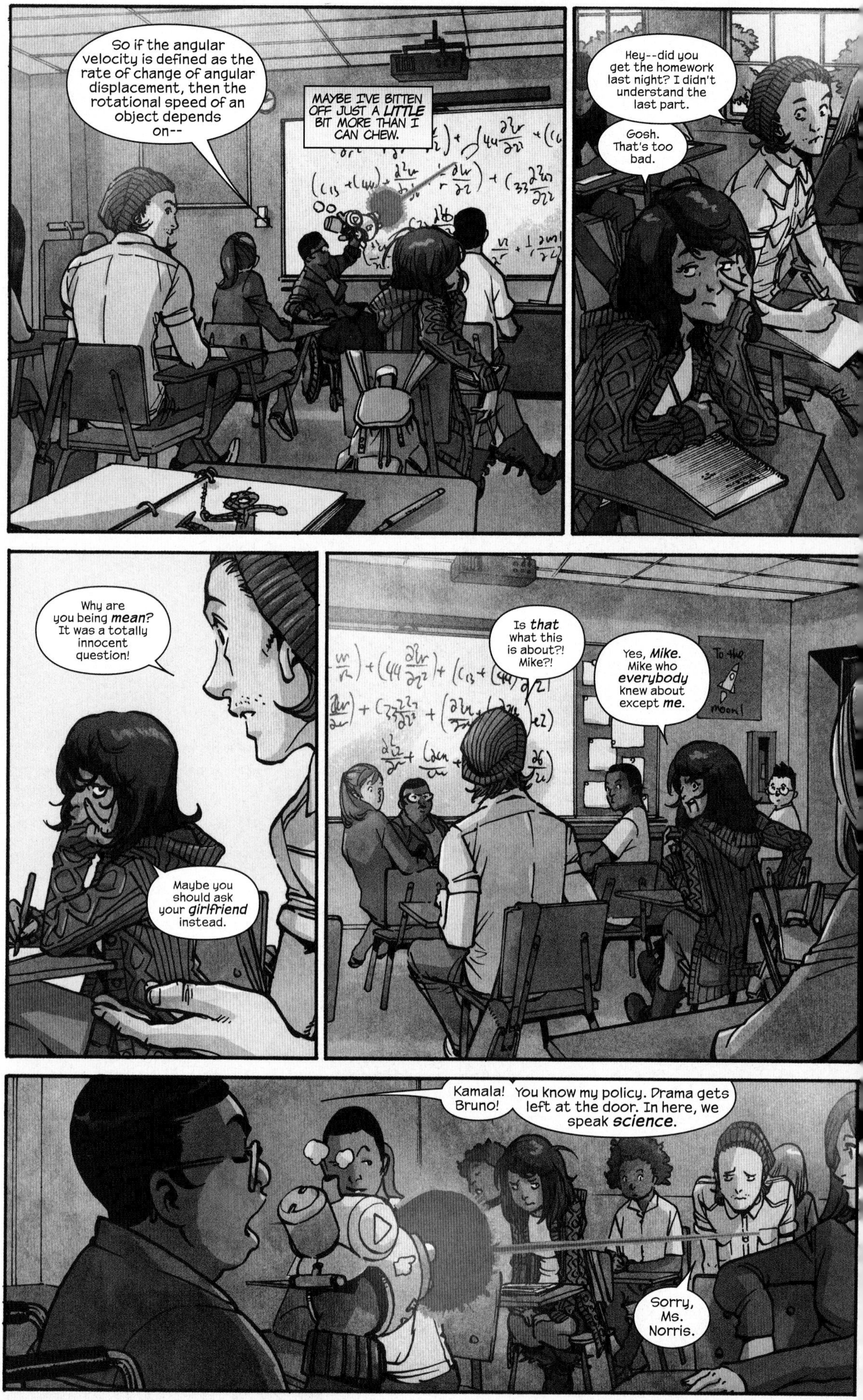
So if the angular velocity is defined as the rate of change of angular displacement, then the rotational speed of an object depends on--
MAYBE I'VE BITTEN OFF JUST A LITTLE BIT MORE THAN I CAN CHEW.
Hey--did you get the homework last night? I didn't understand the last part.
Gosh. That's too bad.
Why are you being mean? It was a totally innocent question!
Maybe you should ask your girlfriend instead.
Is that what this is about?! Mike?!
Yes, Mike. Mike who everybody knew about except me.
To the moon!
Kamala! Bruno!
You know my policy. Drama gets left at the door. In here, we speak science.
Sorry, Ms. Norris.

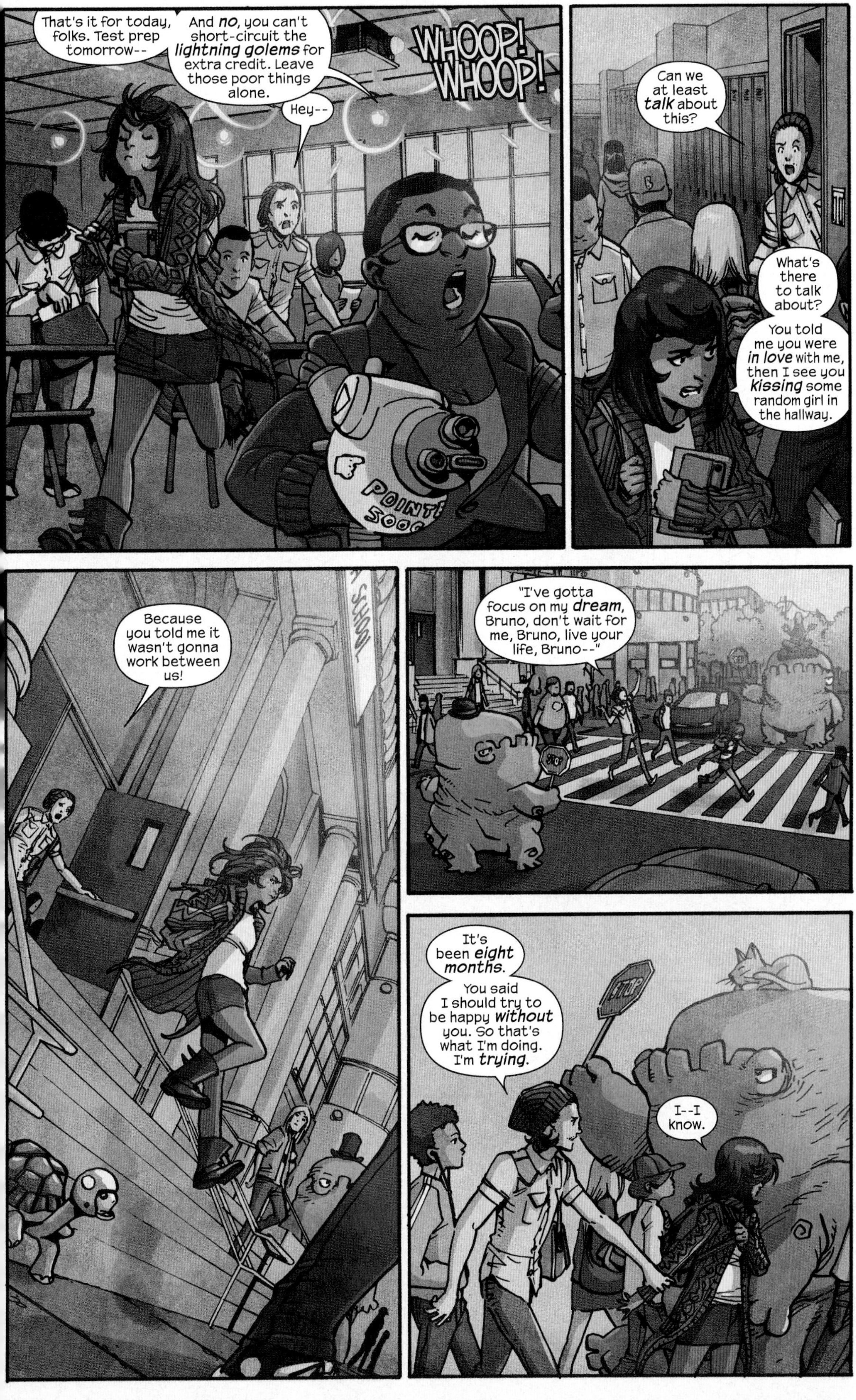

That's it for today, folks. Test prep tomorrow--
And *no*, you can't short-circuit the *lightning golems* for extra credit. Leave those poor things alone.
WHOOP! WHOOP!
Hey--
POINTE 500
Can we at least *talk* about this?
What's there to talk about?
You told me you were *in love* with me, then I see you *kissing* some random girl in the hallway.
Because you told me it wasn't gonna work between us!
"I've gotta focus on my *dream*, Bruno, don't wait for me, Bruno, live your life, Bruno--"
It's been *eight months*.
You said I should try to be happy *without* you. So that's what I'm doing. I'm *trying*.
STOP
I--I know.

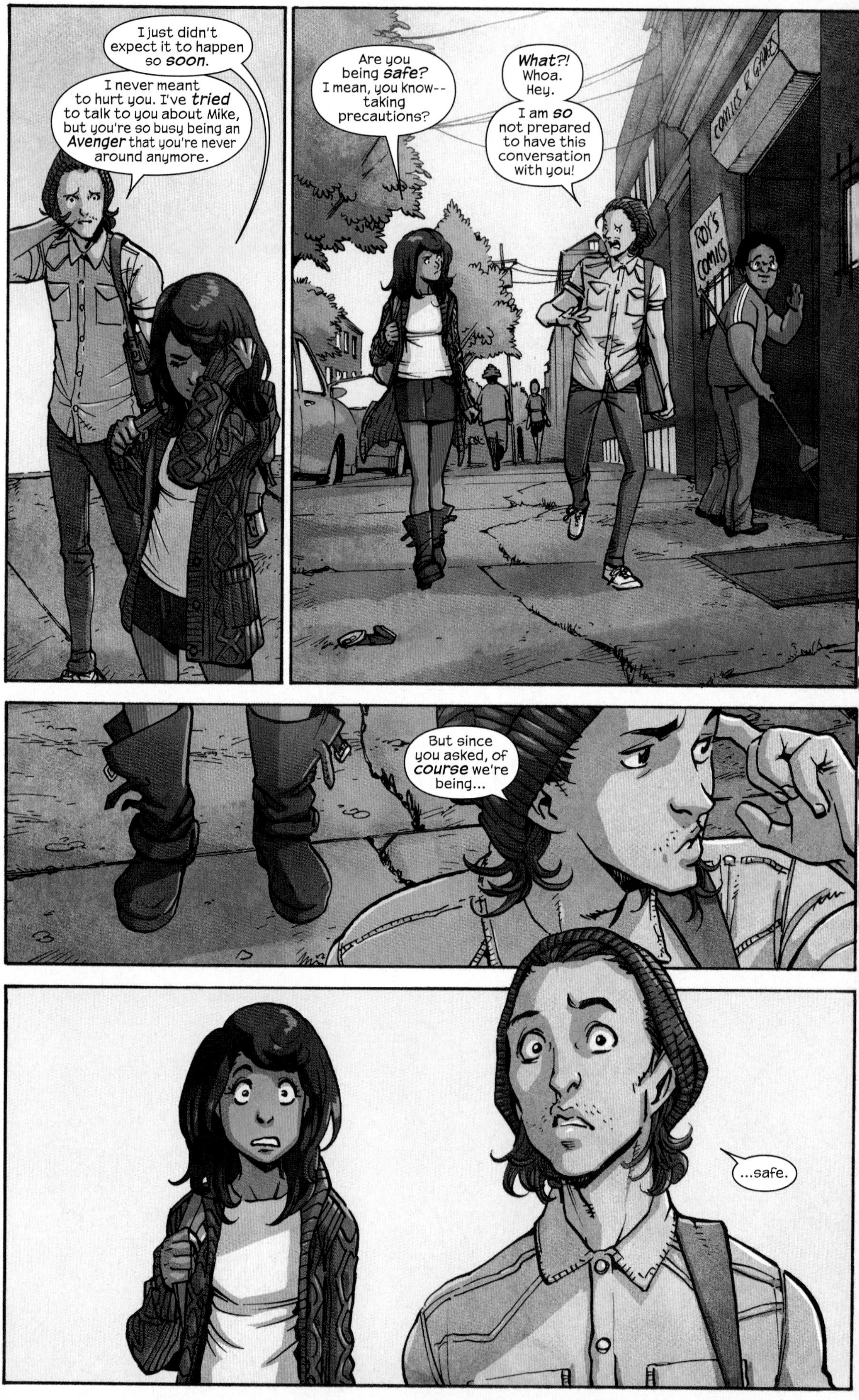
I just didn't expect it to happen so soon.
I never meant to hurt you. I've tried to talk to you about Mike, but you're so busy being an Avenger that you're never around anymore.
Are you being safe? I mean, you know-- taking precautions?
What?! Whoa. Hey.
I am so not prepared to have this conversation with you!
COMICS & GAMES
ROY'S COMICS
But since you asked, of course we're being...
...safe.

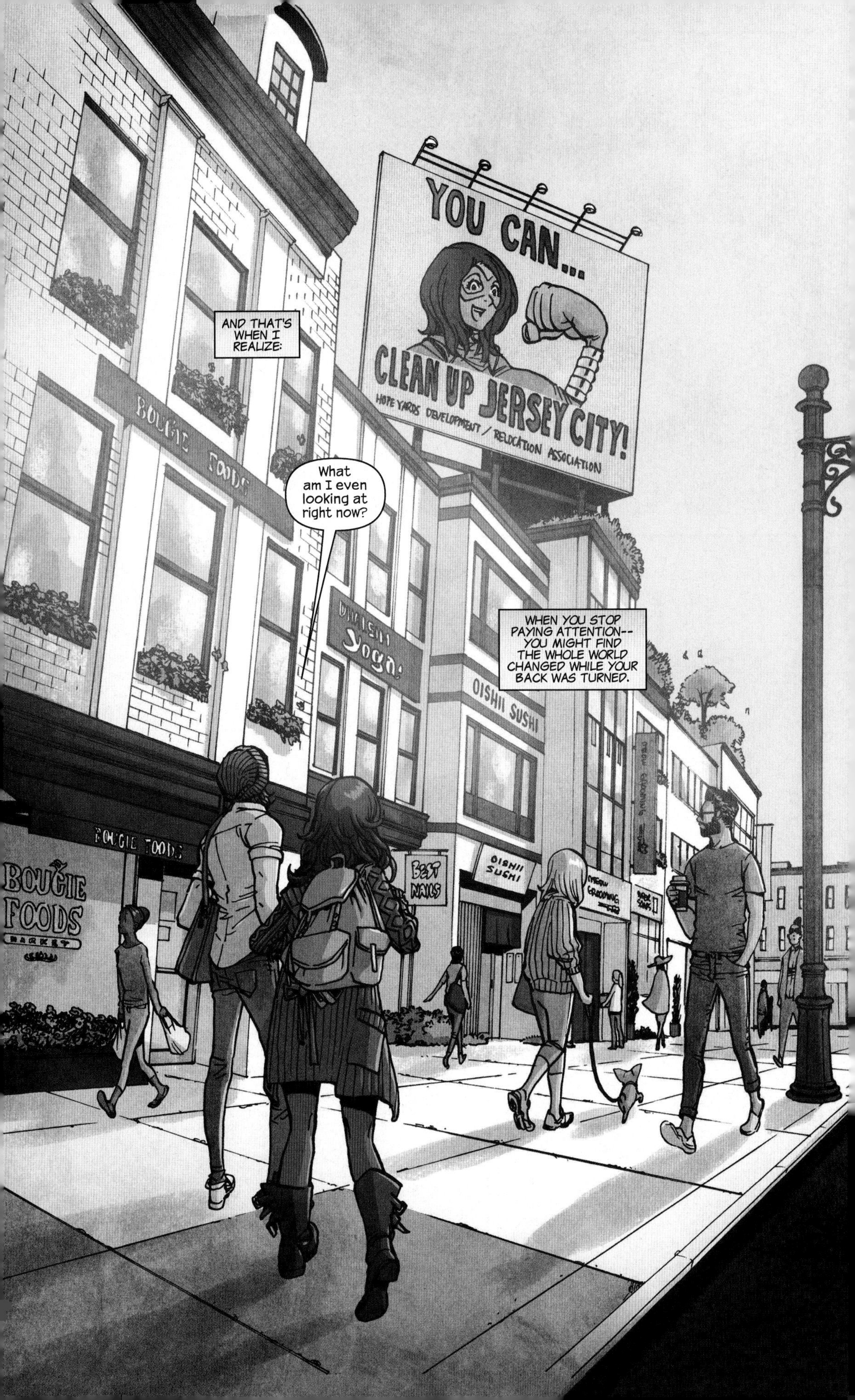
YOU CAN...
CLEAN UP JERSEY CITY!
HOPE YARDS DEVELOPMENT / RELOCATION ASSOCIATION
AND THAT'S WHEN I REALIZE:
What am I even looking at right now?
WHEN YOU STOP PAYING ATTENTION-- YOU MIGHT FIND THE WHOLE WORLD CHANGED WHILE YOUR BACK WAS TURNED.
BOUGIE FOODS
Yoga
OISHII SUSHI
BOUGIE FOODS
BOUGIE FOODS MARKET
BEST NAILS
OISHII SUSHI

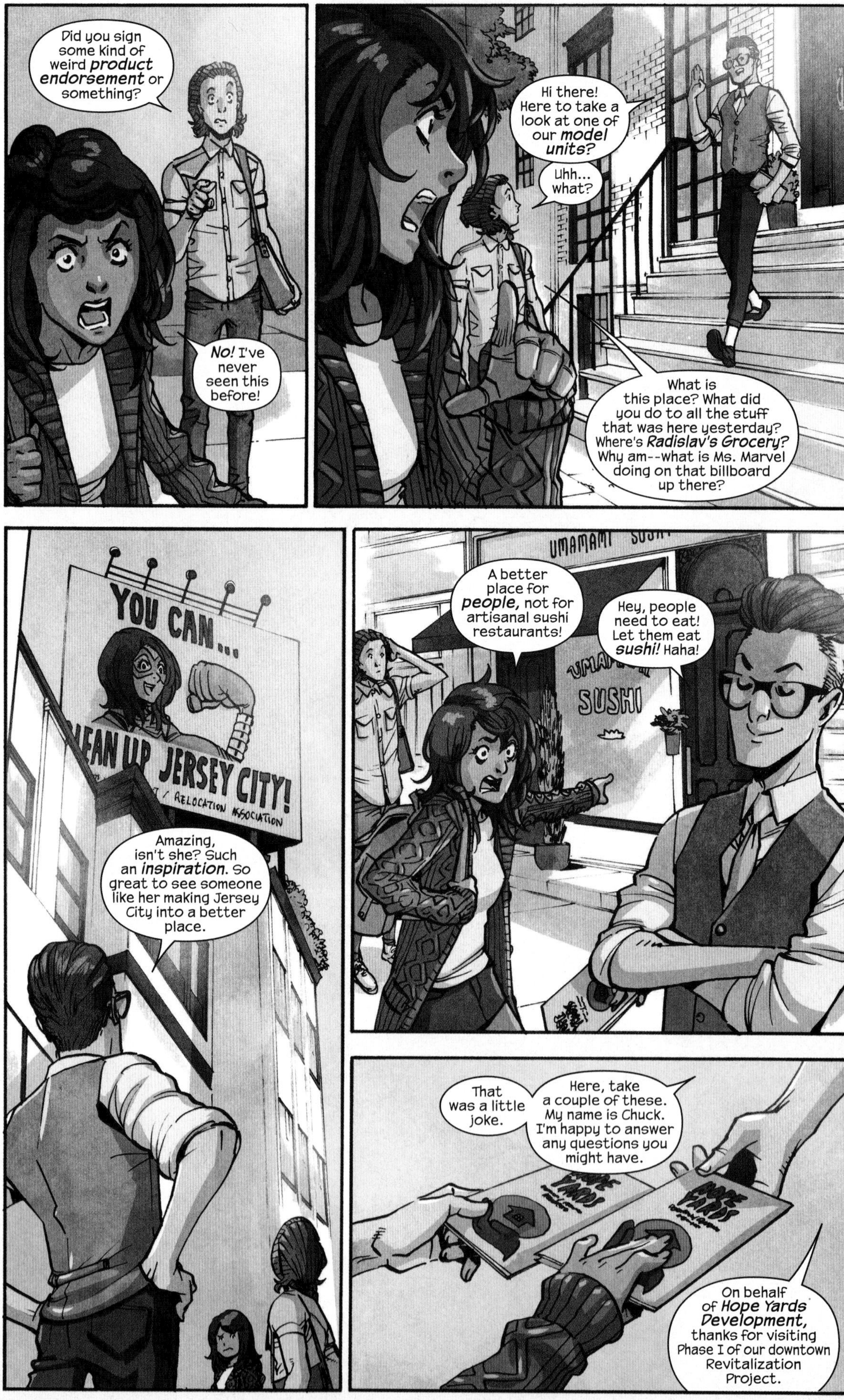
Did you sign some kind of weird *product endorsement* or something?
No! I've never seen this before!
Hi there! Here to take a look at one of our *model units?*
Uhh... what?
What is this place? What did you do to all the stuff that was here yesterday? Where's *Radislav's Grocery?* Why am--what is Ms. Marvel doing on that billboard up there?
YOU CAN...
LEAN UP JERSEY CITY!
RELOCATION ASSOCIATION
Amazing, isn't she? Such an *inspiration*. So great to see someone like her making Jersey City into a better place.
UMAMAMI
SUSHI
A better place for *people,* not for artisanal sushi restaurants!
Hey, people need to eat! Let them eat *sushi!* Haha!
That was a little joke.
Here, take a couple of these. My name is Chuck. I'm happy to answer any questions you might have.
HOPE YARDS
On behalf of *Hope Yards Development,* thanks for visiting Phase I of our downtown Revitalization Project.

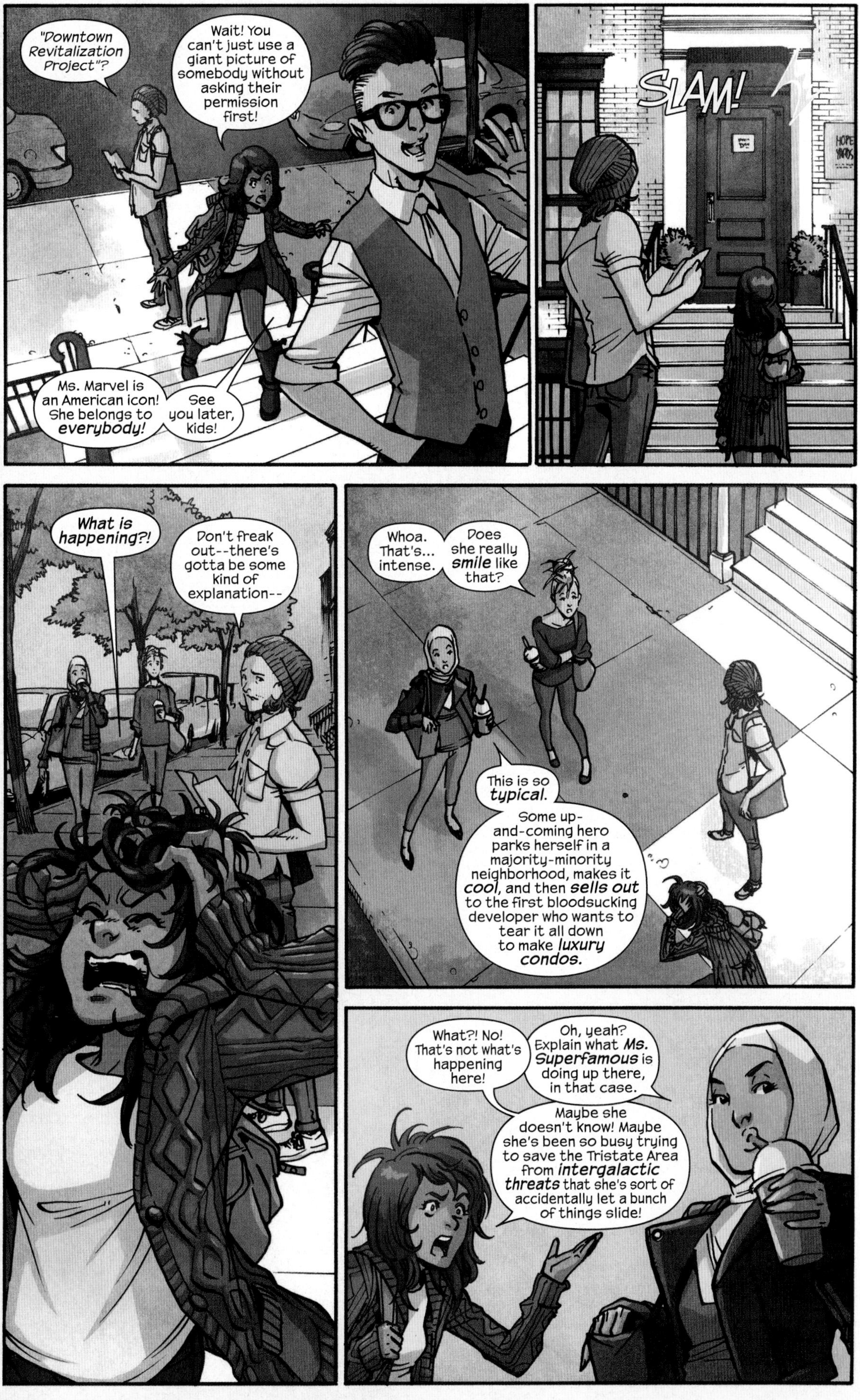

"Downtown Revitalization Project"?
Wait! You can't just use a giant picture of somebody without asking their permission first!
Ms. Marvel is an American icon! She belongs to *everybody!*
See you later, kids!
SLAM!
HOPE YARDS
What is happening?!
Don't freak out--there's gotta be some kind of explanation--
Whoa. That's... intense.
Does she really *smile* like that?
This is so *typical*.
Some up-and-coming hero parks herself in a majority-minority neighborhood, makes it *cool*, and then *sells out* to the first bloodsucking developer who wants to tear it all down to make *luxury condos.*
What?! No! That's not what's happening here!
Oh, yeah? Explain what *Ms. Superfamous* is doing up there, in that case.
Maybe she doesn't know! Maybe she's been so busy trying to save the Tristate Area from *intergalactic threats* that she's sort of accidentally let a bunch of things slide!

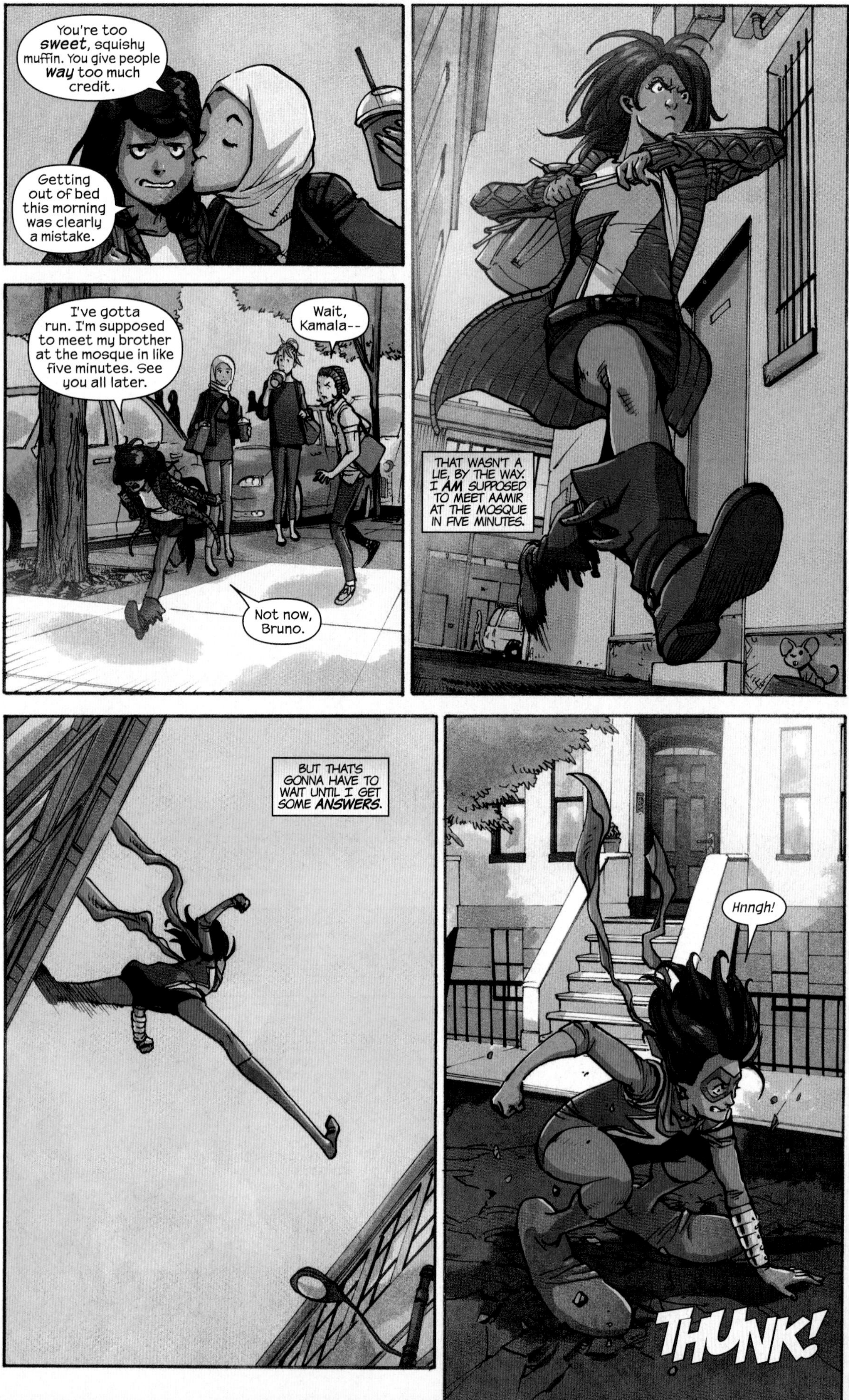
You're too sweet, squishy muffin. You give people way too much credit.
Getting out of bed this morning was clearly a mistake.
THAT WASN'T A LIE, BY THE WAY. I AM SUPPOSED TO MEET AAMIR AT THE MOSQUE IN FIVE MINUTES.
I've gotta run. I'm supposed to meet my brother at the mosque in like five minutes. See you all later.
Wait, Kamala--
Not now, Bruno.
BUT THAT'S GONNA HAVE TO WAIT UNTIL I GET SOME ANSWERS.
Hnngh!
THUNK!

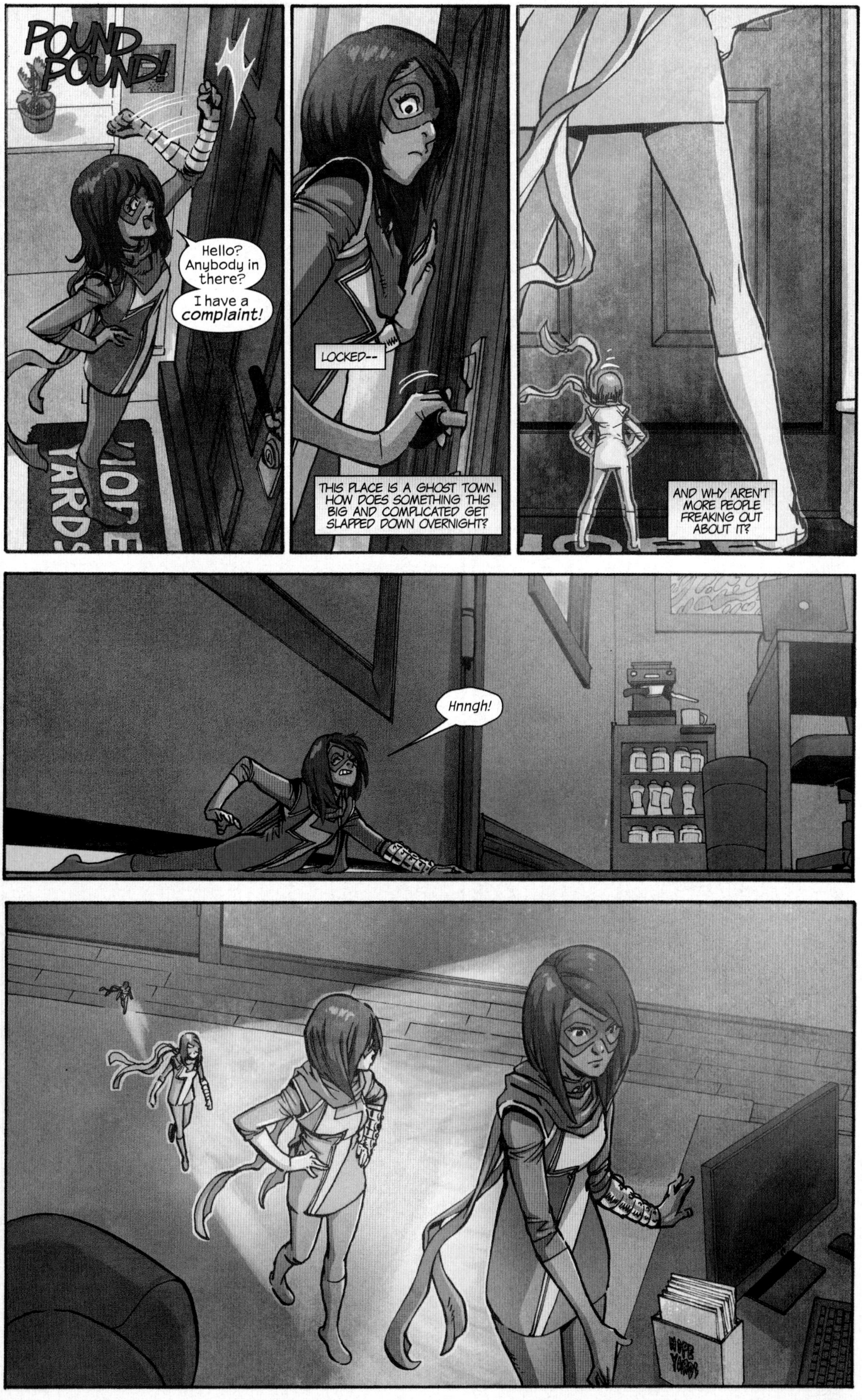

POUND POUND!
Hello? Anybody in there?
I have a *complaint!*
LOCKED--
THIS PLACE IS A GHOST TOWN. HOW DOES SOMETHING THIS BIG AND COMPLICATED GET SLAPPED DOWN OVERNIGHT?
AND WHY AREN'T MORE PEOPLE FREAKING OUT ABOUT IT?
Hnngh!

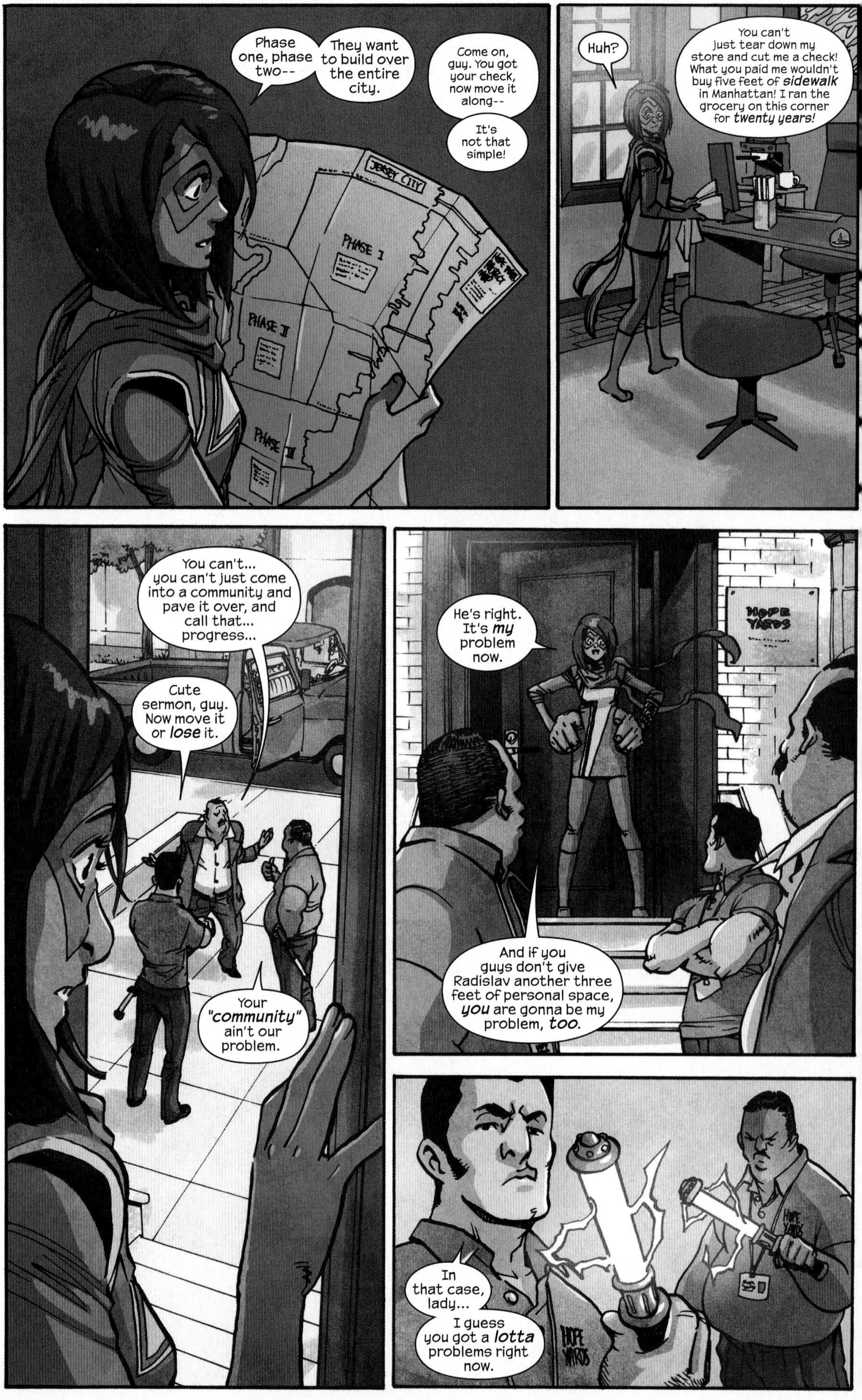
Phase one, phase two--
They want to build over the entire city.
JERSEY CITY
PHASE I
PHASE II
PHASE III
Come on, guy. You got your check, now move it along--
It's not that simple!
Huh?
You can't just tear down my store and cut me a check! What you paid me wouldn't buy five feet of ***sidewalk*** in Manhattan! I ran the grocery on this corner for ***twenty years!***
You can't... you can't just come into a community and pave it over, and call that... progress...
Cute sermon, guy. Now move it or *lose* it.
Your ***"community"*** ain't our problem.
He's right. It's ***my*** problem now.
HOPE YARDS
And if you guys don't give Radislav another three feet of personal space, ***you*** are gonna be my problem, ***too***.
In that case, lady...
I guess you got a ***lotta*** problems right now.
HOPE YARDS

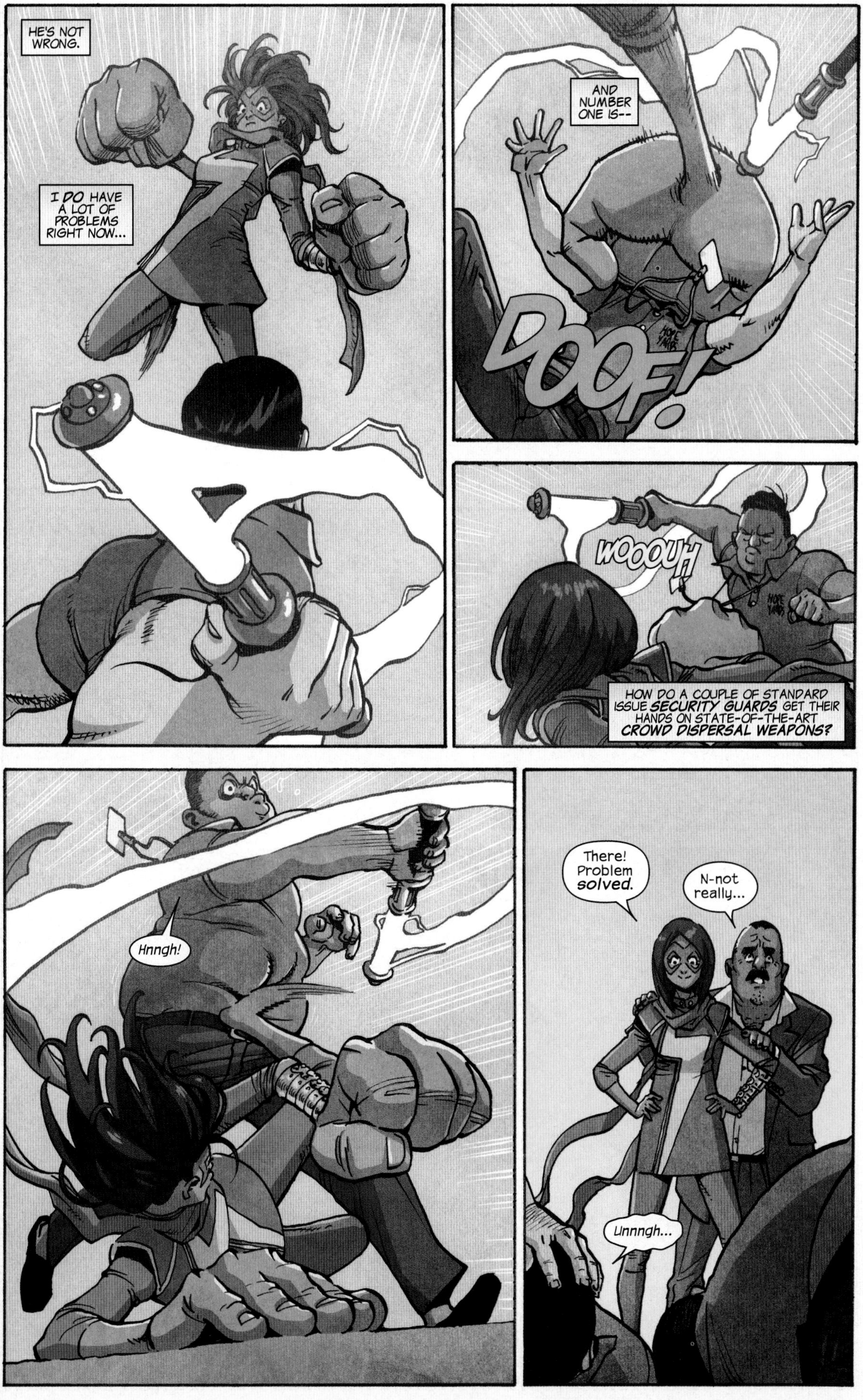
HE'S NOT WRONG.
I DO HAVE A LOT OF PROBLEMS RIGHT NOW...
AND NUMBER ONE IS--
DOOF!
WOOOUH
HOW DO A COUPLE OF STANDARD ISSUE SECURITY GUARDS GET THEIR HANDS ON STATE-OF-THE-ART CROWD DISPERSAL WEAPONS?
Hnngh!
There! Problem solved.
N-not really...
Unnngh...

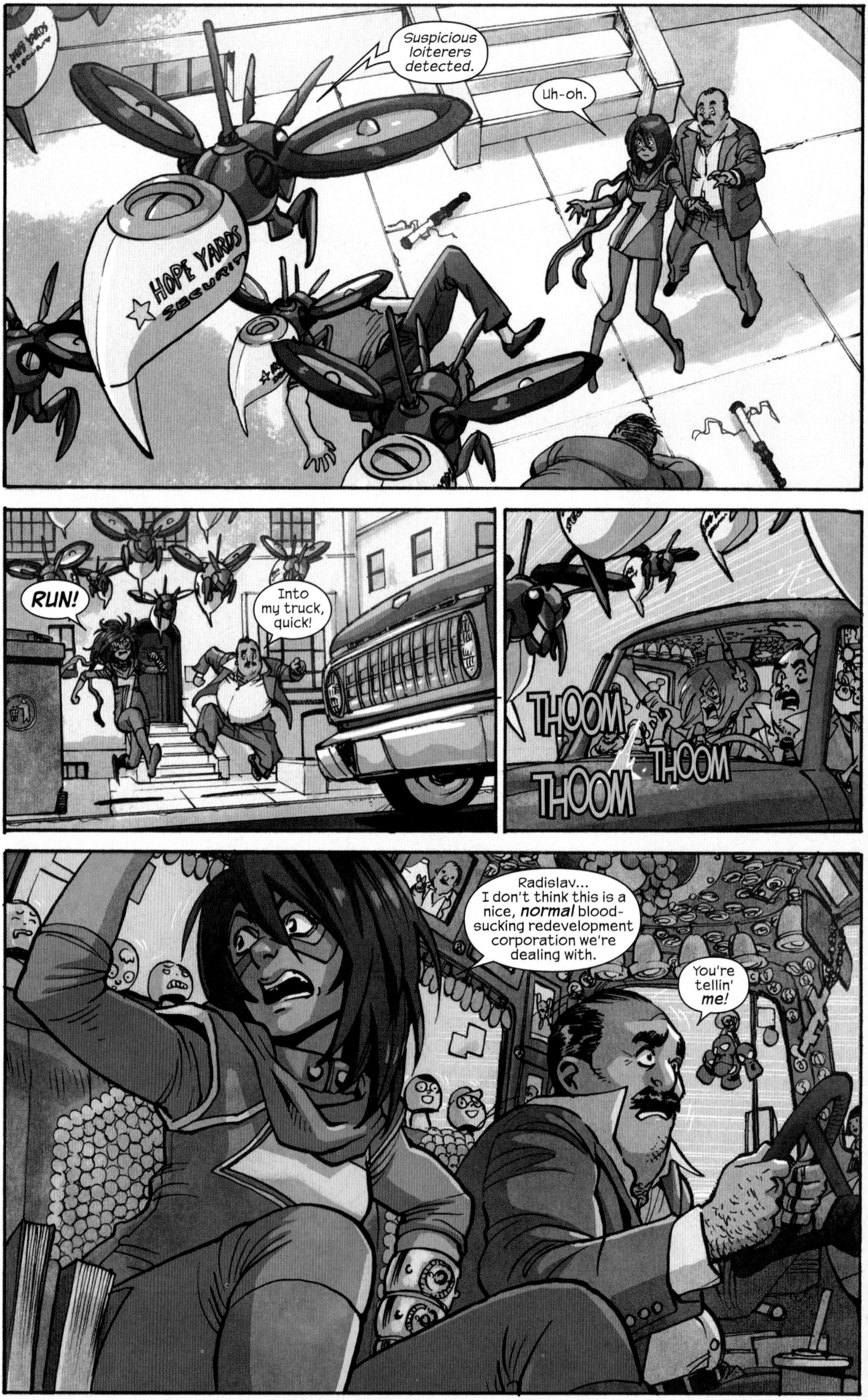

HOPE YARDS SECURITY
Suspicious loiterers detected.
Uh-oh.
RUN!
Into my truck, quick!
THOOM
THOOM
THOOM
Radislav... I don't think this is a nice, *normal* blood-sucking redevelopment corporation we're dealing with.
You're tellin' *me!*

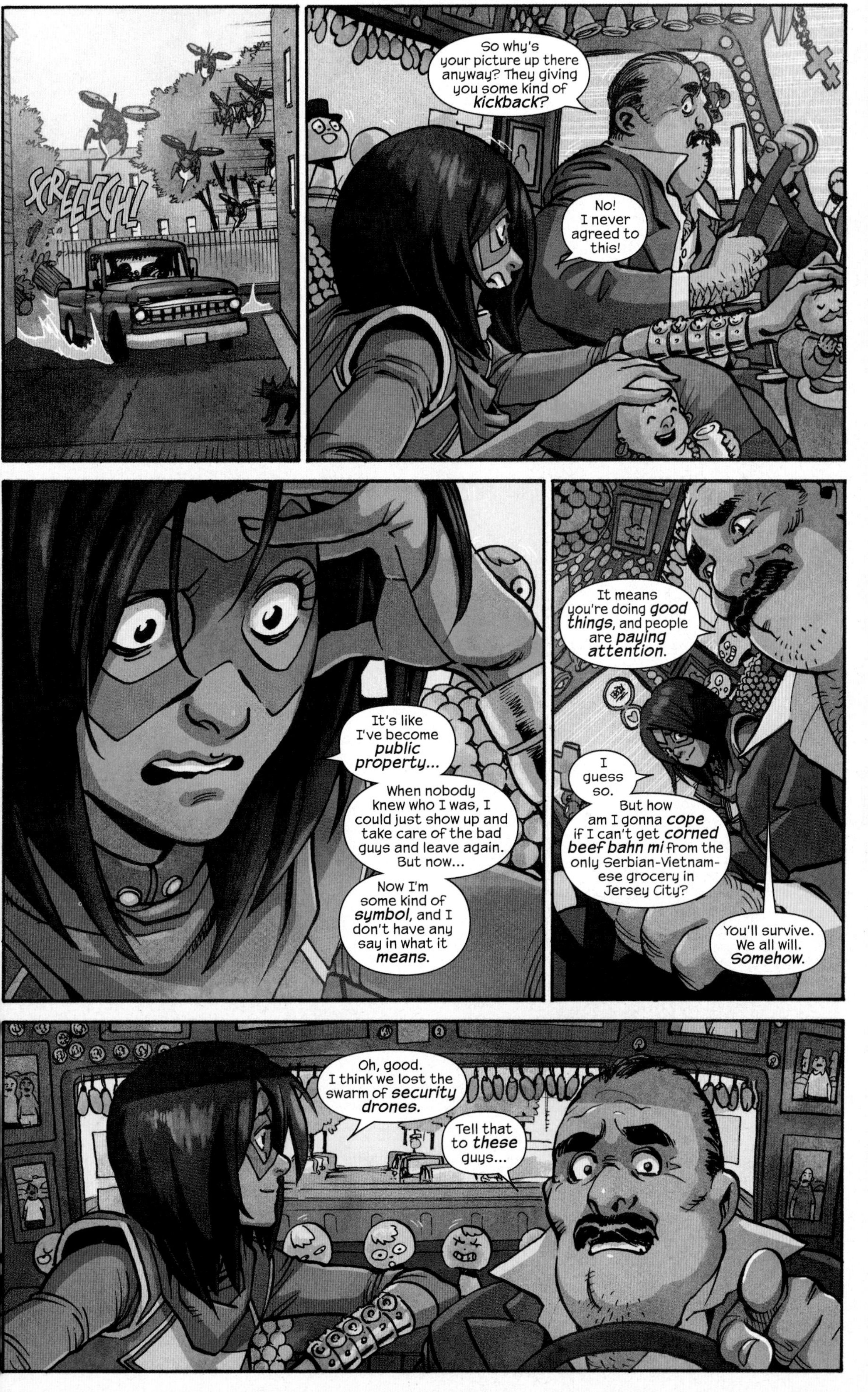
SCREEECH!
So why's your picture up there anyway? They giving you some kind of kickback?
No! I never agreed to this!
It's like I've become public property...
When nobody knew who I was, I could just show up and take care of the bad guys and leave again. But now...
Now I'm some kind of symbol, and I don't have any say in what it means.
It means you're doing good things, and people are paying attention.
I guess so.
But how am I gonna cope if I can't get corned beef bahn mi from the only Serbian-Vietnamese grocery in Jersey City?
You'll survive. We all will. Somehow.
Oh, good. I think we lost the swarm of security drones.
Tell that to these guys...

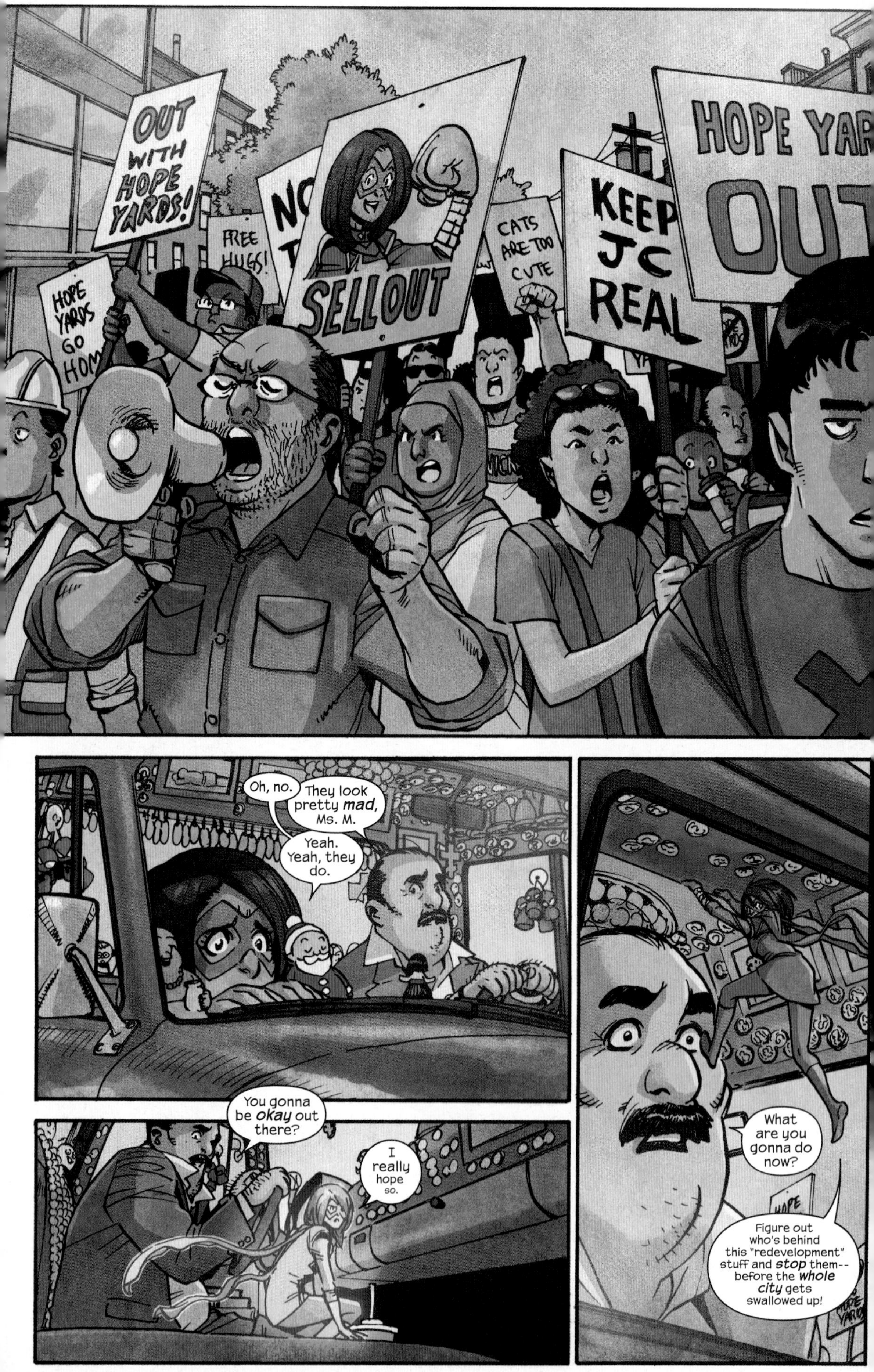
OUT WITH HOPE YARDS!
FREE HUGS!
HOPE YARDS GO HOM
SELLOUT
CATS ARE TOO CUTE
KEEP JC REAL
HOPE YAR OUT
Oh, no.
They look pretty *mad*, Ms. M.
Yeah. Yeah, they do.
What are you gonna do now?
Figure out who's behind this "redevelopment" stuff and *stop* them--before the *whole city* gets swallowed up!
You gonna be *okay* out there?
I really hope so.

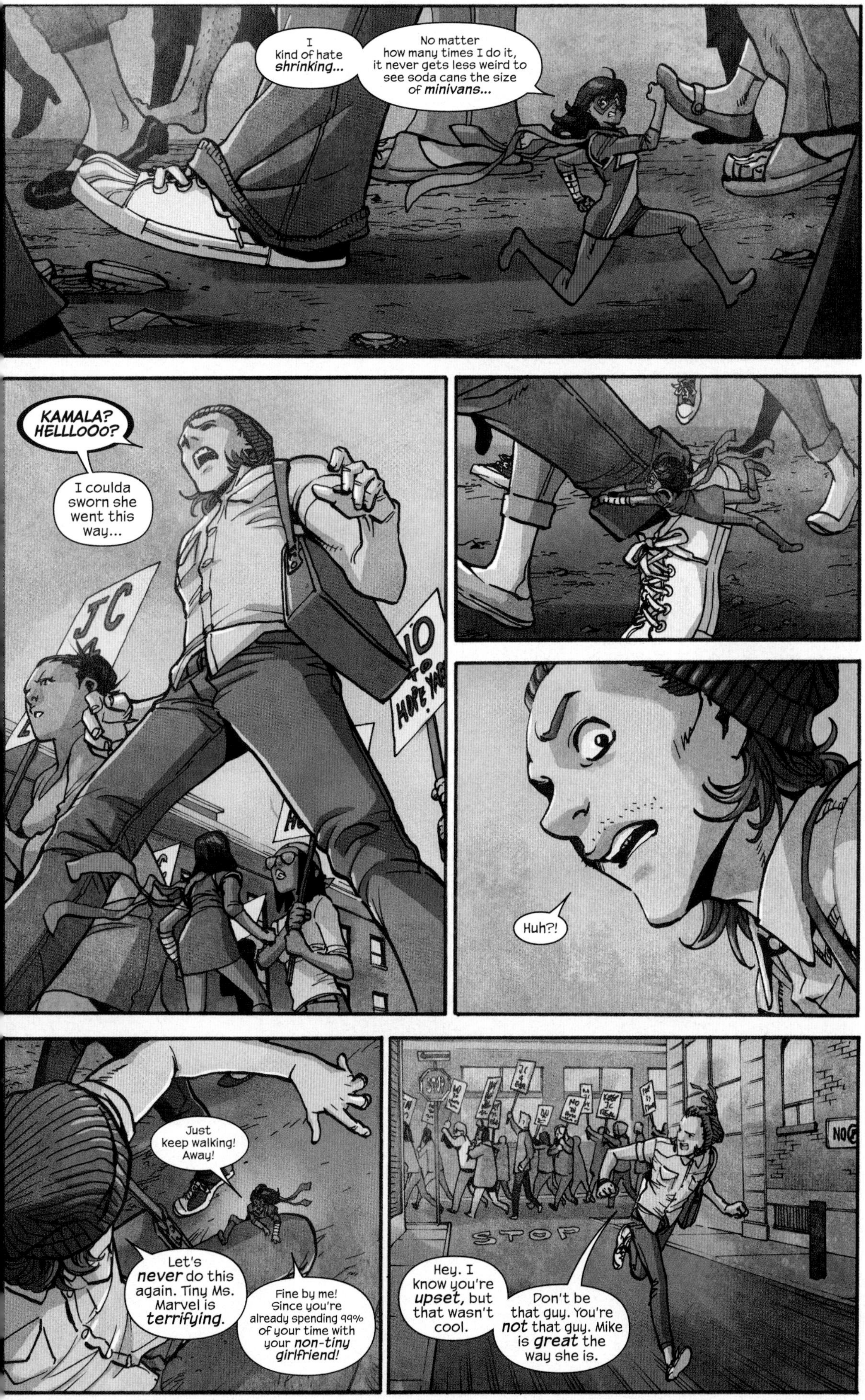
I kind of hate *shrinking...*
No matter how many times I do it, it never gets less weird to see soda cans the size of *minivans...*
KAMALA? HELLLOOo?
I coulda sworn she went this way...
Huh?!
Just keep walking! Away!
Let's *never* do this again. Tiny Ms. Marvel is *terrifying*.
Fine by me! Since you're already spending 99% of your time with your *non-tiny girlfriend!*
Hey. I know you're *upset*, but that wasn't cool.
Don't be that guy. You're *not* that guy. Mike is *great* the way she is.
STOP

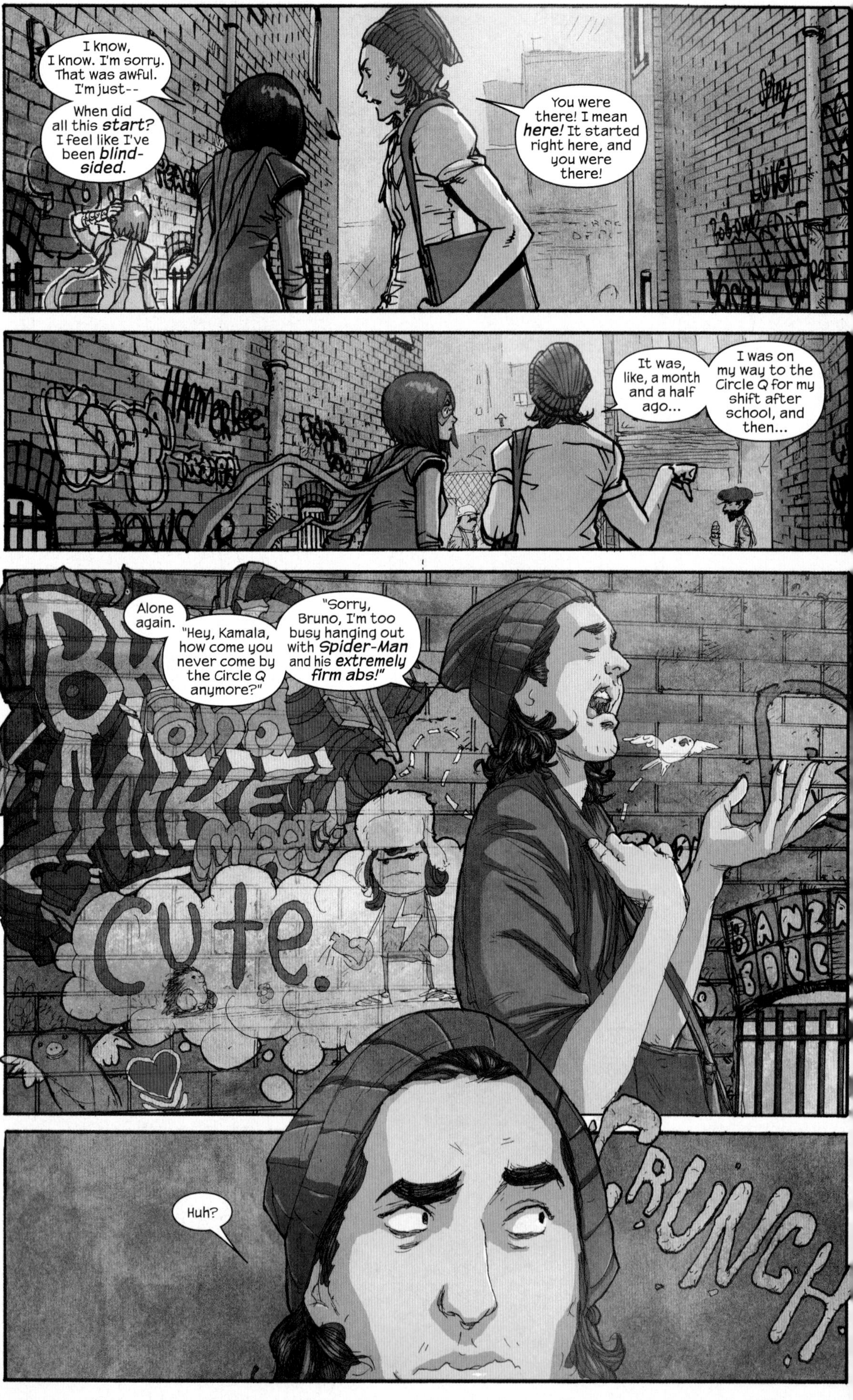
I know, I know. I'm sorry. That was awful. I'm just--
When did all this start? I feel like I've been blind-sided.
You were there! I mean here! It started right here, and you were there!
It was, like, a month and a half ago...
I was on my way to the Circle Q for my shift after school, and then...
Alone again.
"Hey, Kamala, how come you never come by the Circle Q anymore?"
"Sorry, Bruno, I'm too busy hanging out with Spider-Man and his extremely firm abs!"
Cute.
Huh?
RUNCH

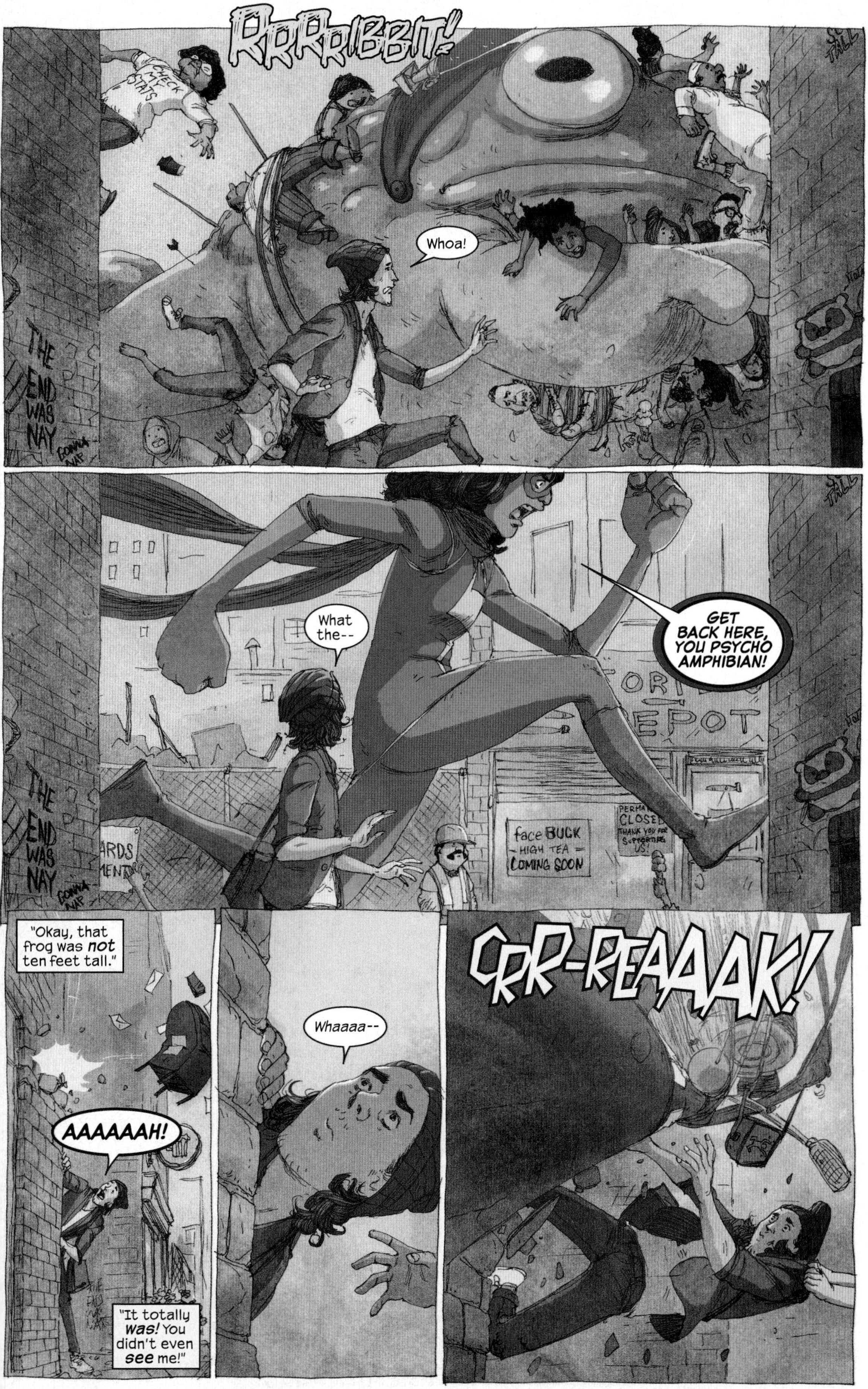
RRRIBBIT!
CHECK MY STATS
Whoa!
THE END WAS NAY
GONNA NAP
What the--
GET BACK HERE, YOU PSYCHO AMPHIBIAN!
face BUCK
HIGH TEA
COMING SOON
CLOSED
THANK YOU FOR SUPPORTING US!
"Okay, that frog was not ten feet tall."
AAAAAAH!
"It totally was! You didn't even see me!"
Whaaaa--
CRR-REAAAK!

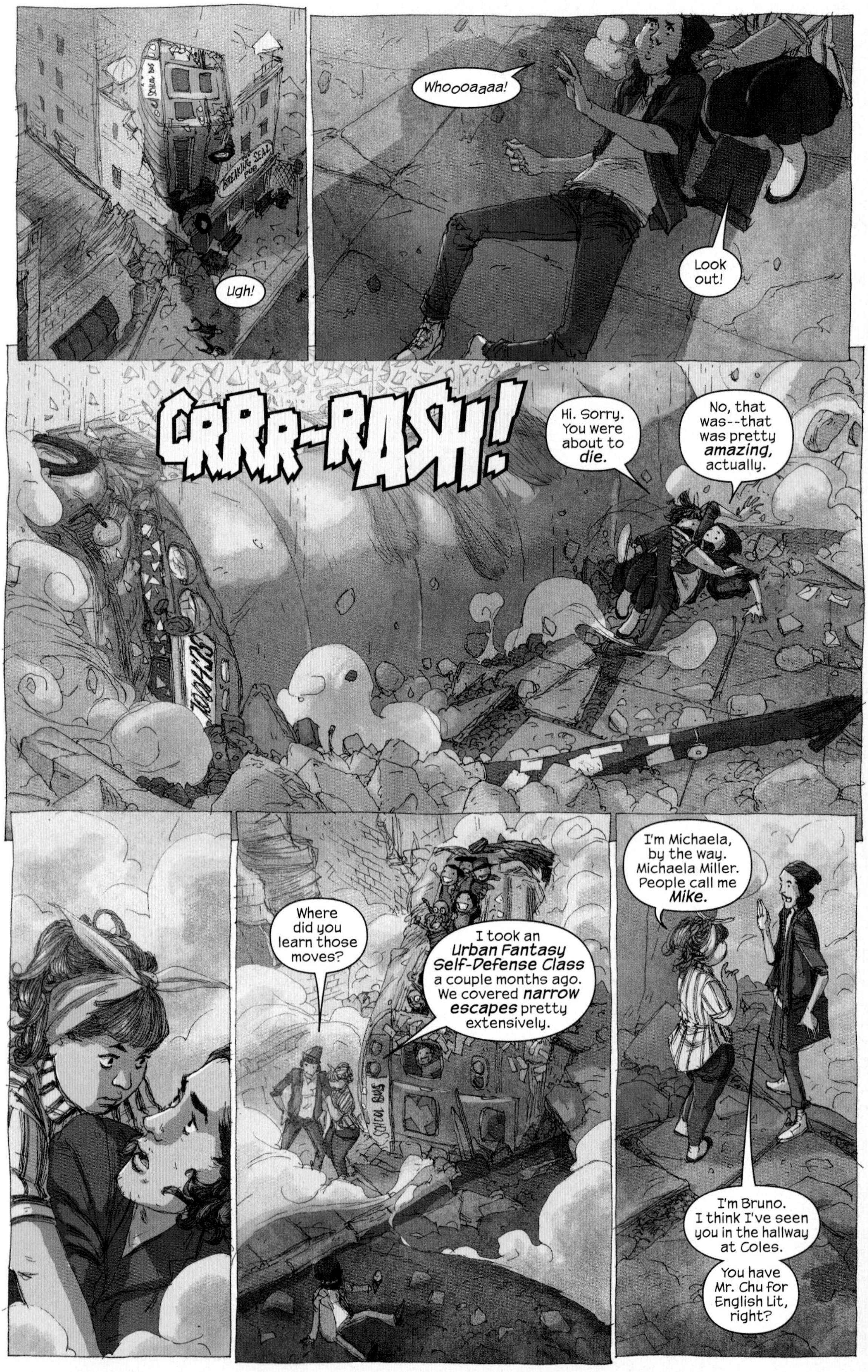

SCHOOL BUS
BREAKING SEAL PUB
Ugh!
Whoooaaaa!
Look out!
CRRR-RASH!
Hi. Sorry. You were about to *die.*
No, that was--that was pretty ***amazing,*** actually.
SCHOOL
Where did you learn those moves?
I took an *Urban Fantasy Self-Defense Class* a couple months ago. We covered *narrow **escapes*** pretty extensively.
SCHOOL BUS
I'm Michaela, by the way. Michaela Miller. People call me ***Mike.***
I'm Bruno. I think I've seen you in the hallway at Coles.
You have Mr. Chu for English Lit, right?

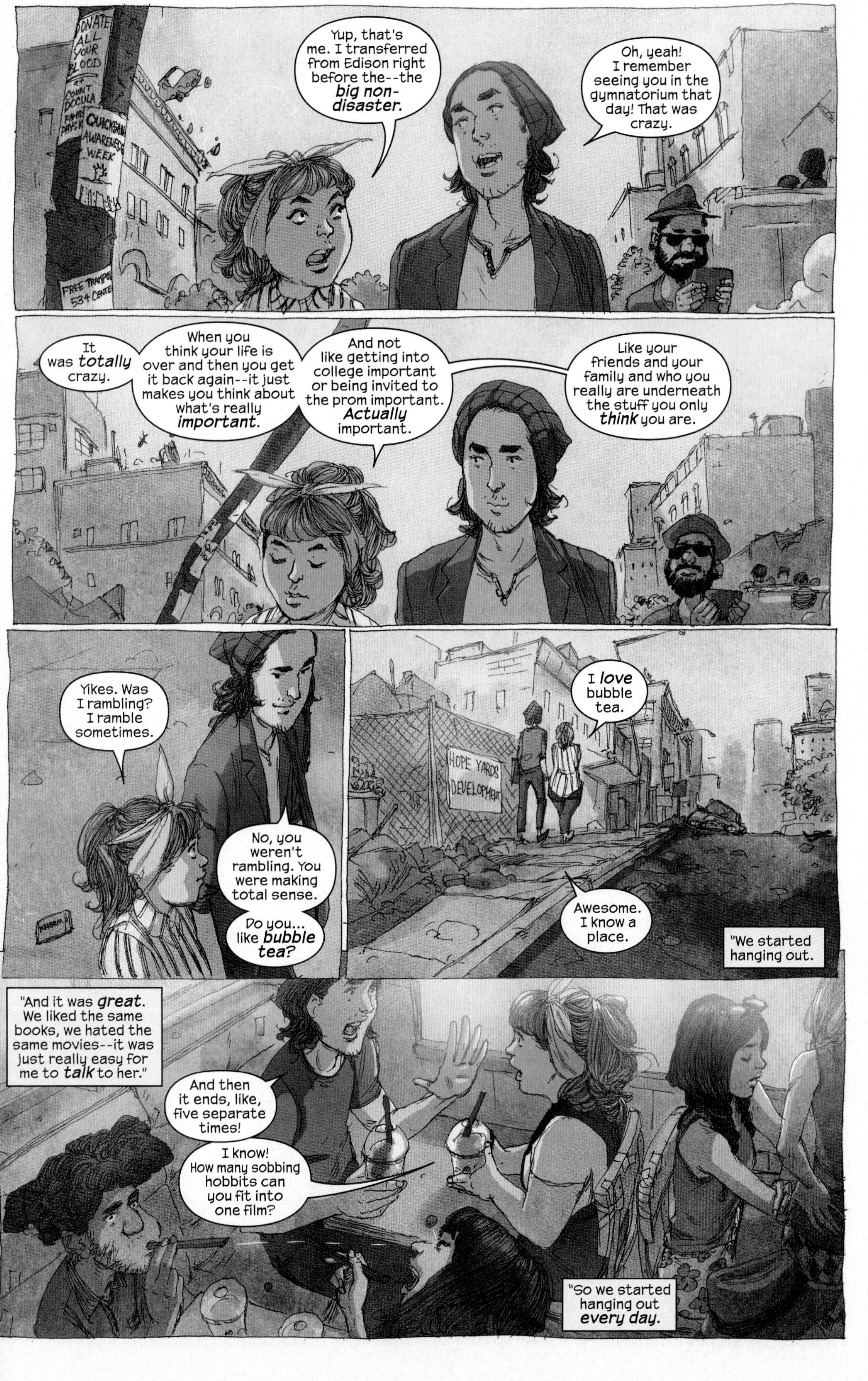
DONATE ALL YOUR BLOOD
COUNT DOCULA
QUICKSAND AWARENESS WEEK
Yup, that's me. I transferred from Edison right before the--the *big non-disaster.*
Oh, yeah! I remember seeing you in the gymnatorium that day! That was crazy.
It was *totally* crazy.
When you think your life is over and then you get it back again--it just makes you think about what's really *important*.
And not like getting into college important or being invited to the prom important. *Actually* important.
Like your friends and your family and who you really are underneath the stuff you only *think* you are.
Yikes. Was I rambling? I ramble sometimes.
No, you weren't rambling. You were making total sense.
Do you... like *bubble tea?*
I *love* bubble tea.
HOPE YARDS DEVELOPMENT
Awesome. I know a place.
"We started hanging out.
"And it was *great*. We liked the same books, we hated the same movies--it was just really easy for me to *talk* to her."
And then it ends, like, five separate times!
I know! How many sobbing hobbits can you fit into one film?
"So we started hanging out *every day*.

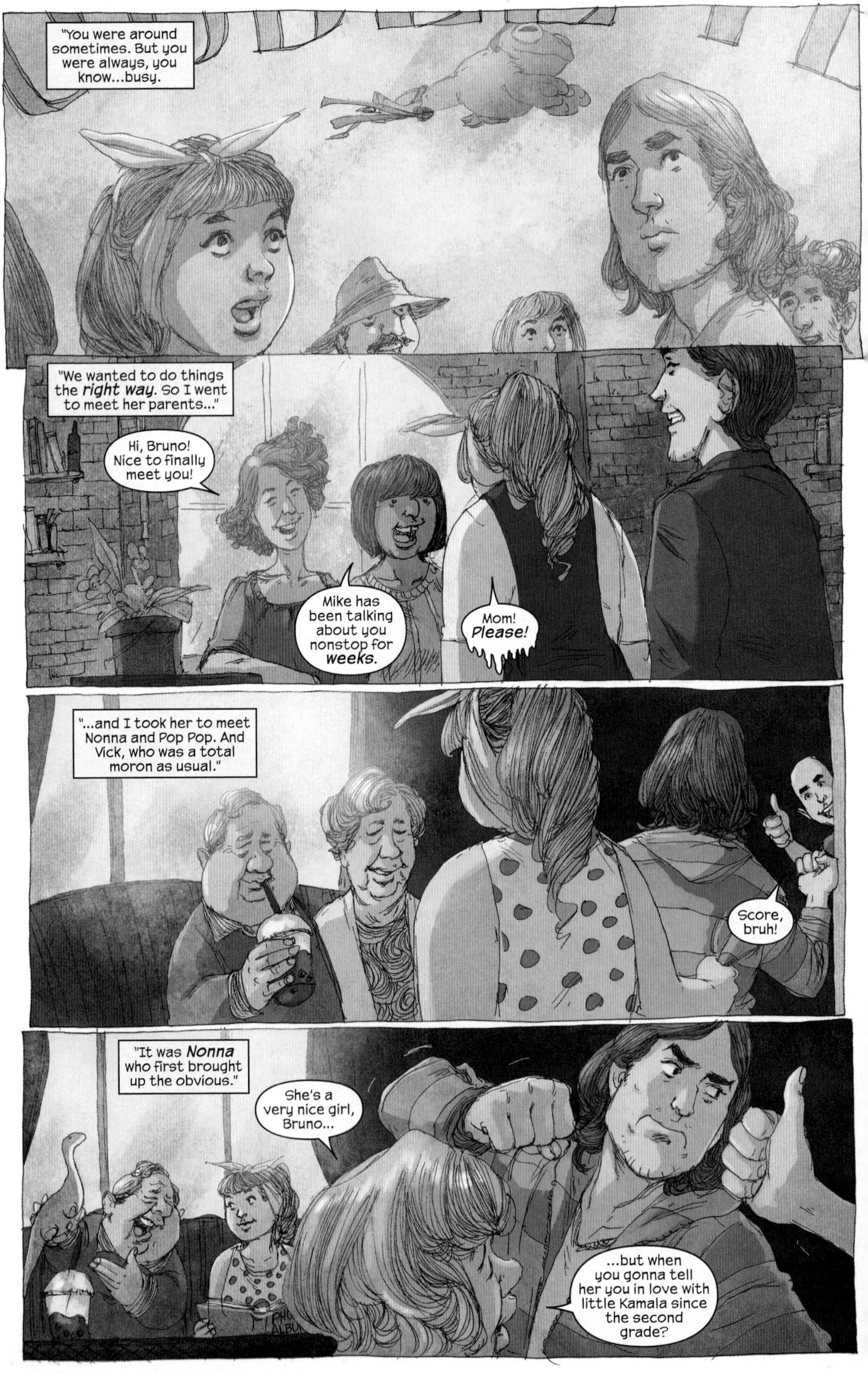
"You were around sometimes. But you were always, you know...busy.
"We wanted to do things the *right way*. So I went to meet her parents..."
Hi, Bruno! Nice to finally meet you!
Mike has been talking about you nonstop for *weeks*.
Mom! *Please!*
"...and I took her to meet Nonna and Pop Pop. And Vick, who was a total moron as usual."
Score, bruh!
"It was *Nonna* who first brought up the obvious."
She's a very nice girl, Bruno...
...but when you gonna tell her you in love with little Kamala since the second grade?

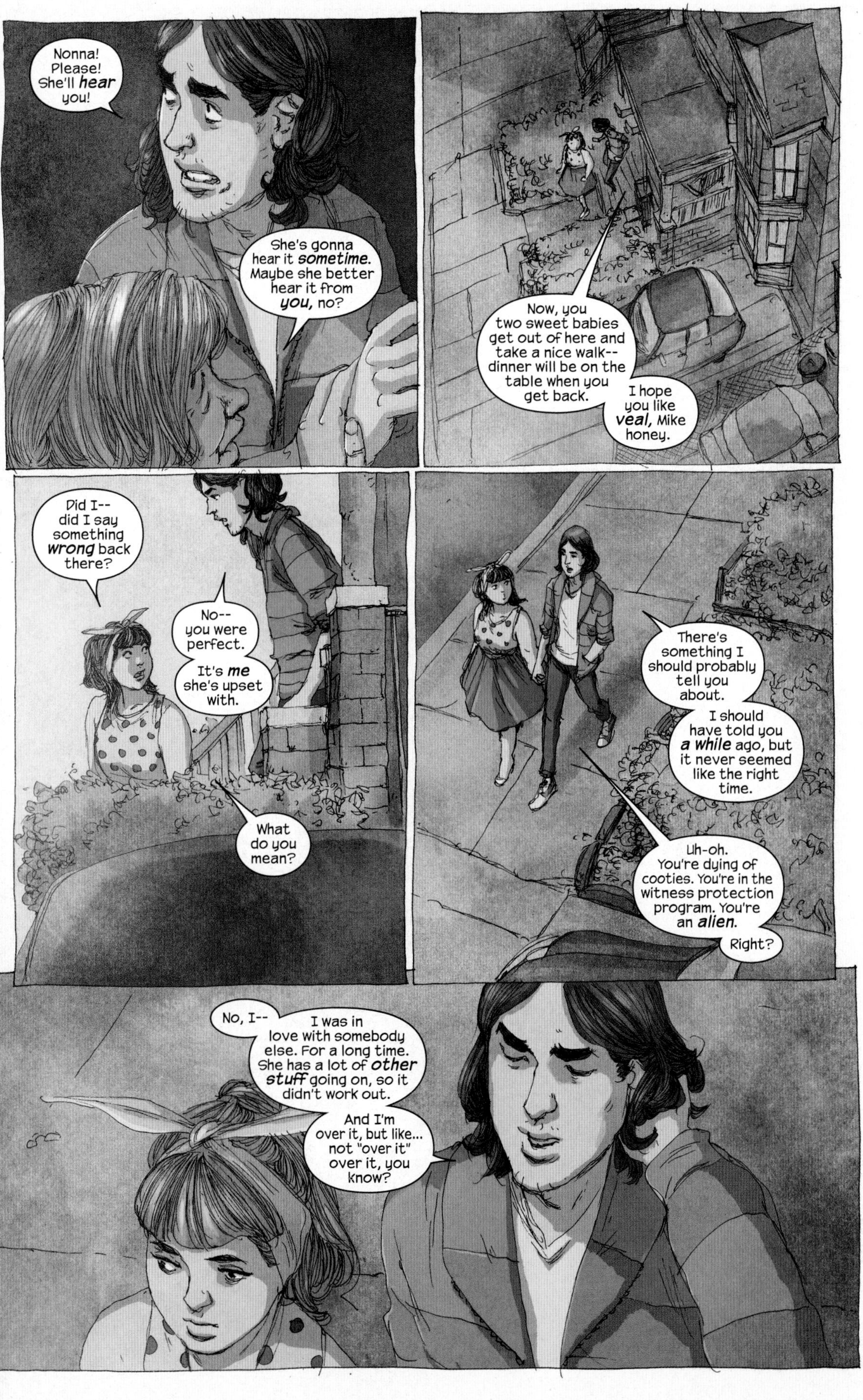
Nonna! Please! She'll hear you!
She's gonna hear it sometime. Maybe she better hear it from you, no?
Now, you two sweet babies get out of here and take a nice walk-- dinner will be on the table when you get back.
I hope you like veal, Mike honey.
Did I-- did I say something wrong back there?
No-- you were perfect.
It's me she's upset with.
What do you mean?
There's something I should probably tell you about.
I should have told you a while ago, but it never seemed like the right time.
Uh-oh. You're dying of cooties. You're in the witness protection program. You're an alien.
Right?
No, I--
I was in love with somebody else. For a long time. She has a lot of other stuff going on, so it didn't work out.
And I'm over it, but like... not "over it" over it, you know?

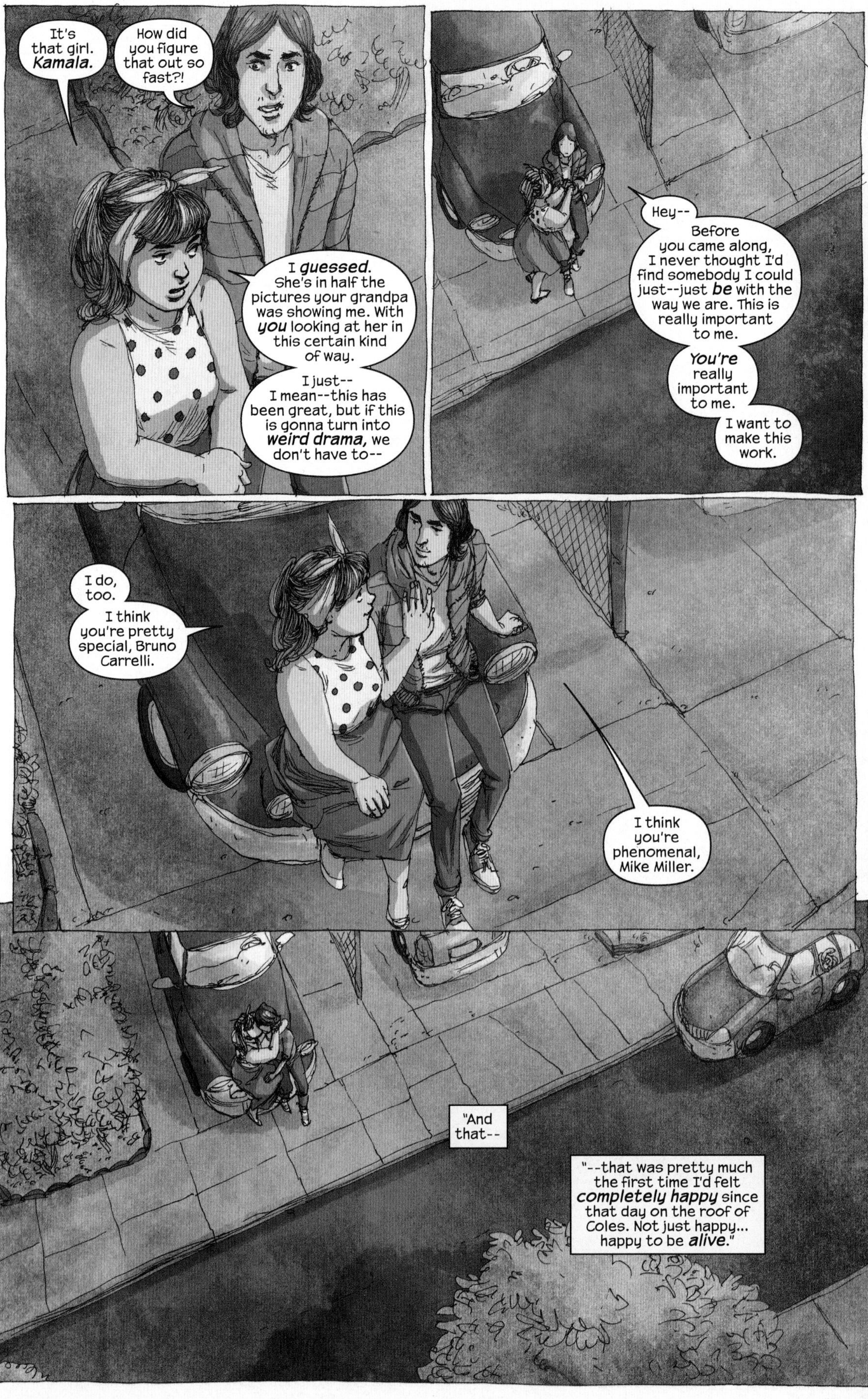
It's that girl. *Kamala.*
How did you figure that out so fast?!
I *guessed.* She's in half the pictures your grandpa was showing me. With *you* looking at her in this certain kind of way.
I just-- I mean--this has been great, but if this is gonna turn into *weird drama,* we don't have to--
Hey--
Before you came along, I never thought I'd find somebody I could just--just *be* with the way we are. This is really important to me.
You're really important to me.
I want to make this work.
I do, too.
I think you're pretty special, Bruno Carrelli.
I think you're phenomenal, Mike Miller.
"And that--
"--that was pretty much the first time I'd felt *completely happy* since that day on the roof of Coles. Not just happy... happy to be *alive.*"

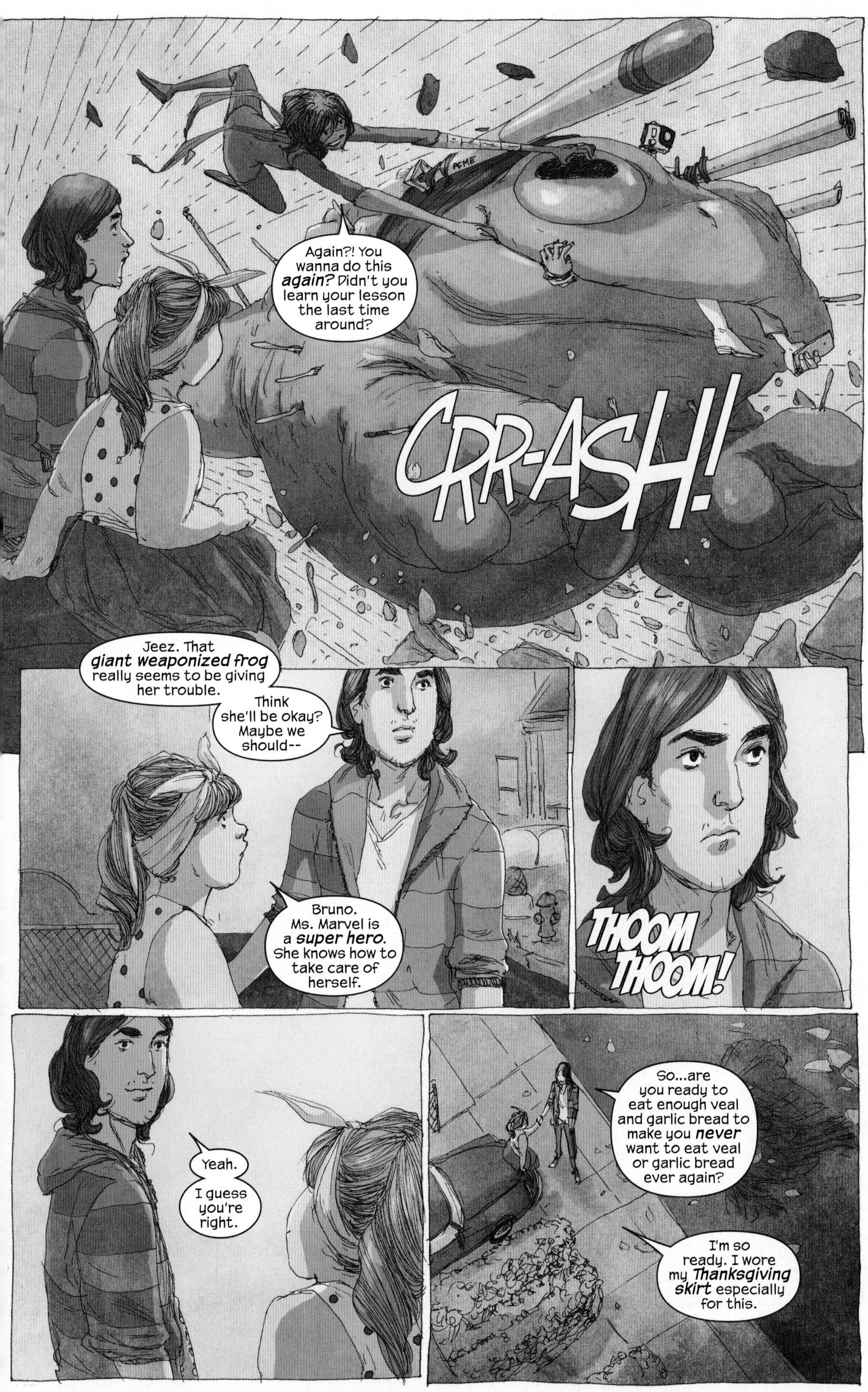
Again?! You wanna do this *again?* Didn't you learn your lesson the last time around?
CRR-ASH!!
Jeez. That *giant weaponized frog* really seems to be giving her trouble.
Think she'll be okay? Maybe we should--
Bruno. Ms. Marvel is a *super hero*. She knows how to take care of herself.
THOOM THOOM!
Yeah.
I guess you're right.
So...are you ready to eat enough veal and garlic bread to make you *never* want to eat veal or garlic bread ever again?
I'm so ready. I wore my *Thanksgiving skirt* especially for this.

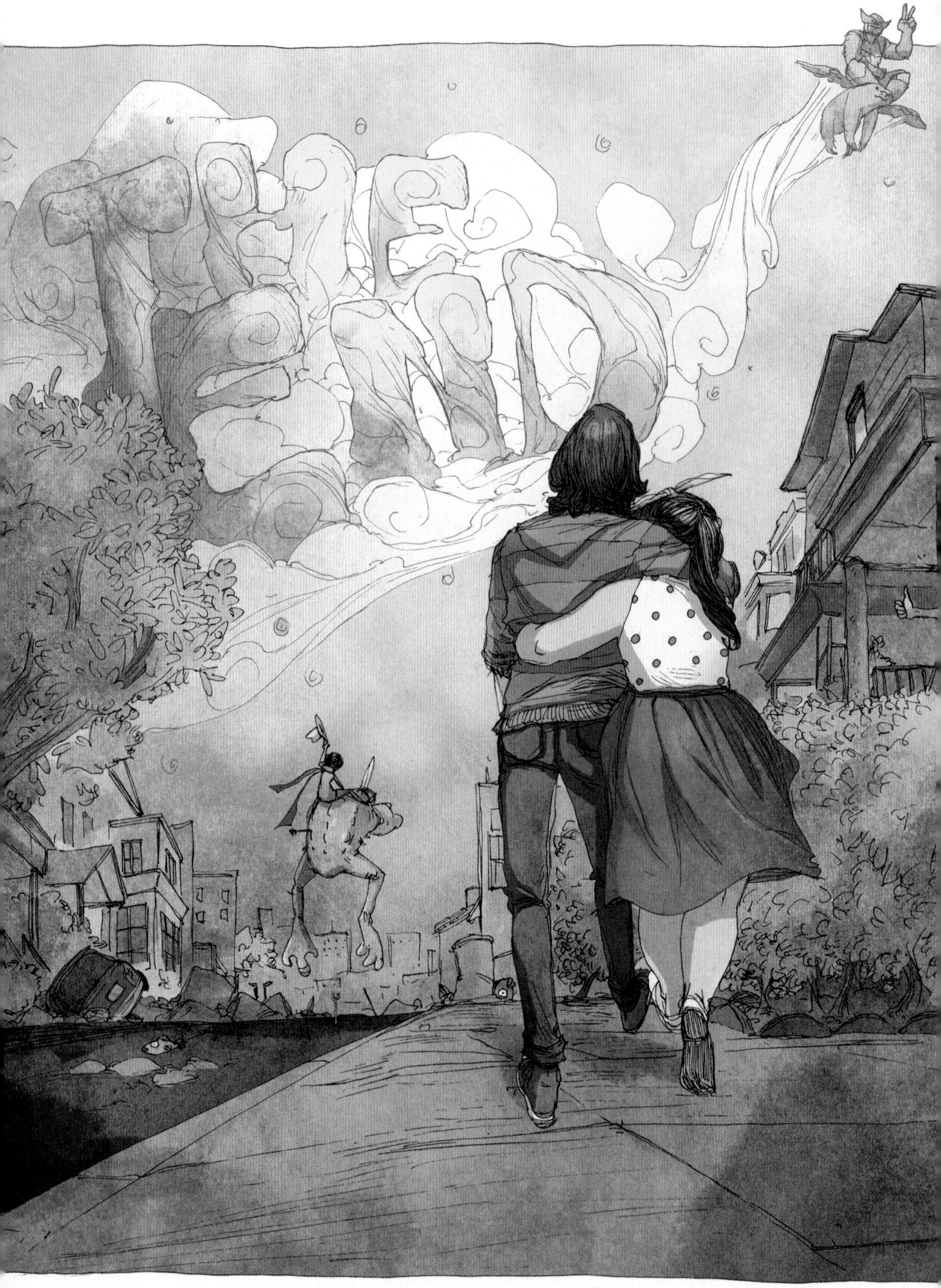
THE END

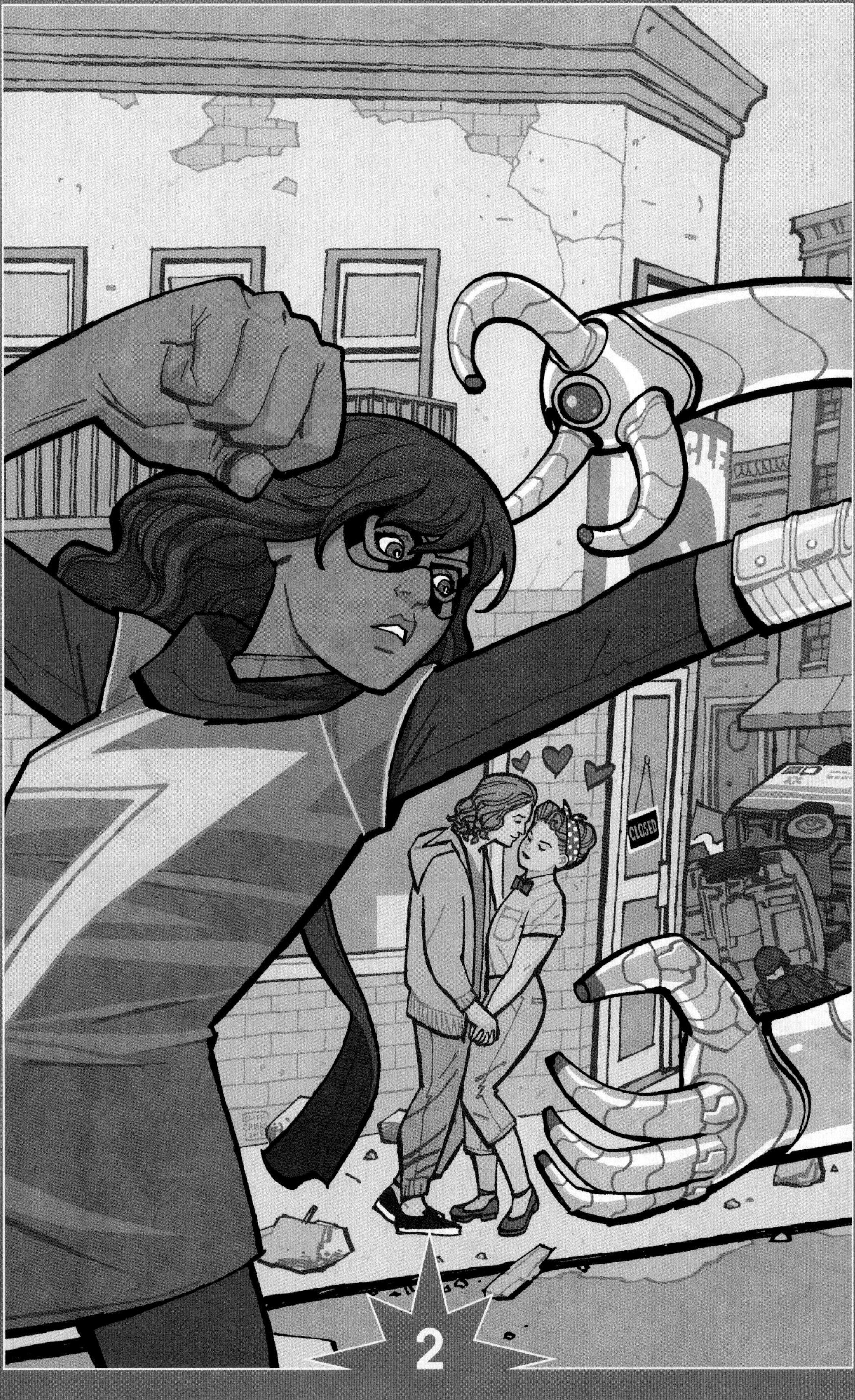
CLOSED
2

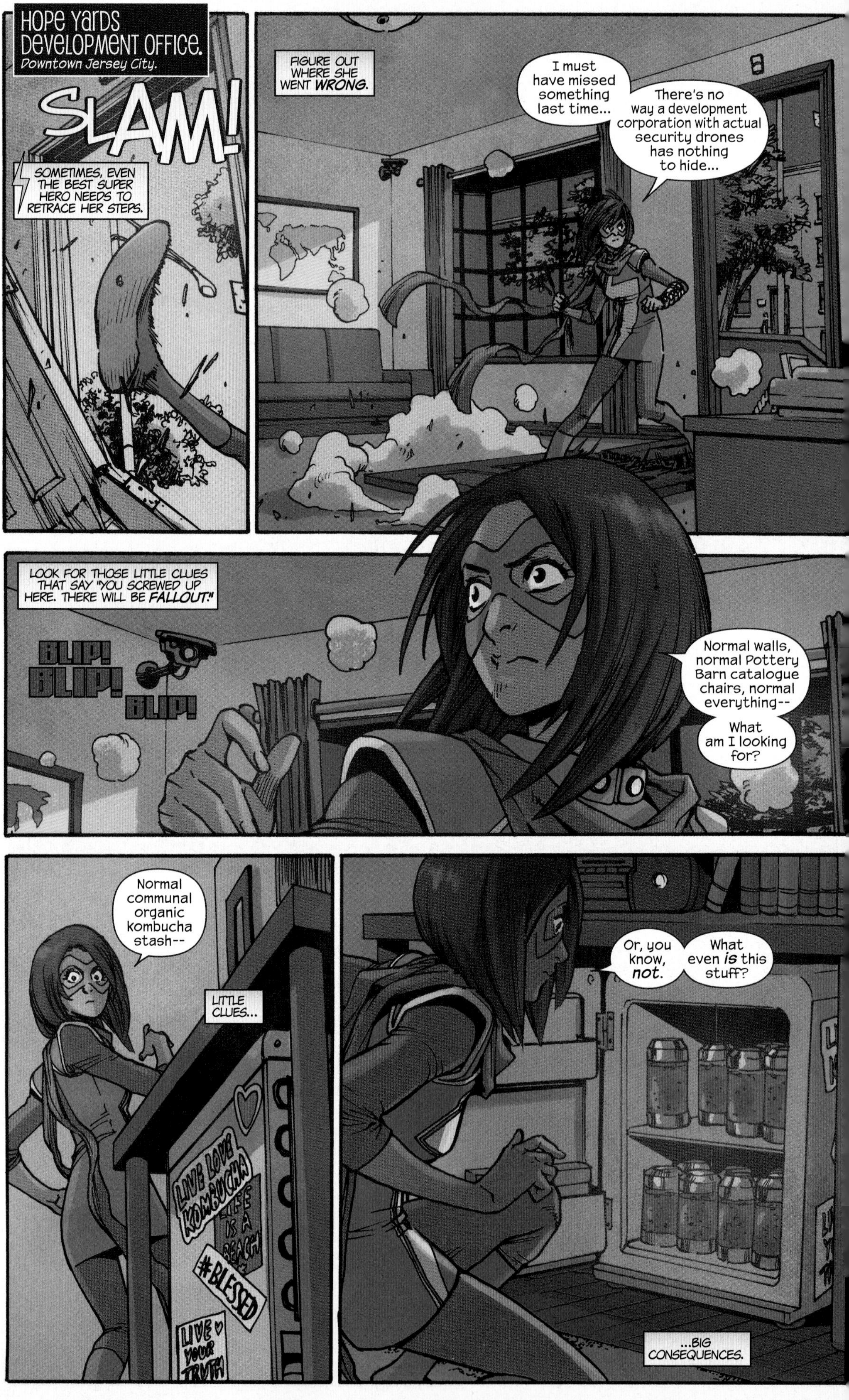

HOPE YARDS DEVELOPMENT OFFICE.
Downtown Jersey City.
SLAM!
SOMETIMES, EVEN THE BEST SUPER HERO NEEDS TO RETRACE HER STEPS.
FIGURE OUT WHERE SHE WENT WRONG.
I must have missed something last time...
There's no way a development corporation with actual security drones has nothing to hide...
LOOK FOR THOSE LITTLE CLUES THAT SAY "YOU SCREWED UP HERE. THERE WILL BE FALLOUT."
BLIP! BLIP! BLIP!
Normal walls, normal Pottery Barn catalogue chairs, normal everything--
What am I looking for?
Normal communal organic kombucha stash--
LITTLE CLUES...
LIVE LOVE KOMBUCHA
LIFE IS A BEACH
#BLESSED
LIVE YOUR TRUTH
Or, you know, not.
What even is this stuff?
...BIG CONSEQUENCES.

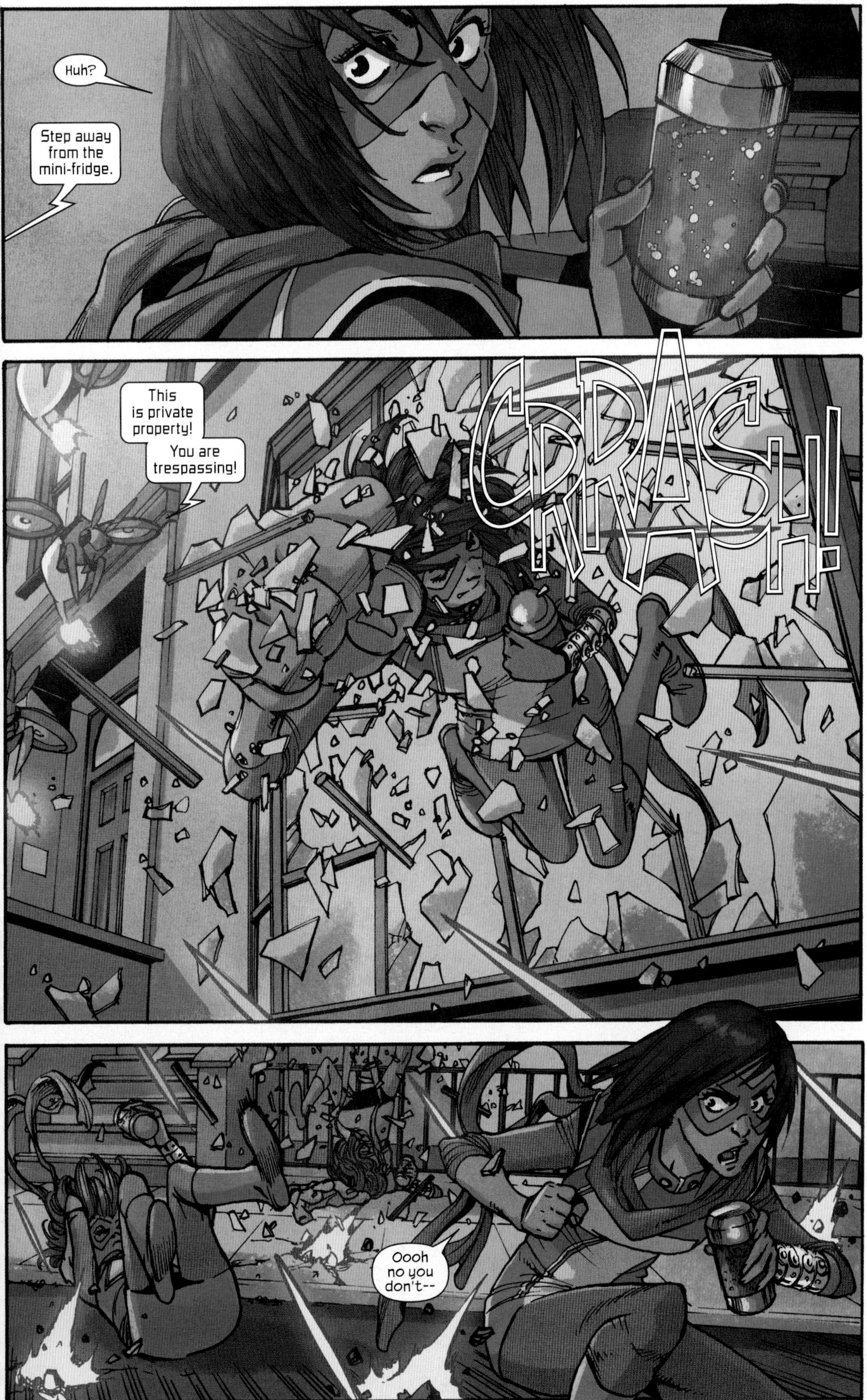
Huh?
Step away from the mini-fridge.
This is private property!
You are trespassing!
CRASH!
KRAAASH!
Oooh no you don't--

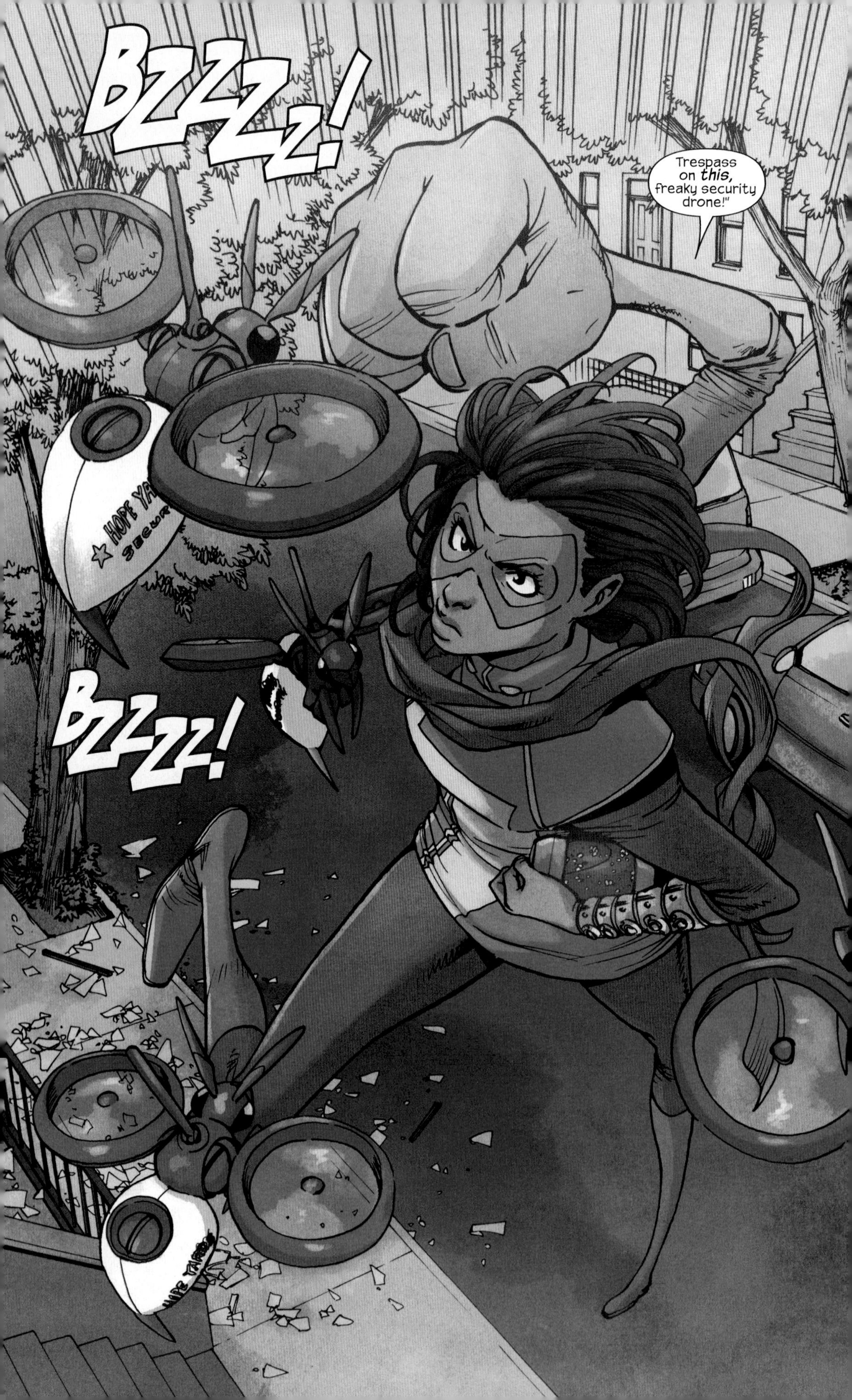
BZZZZz!
Trespass on this, freaky security drone!"
BZZZZ!

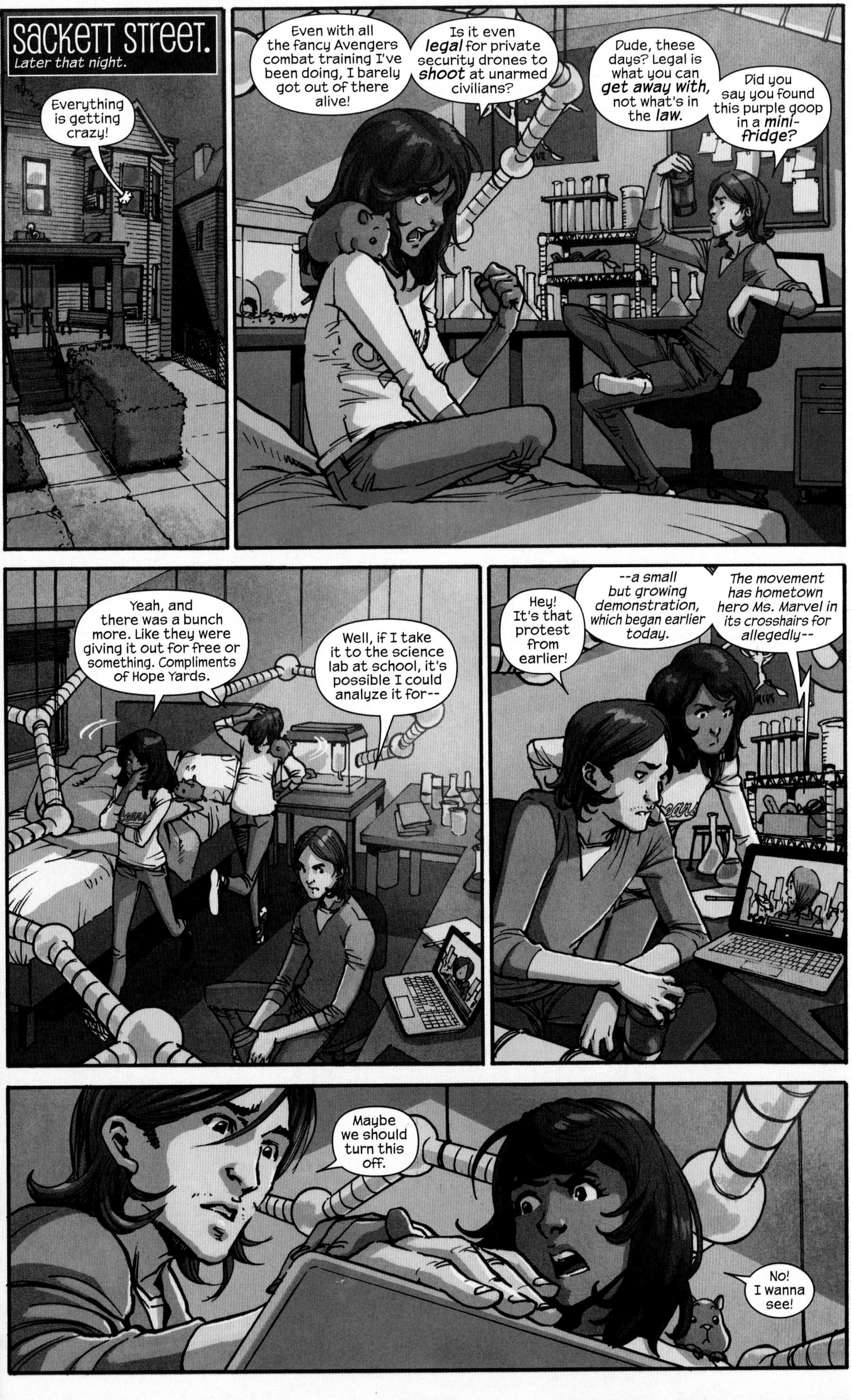
SACKETT STREET.
Later that night.
Everything is getting crazy!
Even with all the fancy Avengers combat training I've been doing, I barely got out of there alive!
Is it even legal for private security drones to shoot at unarmed civilians?
Dude, these days? Legal is what you can get away with, not what's in the law.
Did you say you found this purple goop in a mini-fridge?
Yeah, and there was a bunch more. Like they were giving it out for free or something. Compliments of Hope Yards.
Well, if I take it to the science lab at school, it's possible I could analyze it for--
Hey! It's that protest from earlier!
--a small but growing demonstration, which began earlier today.
The movement has hometown hero Ms. Marvel in its crosshairs for allegedly--
Maybe we should turn this off.
No! I wanna see!

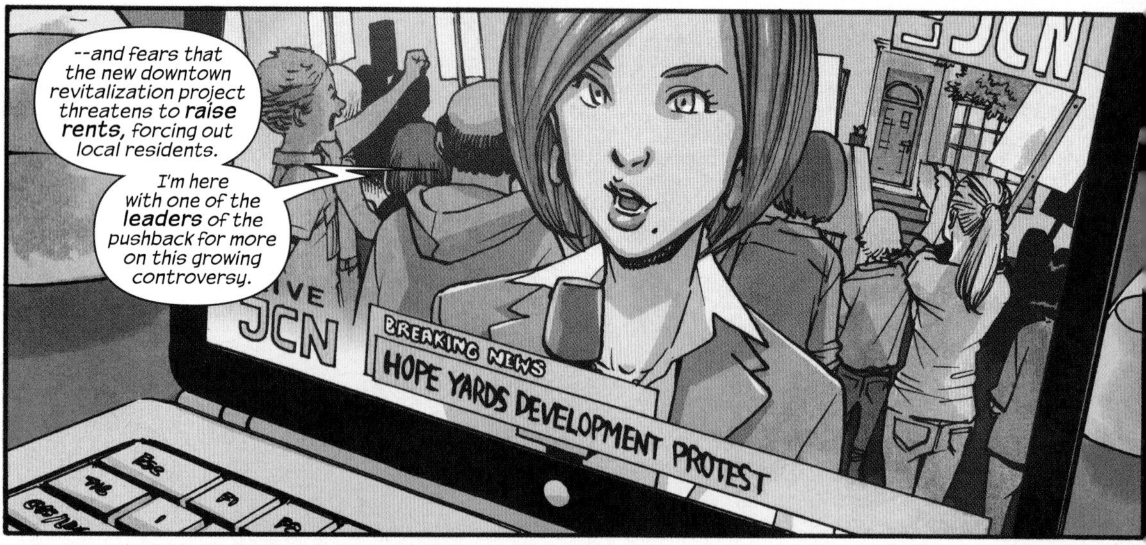
--and fears that the new downtown revitalization project threatens to **raise rents,** forcing out local residents.
I'm here with one of the **leaders** of the pushback for more on this growing controversy.
LIVE JCN
BREAKING NEWS
HOPE YARDS DEVELOPMENT PROTEST

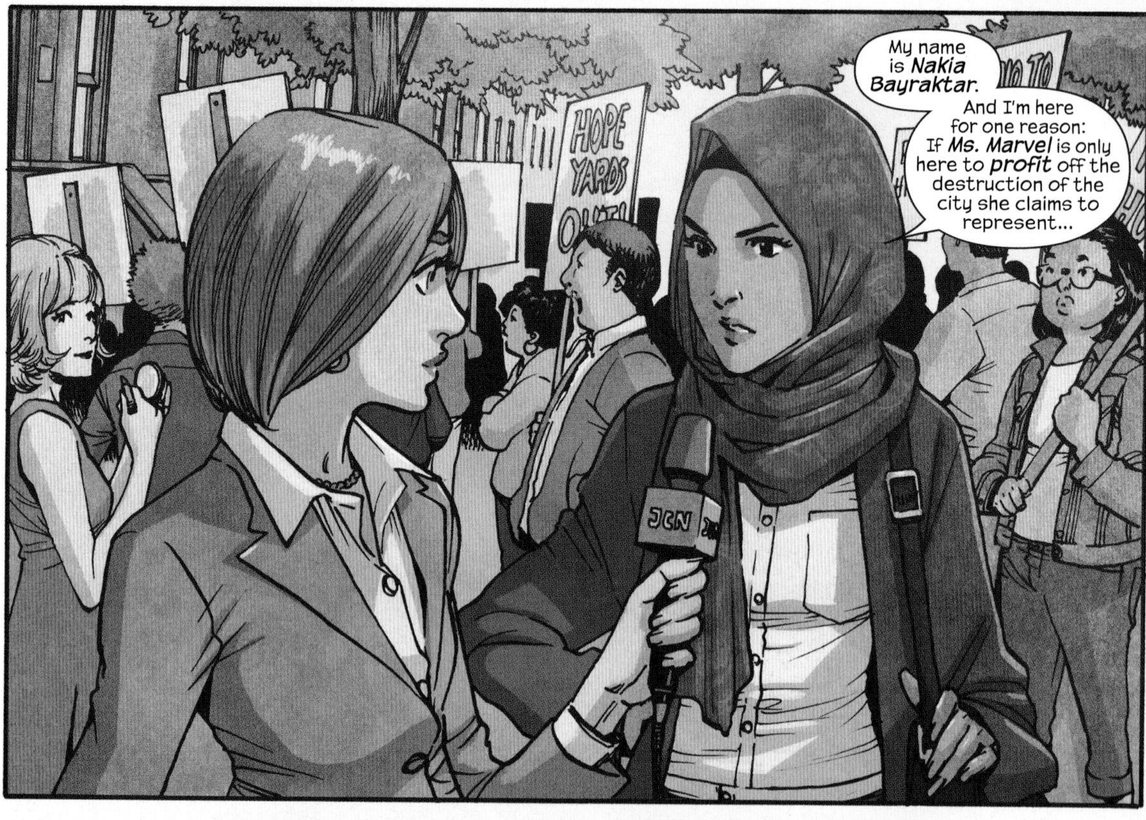
My name is *Nakia Bayraktar.*
And I'm here for one reason: If *Ms. Marvel* is only here to ***profit*** off the destruction of the city she claims to represent...
HOPE YARDS OUT!
JCN

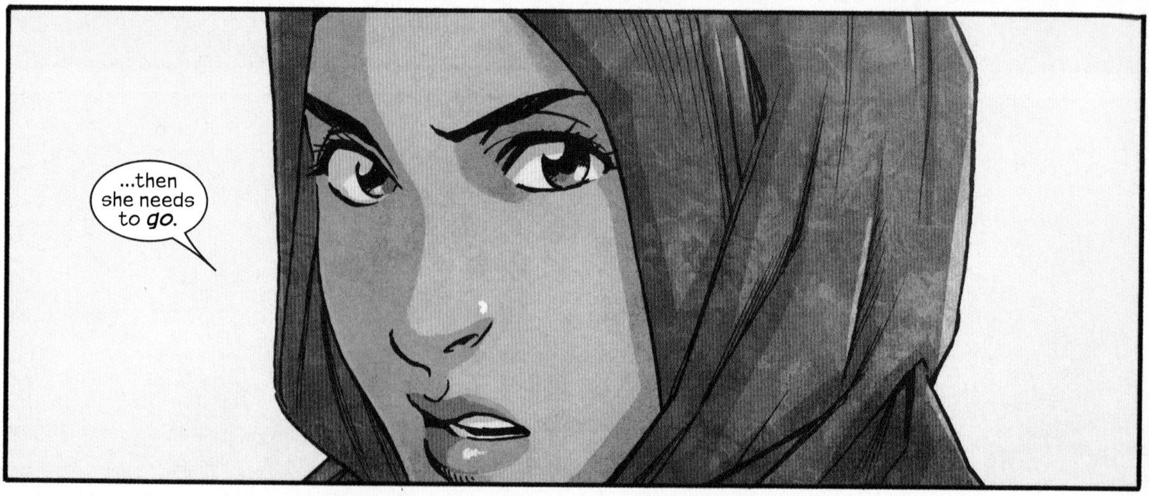
...then she needs to ***go.***

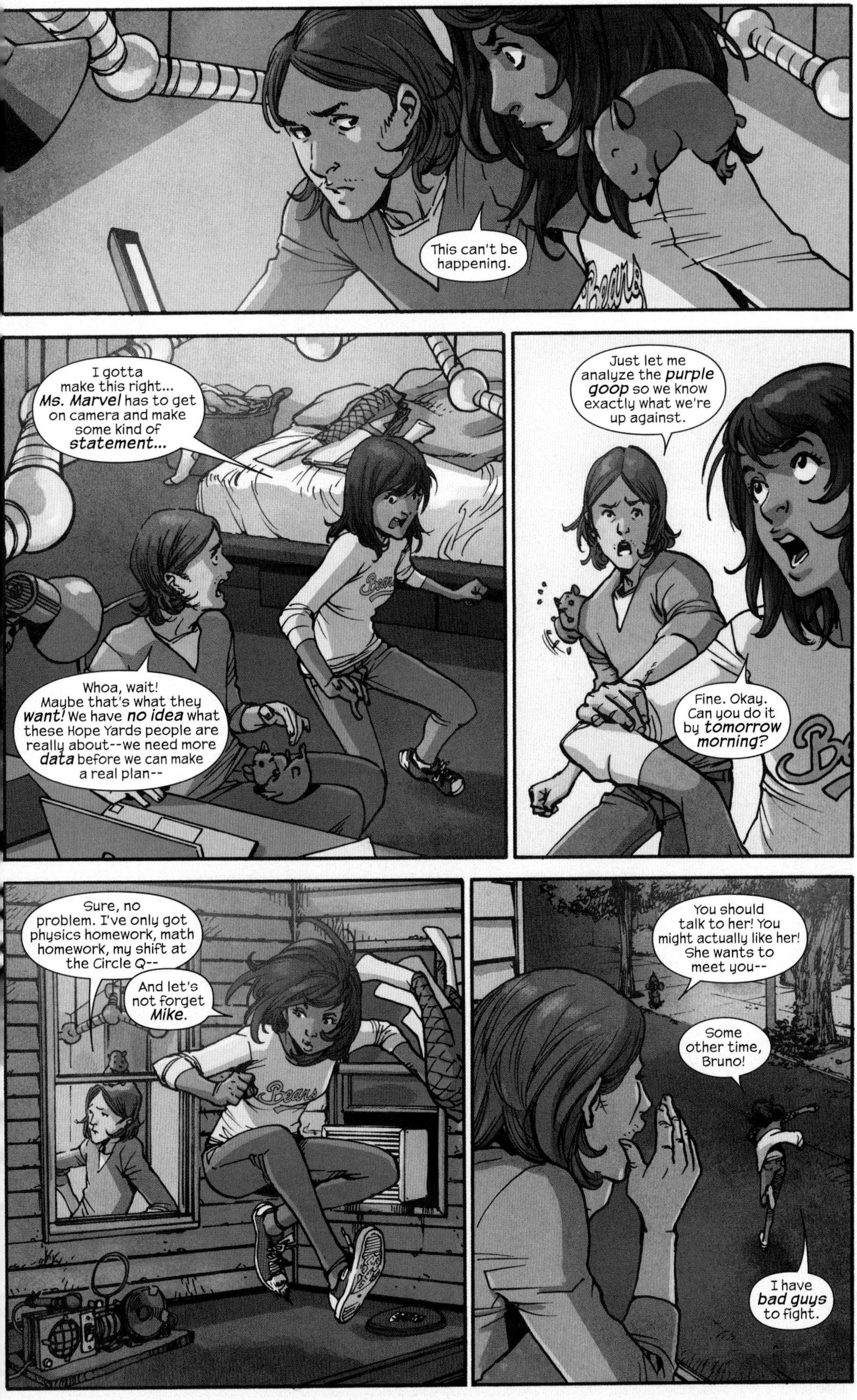
This can't be happening.
I gotta make this right... Ms. Marvel has to get on camera and make some kind of statement...
Whoa, wait! Maybe that's what they want! We have no idea what these Hope Yards people are really about--we need more data before we can make a real plan--
Just let me analyze the purple goop so we know exactly what we're up against.
Fine. Okay. Can you do it by tomorrow morning?
Sure, no problem. I've only got physics homework, math homework, my shift at the Circle Q--
And let's not forget Mike.
You should talk to her! You might actually like her! She wants to meet you--
Some other time, Bruno!
I have bad guys to fight.

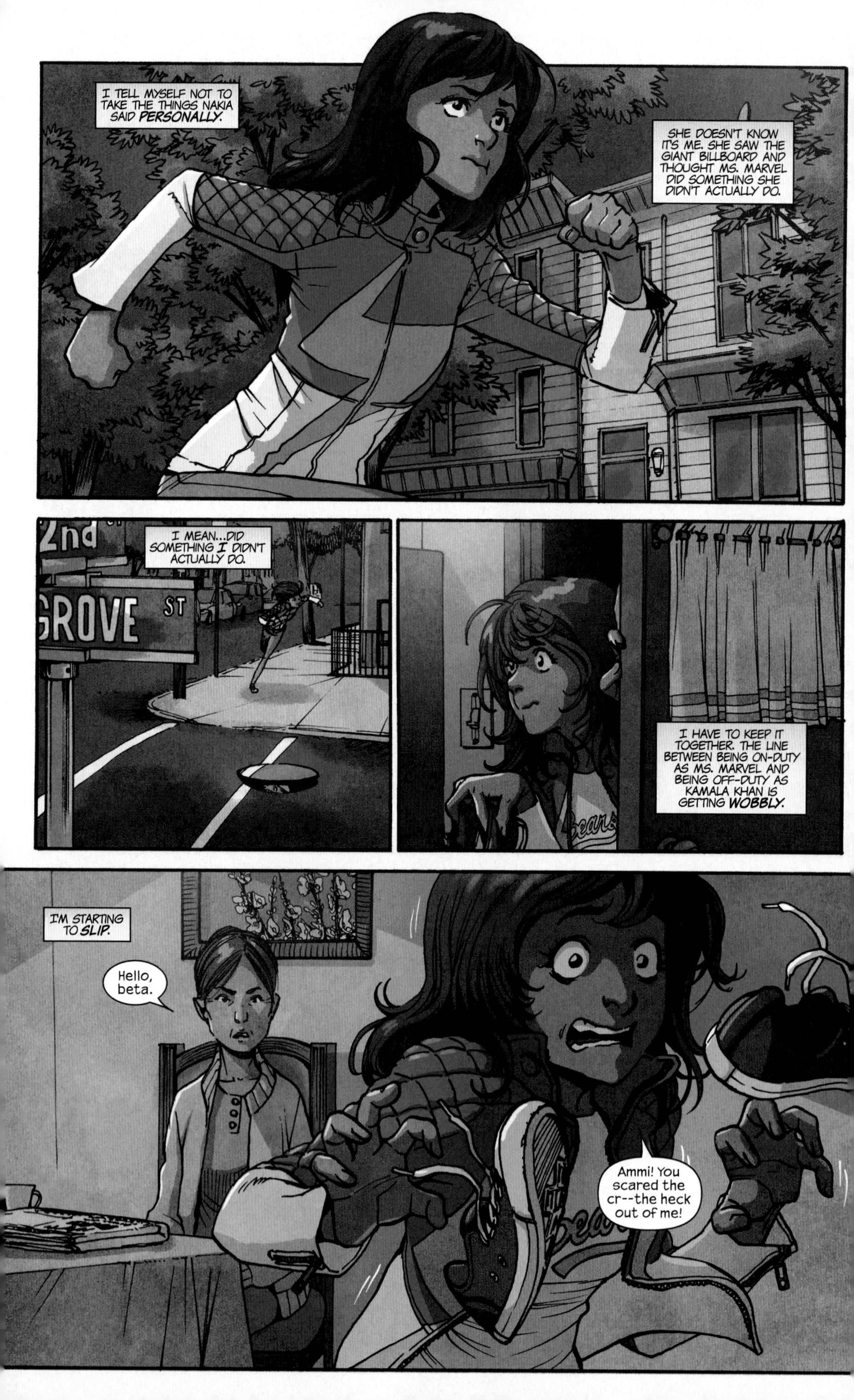
I TELL MYSELF NOT TO TAKE THE THINGS NAKIA SAID PERSONALLY.
SHE DOESN'T KNOW IT'S ME. SHE SAW THE GIANT BILLBOARD AND THOUGHT MS. MARVEL DID SOMETHING SHE DIDN'T ACTUALLY DO.
2nd
GROVE ST
I MEAN...DID SOMETHING I DIDN'T ACTUALLY DO.
I HAVE TO KEEP IT TOGETHER. THE LINE BETWEEN BEING ON-DUTY AS MS. MARVEL AND BEING OFF-DUTY AS KAMALA KHAN IS GETTING WOBBLY.
I'M STARTING TO SLIP.
Hello, beta.
Ammi! You scared the cr--the heck out of me!

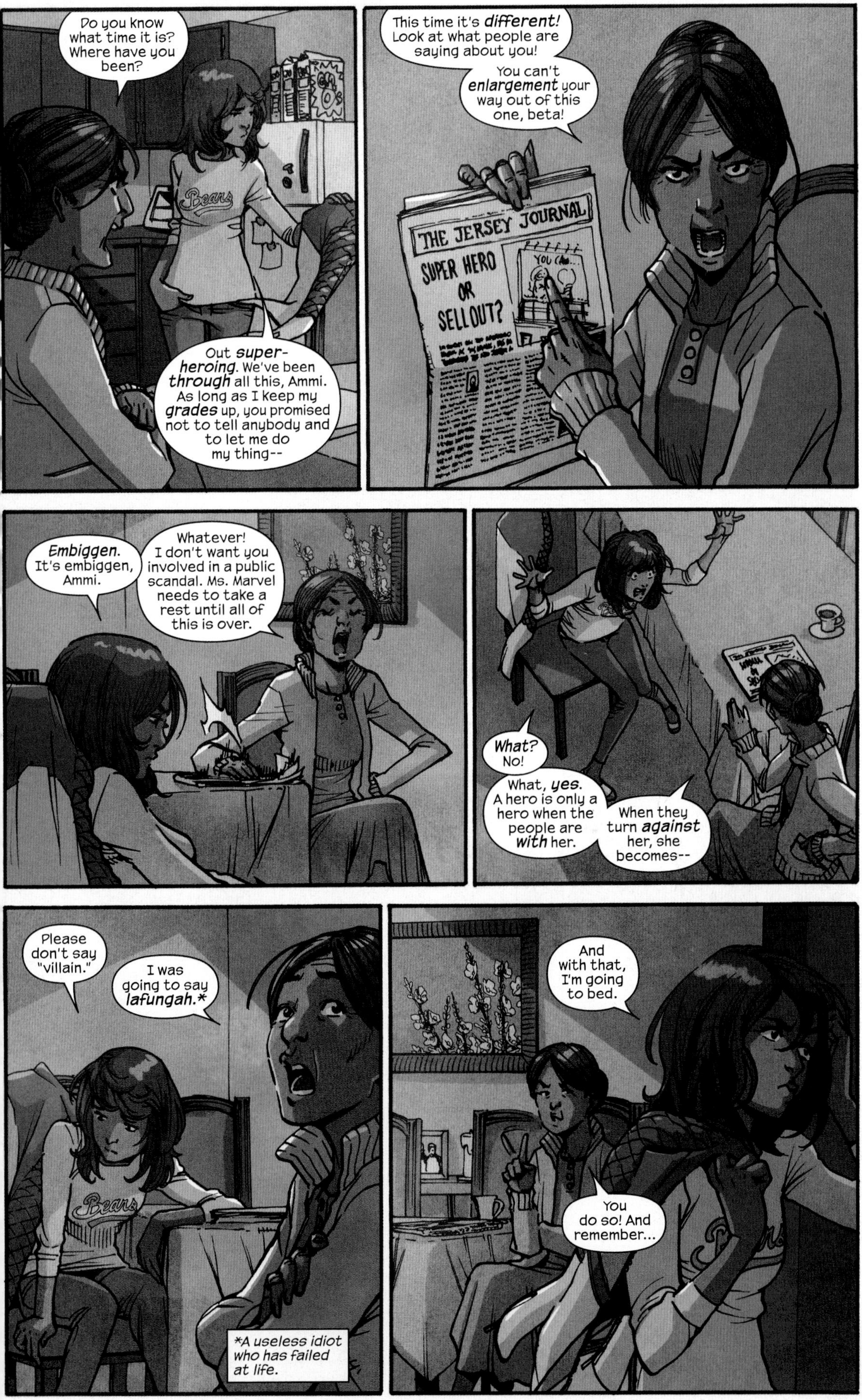

Do you know what time it is? Where have you been?
Out super-heroing. We've been through all this, Ammi. As long as I keep my grades up, you promised not to tell anybody and to let me do my thing--
This time it's different! Look at what people are saying about you!
You can't enlargement your way out of this one, beta!
THE JERSEY JOURNAL
SUPER HERO OR SELL OUT?
Embiggen. It's embiggen, Ammi.
Whatever! I don't want you involved in a public scandal. Ms. Marvel needs to take a rest until all of this is over.
What? No!
What, yes. A hero is only a hero when the people are with her.
When they turn against her, she becomes--
Please don't say "villain."
I was going to say lafungah.*
*A useless idiot who has failed at life.
And with that, I'm going to bed.
You do so! And remember...

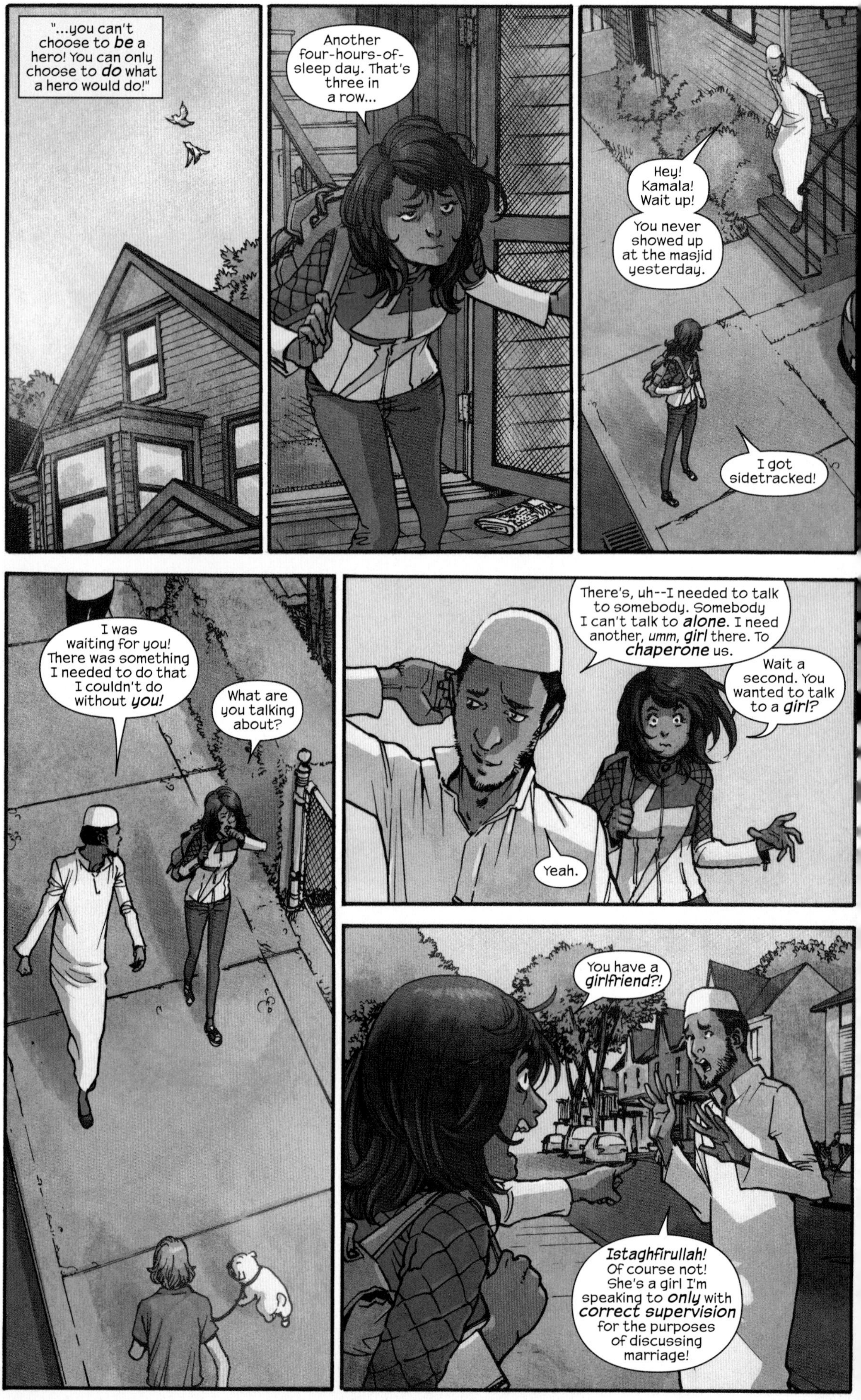
"...you can't choose to **be** a hero! You can only choose to **do** what a hero would do!"
Another four-hours-of-sleep day. That's three in a row...
Hey! Kamala! Wait up!
You never showed up at the masjid yesterday.
I got sidetracked!
I was waiting for you! There was something I needed to do that I couldn't do without **you!**
What are you talking about?
There's, uh--I needed to talk to somebody. Somebody I can't talk to **alone**. I need another, *umm*, *girl* there. To **chaperone** us.
Wait a second. You wanted to talk to a **girl?**
Yeah.
You have a **girlfriend?!**
Istaghfirullah! Of course not! She's a girl I'm speaking to **only** with **correct supervision** for the purposes of discussing marriage!

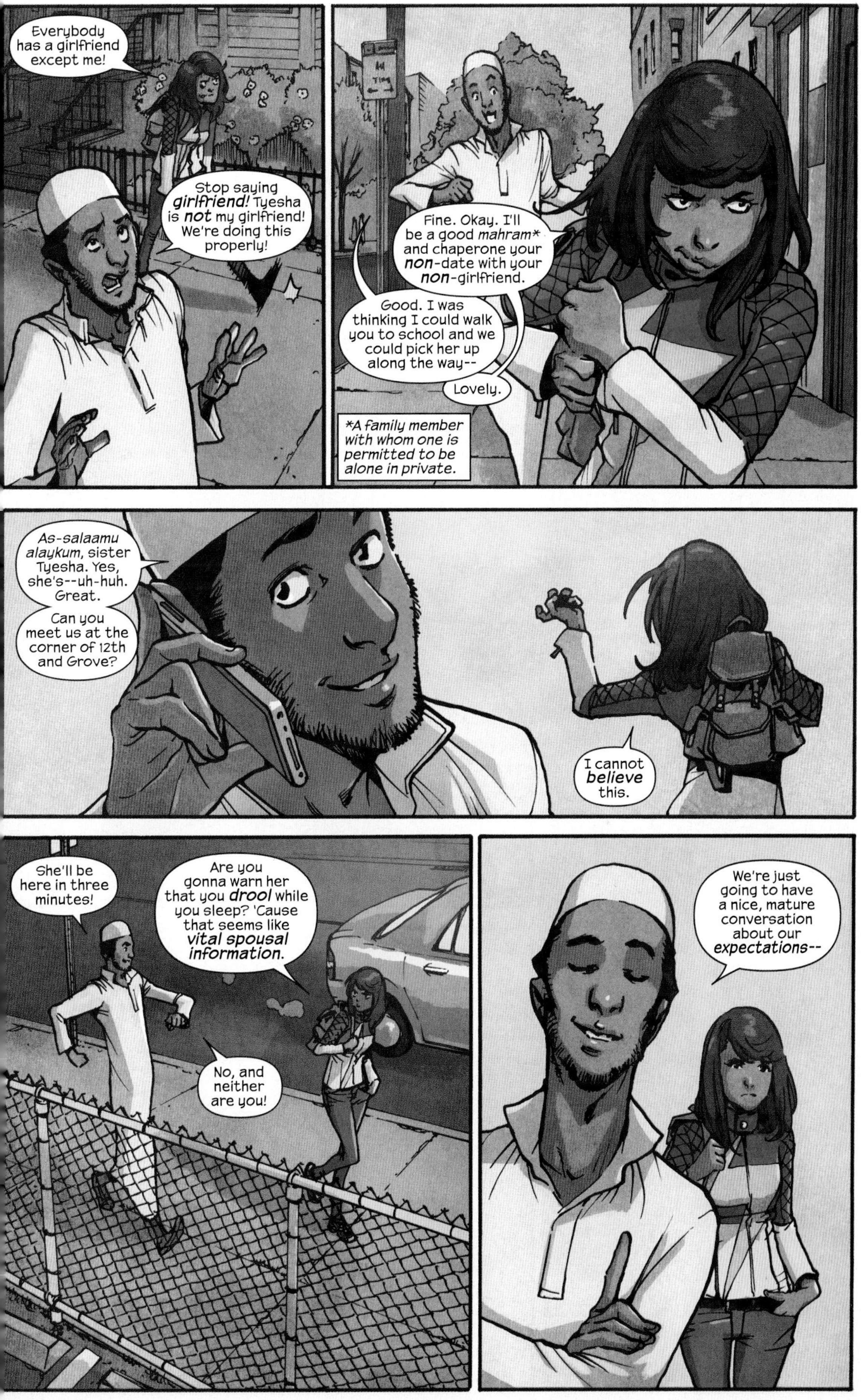
Everybody has a girlfriend except me!
Stop saying girlfriend! Tyesha is not my girlfriend! We're doing this properly!
Fine. Okay. I'll be a good mahram* and chaperone your non-date with your non-girlfriend.
Good. I was thinking I could walk you to school and we could pick her up along the way--
Lovely.
*A family member with whom one is permitted to be alone in private.
As-salaamu alaykum, sister Tyesha. Yes, she's--uh-huh. Great.
Can you meet us at the corner of 12th and Grove?
I cannot believe this.
She'll be here in three minutes!
Are you gonna warn her that you drool while you sleep? 'Cause that seems like vital spousal information.
No, and neither are you!
We're just going to have a nice, mature conversation about our expectations--

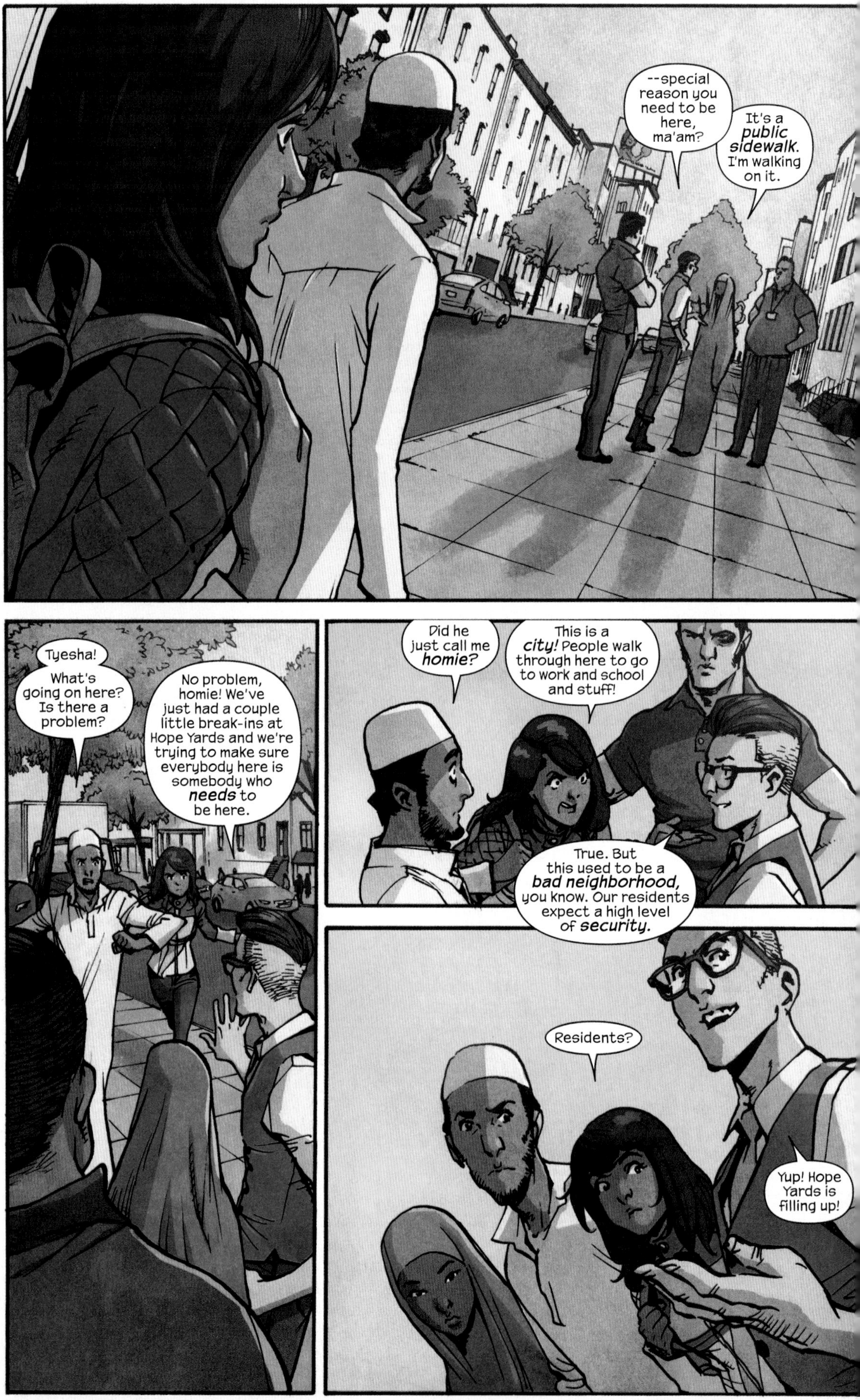
--special reason you need to be here, ma'am?
It's a public sidewalk. I'm walking on it.
Tyesha! What's going on here? Is there a problem?
No problem, homie! We've just had a couple little break-ins at Hope Yards and we're trying to make sure everybody here is somebody who needs to be here.
Did he just call me homie?
This is a city! People walk through here to go to work and school and stuff!
True. But this used to be a bad neighborhood, you know. Our residents expect a high level of security.
Residents?
Yup! Hope Yards is filling up!

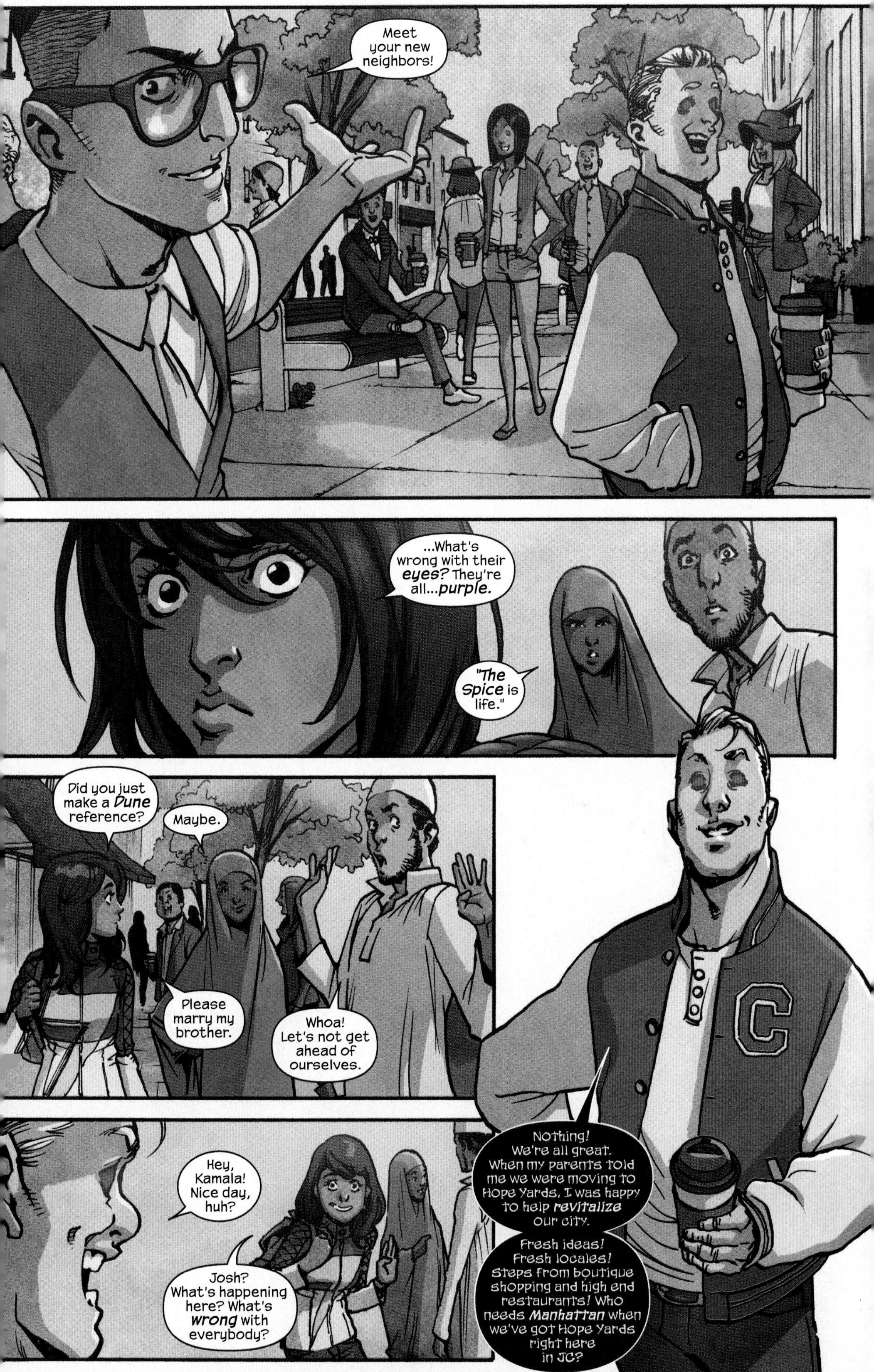
Meet your new neighbors!
...What's wrong with their *eyes?* They're all...*purple.*
"*The Spice* is life."
Did you just make a *Dune* reference?
Maybe.
Please marry my brother.
Whoa! Let's not get ahead of ourselves.
Hey, Kamala! Nice day, huh?
Josh? What's happening here? What's *wrong* with everybody?
Nothing! We're all great. When my parents told me we were moving to Hope Yards, I was happy to help *revitalize* our city.
Fresh ideas! Fresh locales! Steps from boutique shopping and high end restaurants! Who needs *Manhattan* when we've got Hope Yards right here in JC?

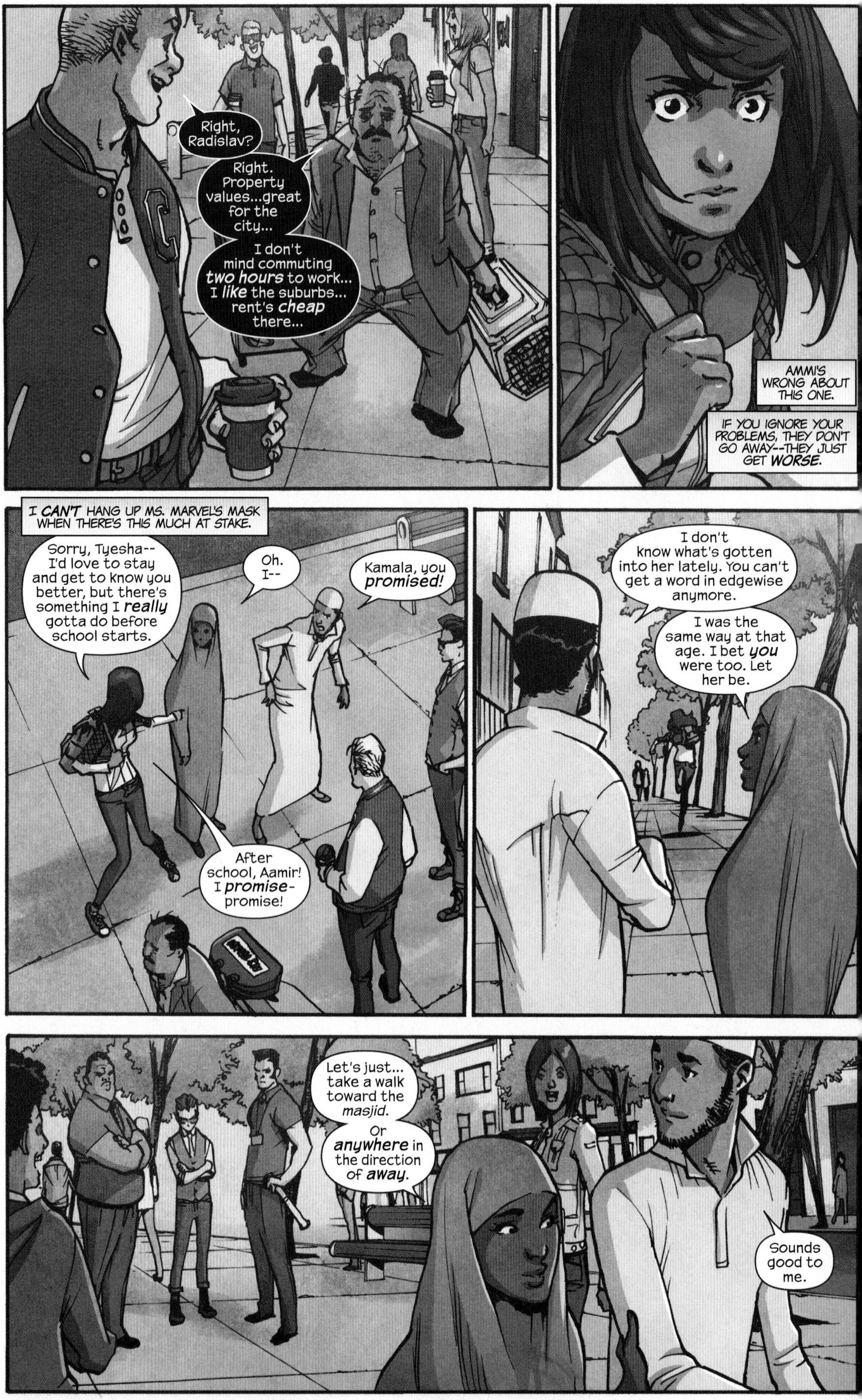
Right, Radislav?
Right. Property values...great for the city...
I don't mind commuting two hours to work... I like the suburbs... rent's cheap there...
AMMI'S WRONG ABOUT THIS ONE.
IF YOU IGNORE YOUR PROBLEMS, THEY DON'T GO AWAY--THEY JUST GET WORSE.
I CAN'T HANG UP MS. MARVEL'S MASK WHEN THERE'S THIS MUCH AT STAKE.
Sorry, Tyesha-- I'd love to stay and get to know you better, but there's something I really gotta do before school starts.
Oh. I--
Kamala, you promised!
After school, Aamir! I promise-promise!
I don't know what's gotten into her lately. You can't get a word in edgewise anymore.
I was the same way at that age. I bet you were too. Let her be.
Let's just... take a walk toward the masjid.
Or anywhere in the direction of away.
Sounds good to me.

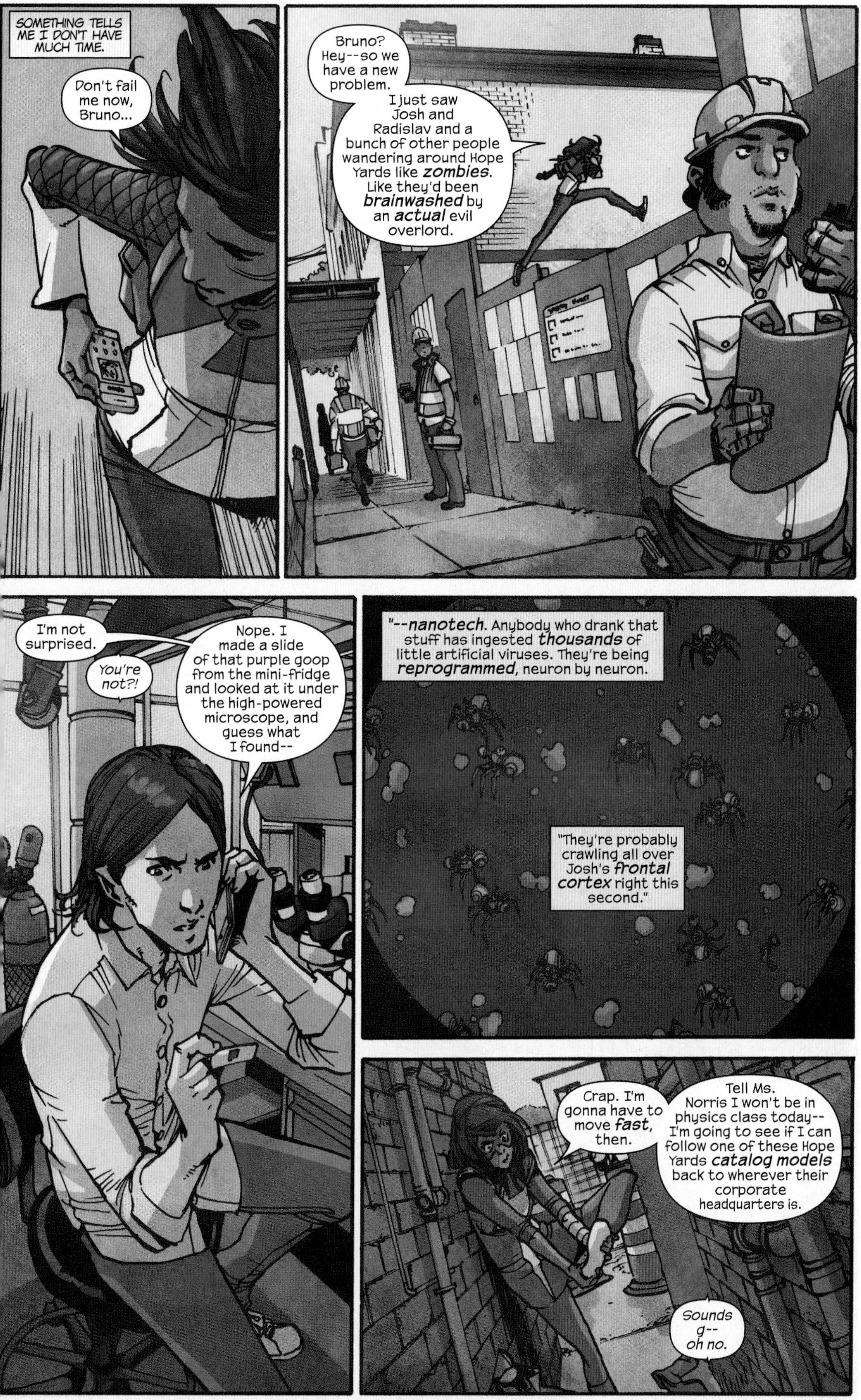

SOMETHING TELLS ME I DON'T HAVE MUCH TIME.
Don't fail me now, Bruno...
Bruno? Hey--so we have a new problem.
I just saw Josh and Radislav and a bunch of other people wandering around Hope Yards like zombies. Like they'd been brainwashed by an actual evil overlord.
I'm not surprised.
You're not?!
Nope. I made a slide of that purple goop from the mini-fridge and looked at it under the high-powered microscope, and guess what I found--
"--nanotech. Anybody who drank that stuff has ingested thousands of little artificial viruses. They're being reprogrammed, neuron by neuron.
"They're probably crawling all over Josh's frontal cortex right this second."
Crap. I'm gonna have to move fast, then.
Tell Ms. Norris I won't be in physics class today--I'm going to see if I can follow one of these Hope Yards catalog models back to wherever their corporate headquarters is.
Sounds g-- oh no.

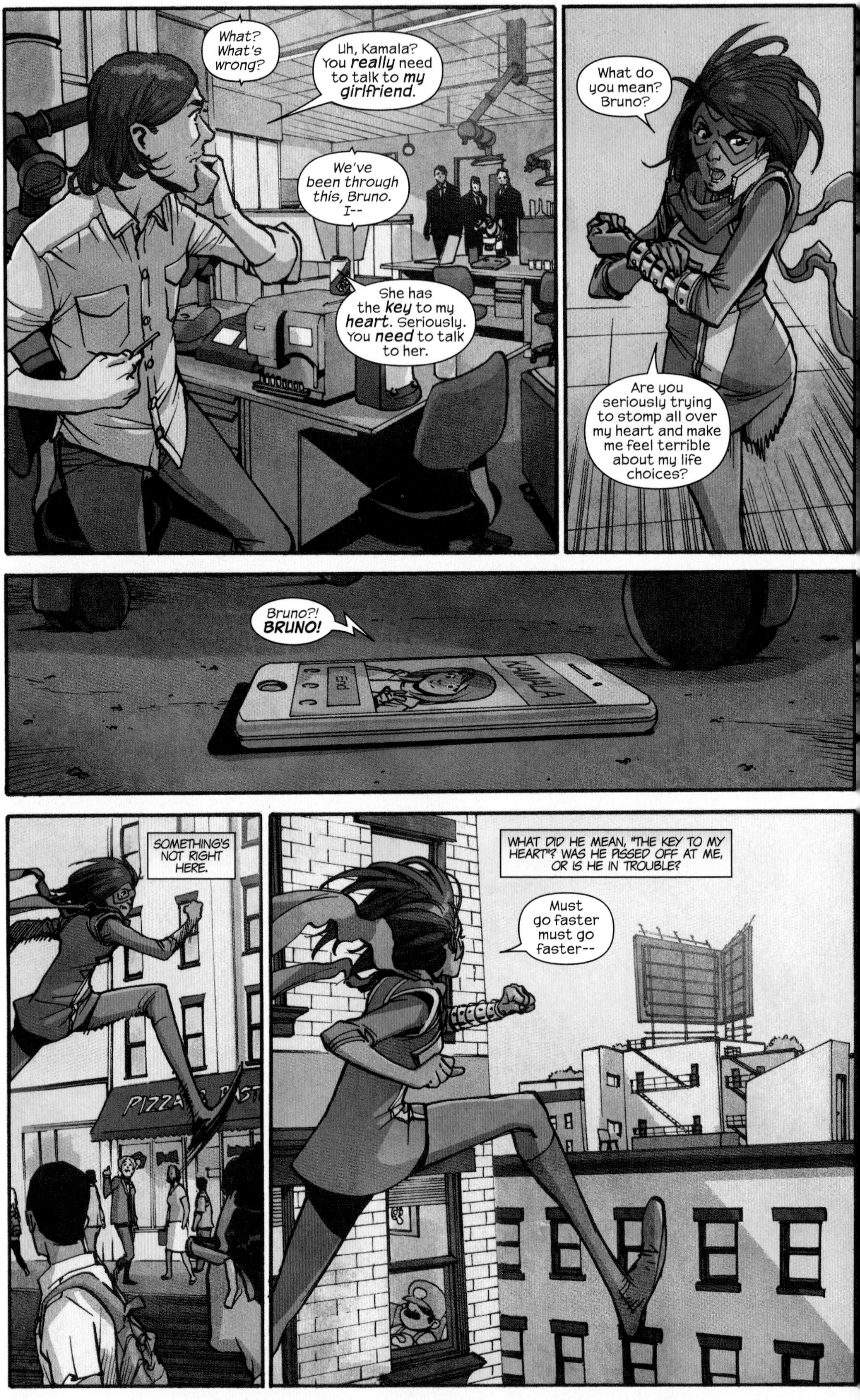
What? What's wrong?
Uh, Kamala? You really need to talk to my girlfriend.
We've been through this, Bruno. I--
She has the key to my heart. Seriously. You need to talk to her.
What do you mean? Bruno?
Are you seriously trying to stomp all over my heart and make me feel terrible about my life choices?
Bruno?! BRUNO!
KAMALA
End
SOMETHING'S NOT RIGHT HERE.
WHAT DID HE MEAN, "THE KEY TO MY HEART"? WAS HE PISSED OFF AT ME, OR IS HE IN TROUBLE?
Must go faster must go faster--

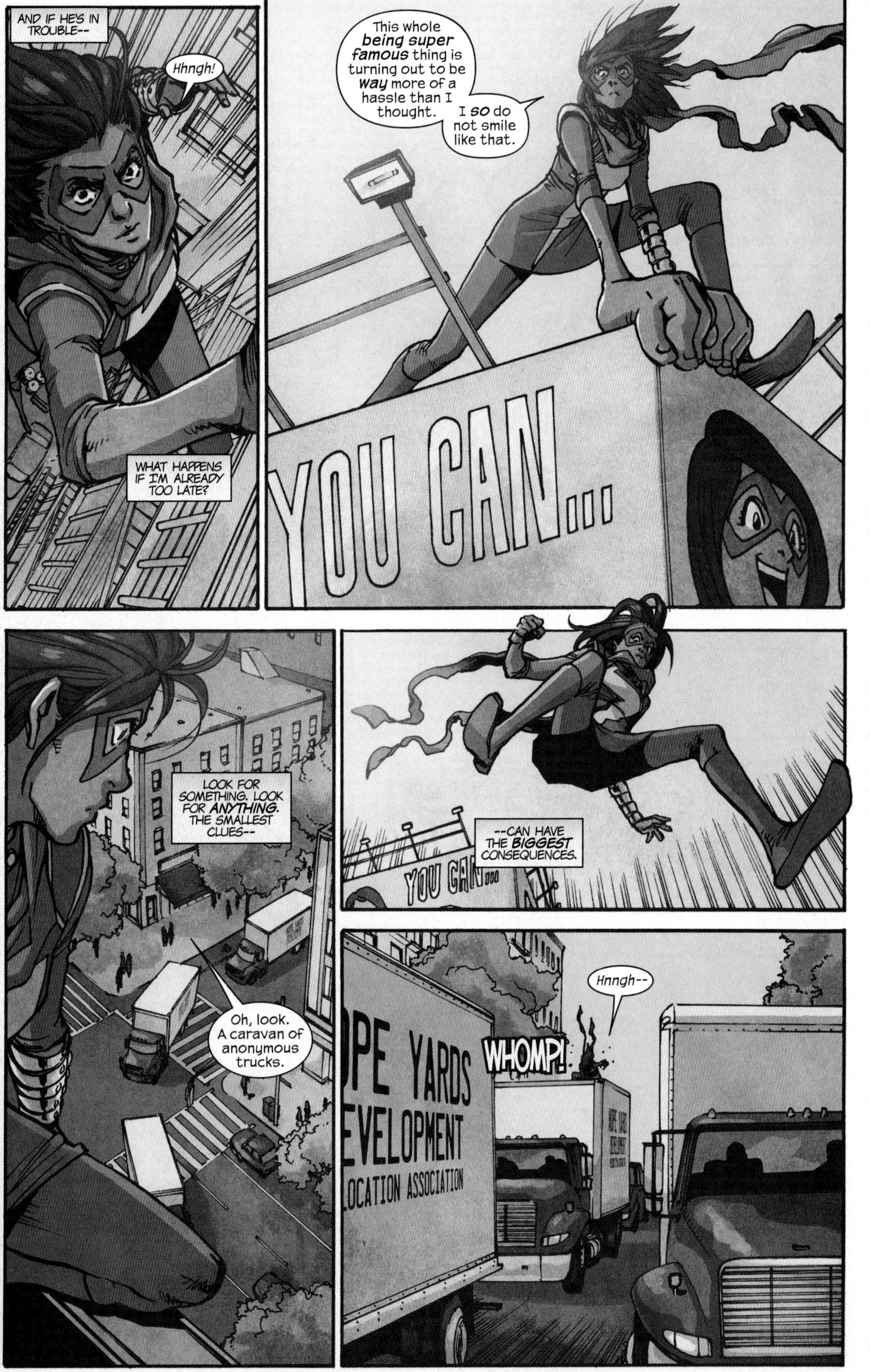

AND IF HE'S IN TROUBLE--
Hhngh!
WHAT HAPPENS IF I'M ALREADY TOO LATE?
This whole **being super famous** thing is turning out to be **way** more of a hassle than I thought.
I **so** do not smile like that.
YOU CAN...
LOOK FOR SOMETHING. LOOK FOR **ANYTHING**. THE SMALLEST CLUES--
Oh, look. A caravan of anonymous trucks.
--CAN HAVE THE **BIGGEST** CONSEQUENCES.
YOU CAN...
Hnngh--
WHOMP!
OPE YARDS
EVELOPMENT
LOCATION ASSOCIATION

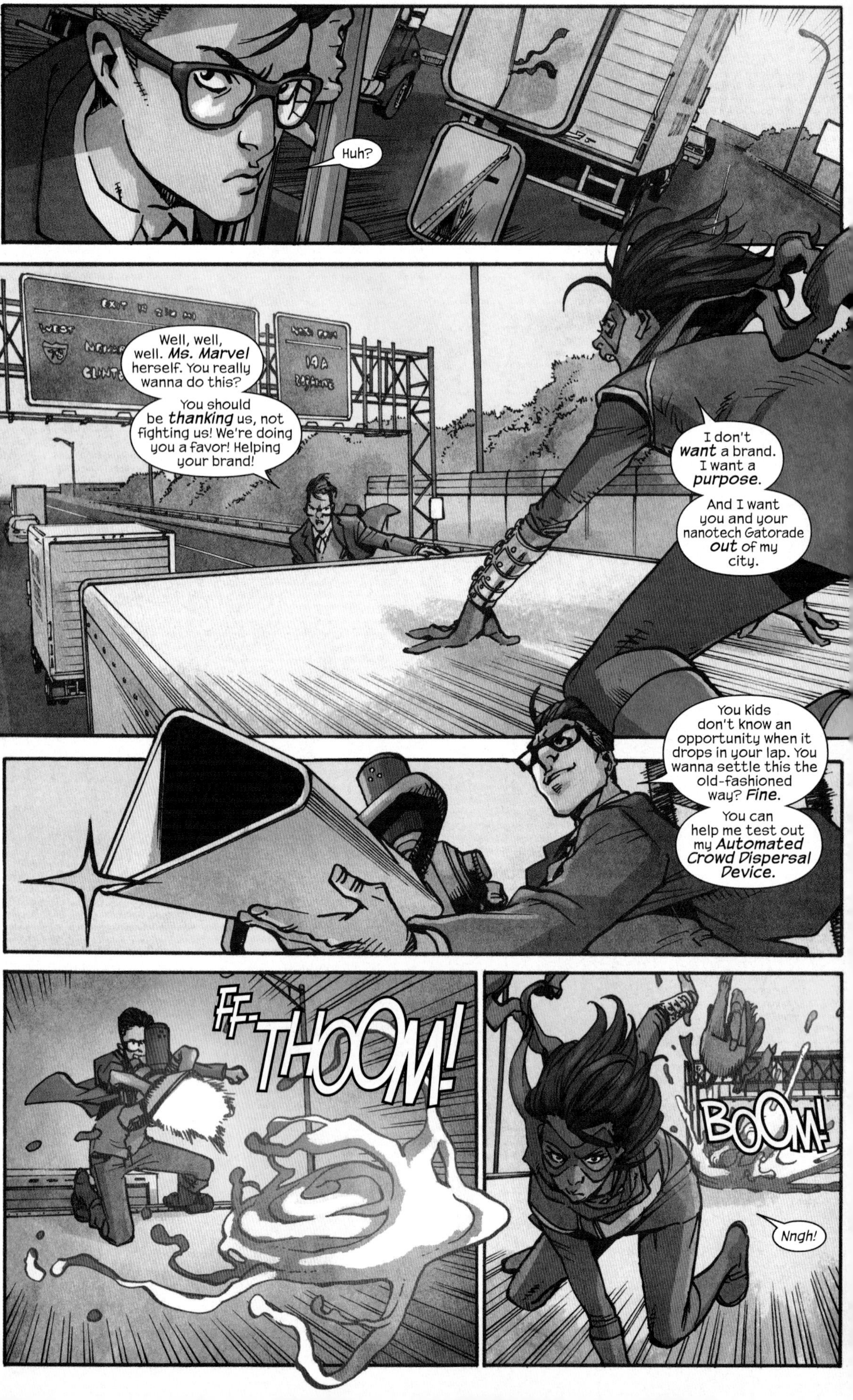
Huh?
Well, well, well. Ms. Marvel herself. You really wanna do this?
You should be thanking us, not fighting us! We're doing you a favor! Helping your brand!
I don't want a brand. I want a purpose.
And I want you and your nanotech Gatorade out of my city.
You kids don't know an opportunity when it drops in your lap. You wanna settle this the old-fashioned way? Fine.
You can help me test out my Automated Crowd Dispersal Device.
FF-THOOM!
BOOM!
Nngh!

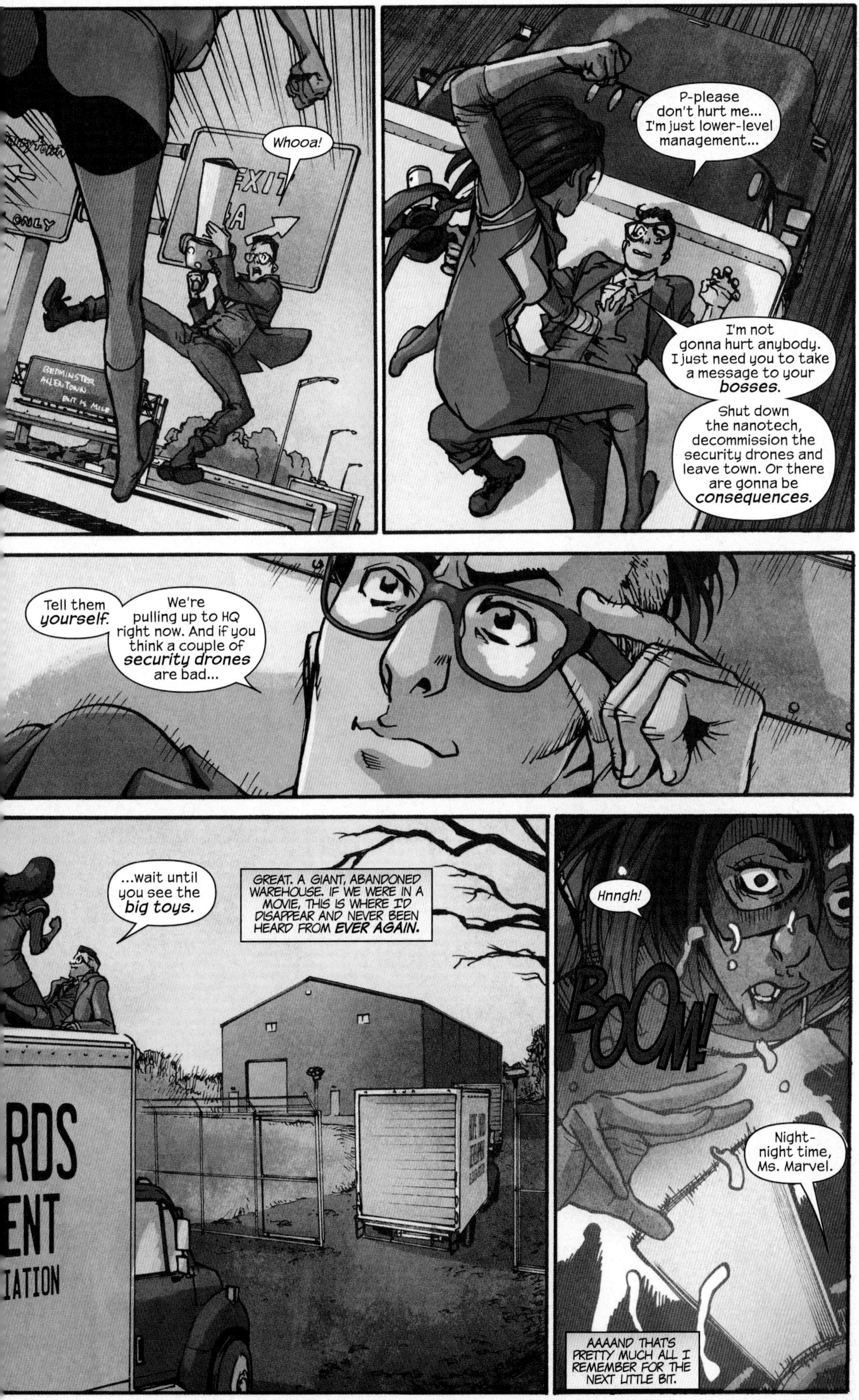
Whooa!
P-please don't hurt me... I'm just lower-level management...
I'm not gonna hurt anybody. I just need you to take a message to your *bosses*.
Shut down the nanotech, decommission the security drones and leave town. Or there are gonna be *consequences*.
Tell them *yourself*.
We're pulling up to HQ right now. And if you think a couple of *security drones* are bad...
...wait until you see the *big toys*.
GREAT. A GIANT, ABANDONED WAREHOUSE. IF WE WERE IN A MOVIE, THIS IS WHERE I'D DISAPPEAR AND NEVER BEEN HEARD FROM *EVER AGAIN*.
Hnngh!
BOOM!
Night-night time, Ms. Marvel.
AAAAND THAT'S PRETTY MUCH ALL I REMEMBER FOR THE NEXT LITTLE BIT.

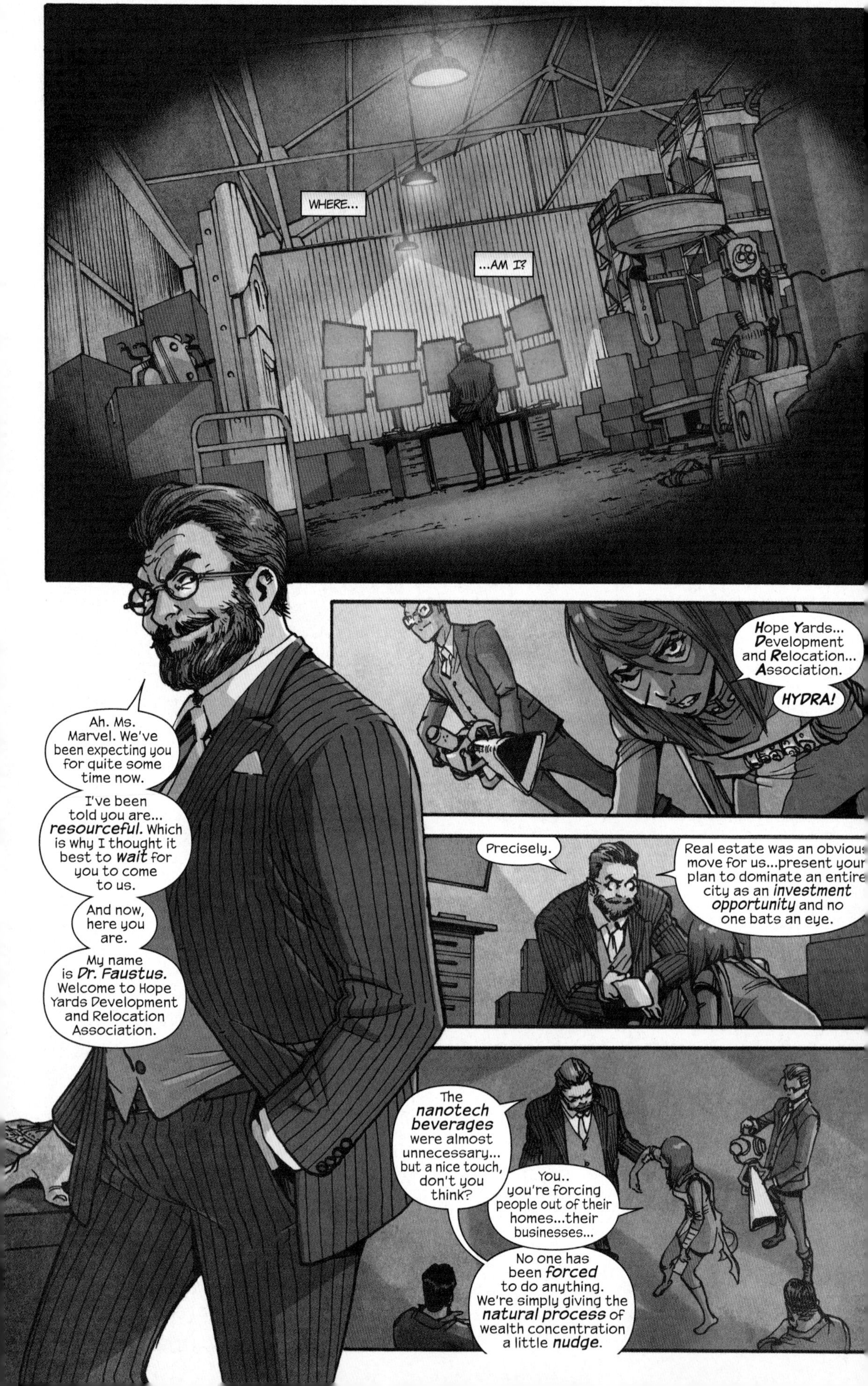
WHERE...
...AM I?
Ah. Ms. Marvel. We've been expecting you for quite some time now.
I've been told you are... resourceful. Which is why I thought it best to wait for you to come to us.
And now, here you are.
My name is Dr. Faustus. Welcome to Hope Yards Development and Relocation Association.
Hope Yards... Development and Relocation... Association.
HYDRA!
Precisely.
Real estate was an obvious move for us...present your plan to dominate an entire city as an investment opportunity and no one bats an eye.
The nanotech beverages were almost unnecessary... but a nice touch, don't you think?
You.. you're forcing people out of their homes...their businesses...
No one has been forced to do anything. We're simply giving the natural process of wealth concentration a little nudge.

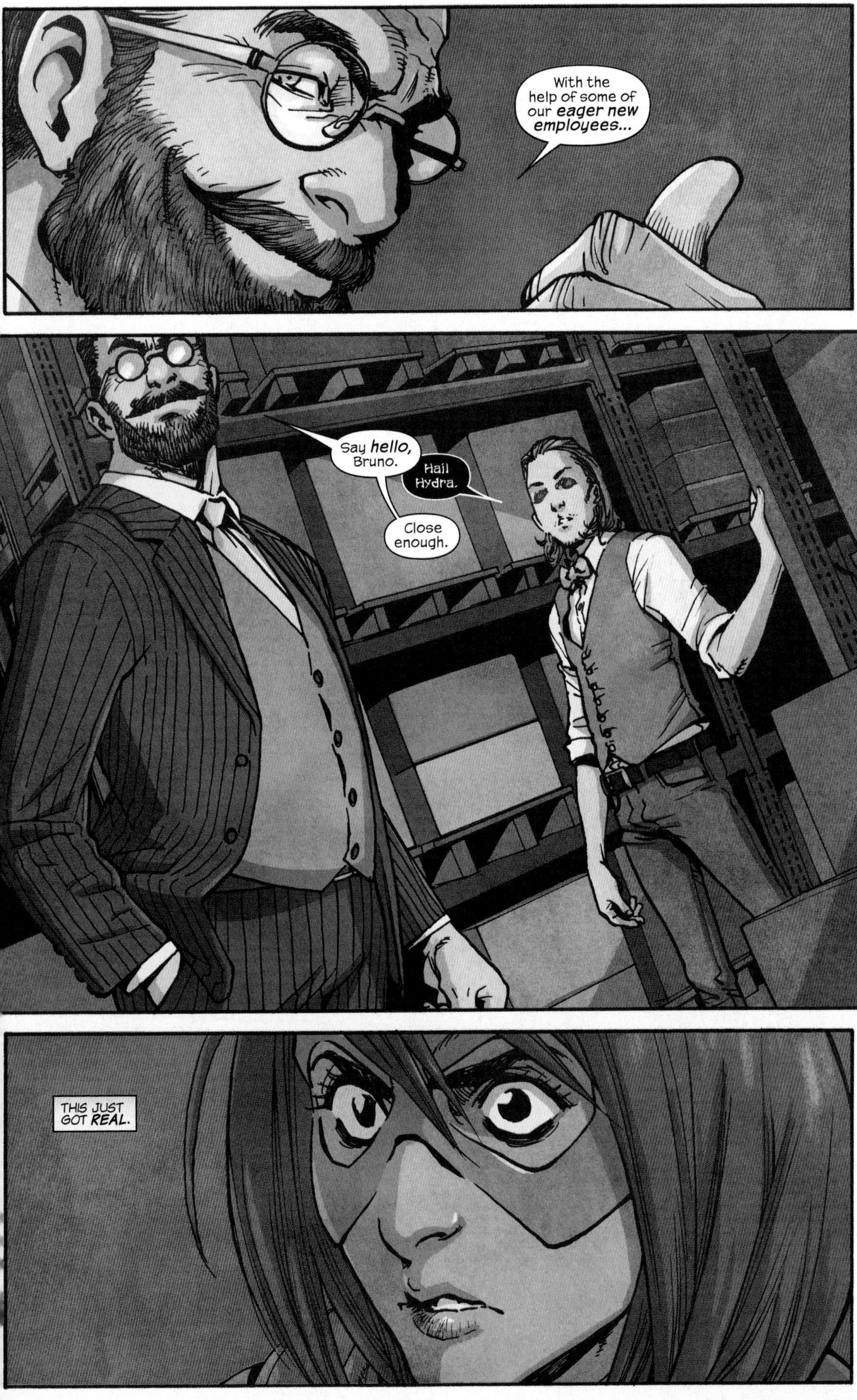

With the help of some of our *eager new employees...*
Say *hello,* Bruno.
Hail Hydra.
Close enough.
THIS JUST GOT *REAL.*

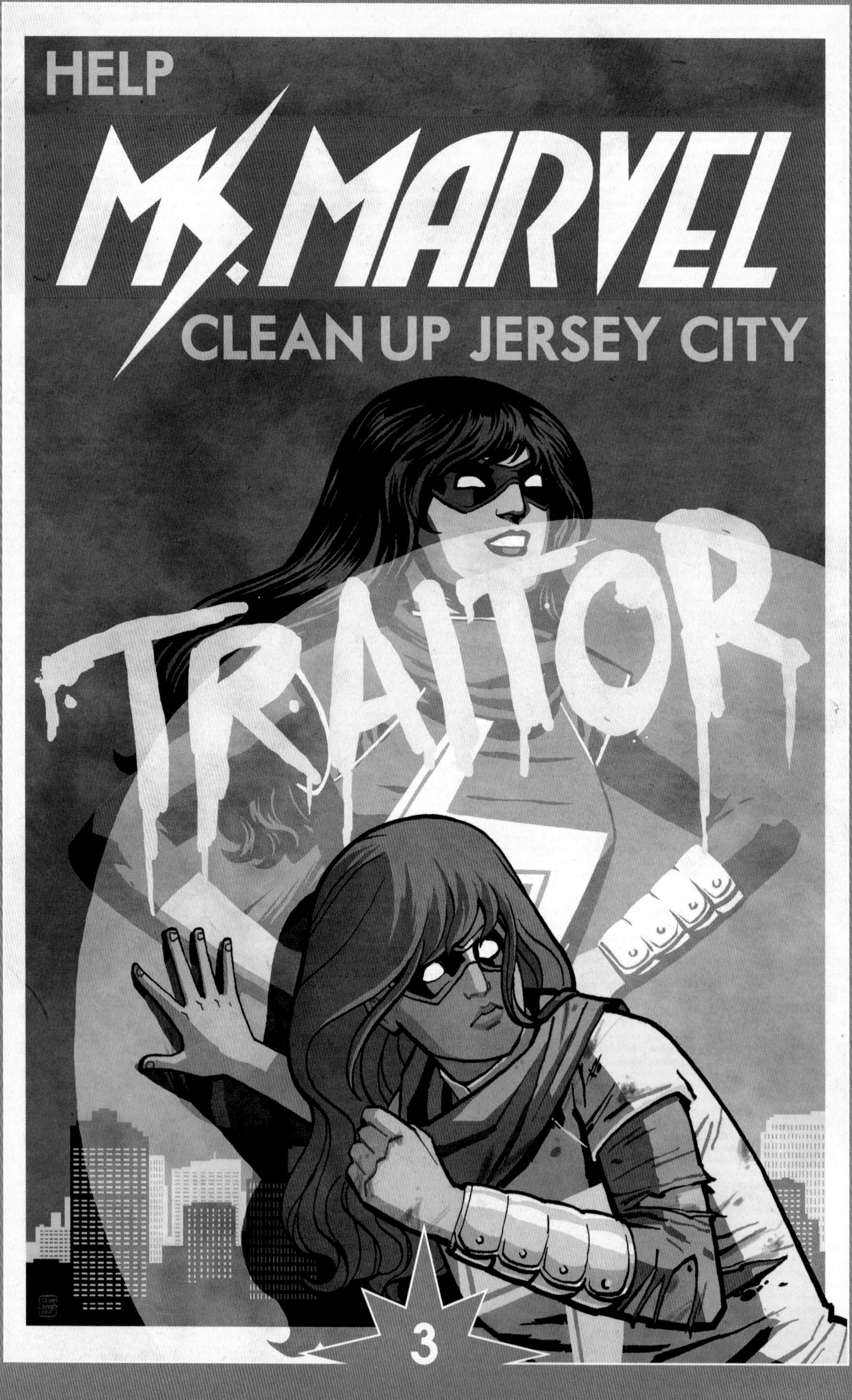
HELP
MS. MARVEL
CLEAN UP JERSEY CITY
TRAITOR
3

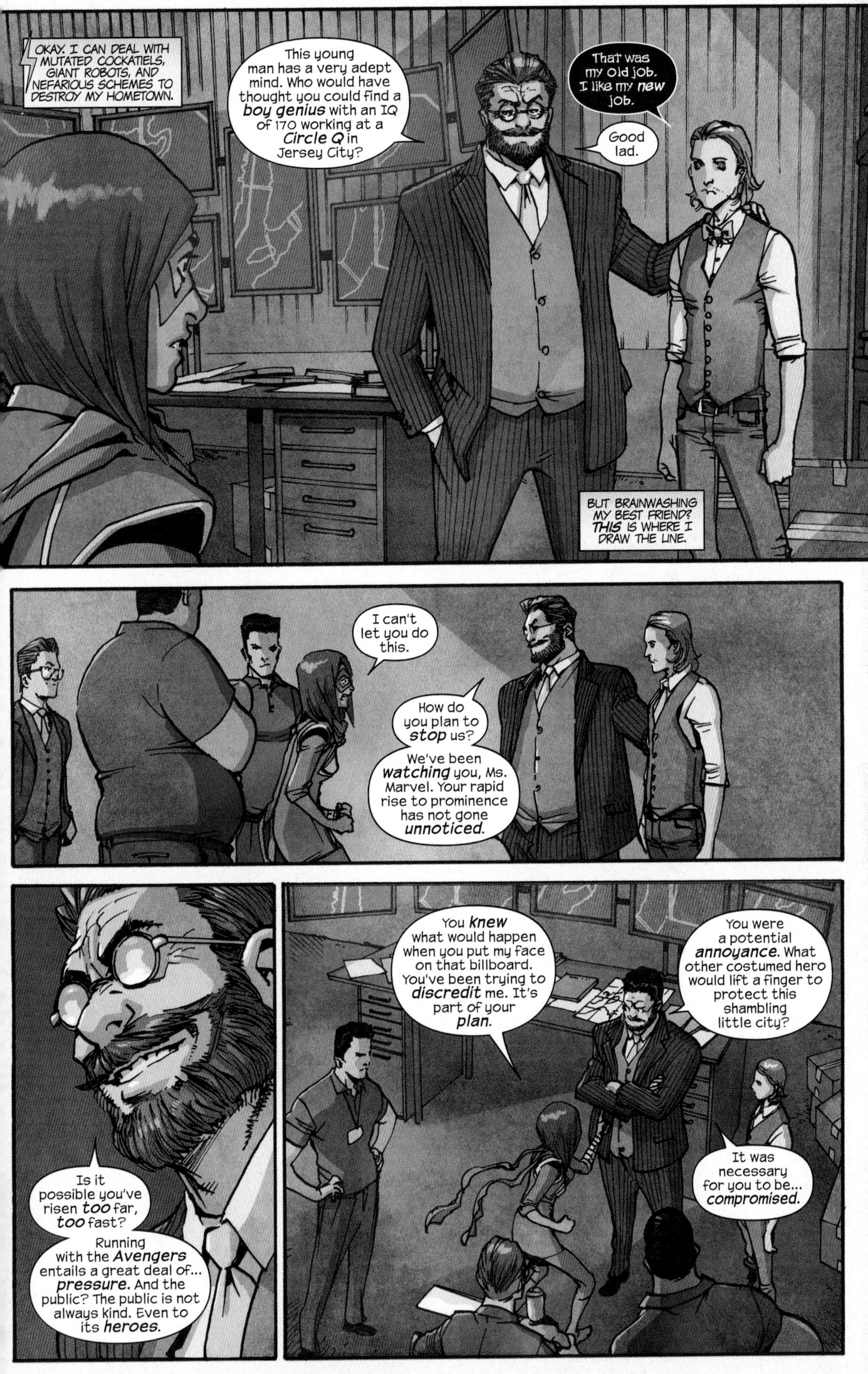
OKAY. I CAN DEAL WITH MUTATED COCKATIELS, GIANT ROBOTS, AND NEFARIOUS SCHEMES TO DESTROY MY HOMETOWN.
This young man has a very adept mind. Who would have thought you could find a boy genius with an IQ of 170 working at a Circle Q in Jersey City?
That was my old job. I like my new job.
Good lad.
BUT BRAINWASHING MY BEST FRIEND? THIS IS WHERE I DRAW THE LINE.
I can't let you do this.
How do you plan to stop us?
We've been watching you, Ms. Marvel. Your rapid rise to prominence has not gone unnoticed.
Is it possible you've risen too far, too fast?
Running with the Avengers entails a great deal of... pressure. And the public? The public is not always kind. Even to its heroes.
You knew what would happen when you put my face on that billboard. You've been trying to discredit me. It's part of your plan.
You were a potential annoyance. What other costumed hero would lift a finger to protect this shambling little city?
It was necessary for you to be... compromised.

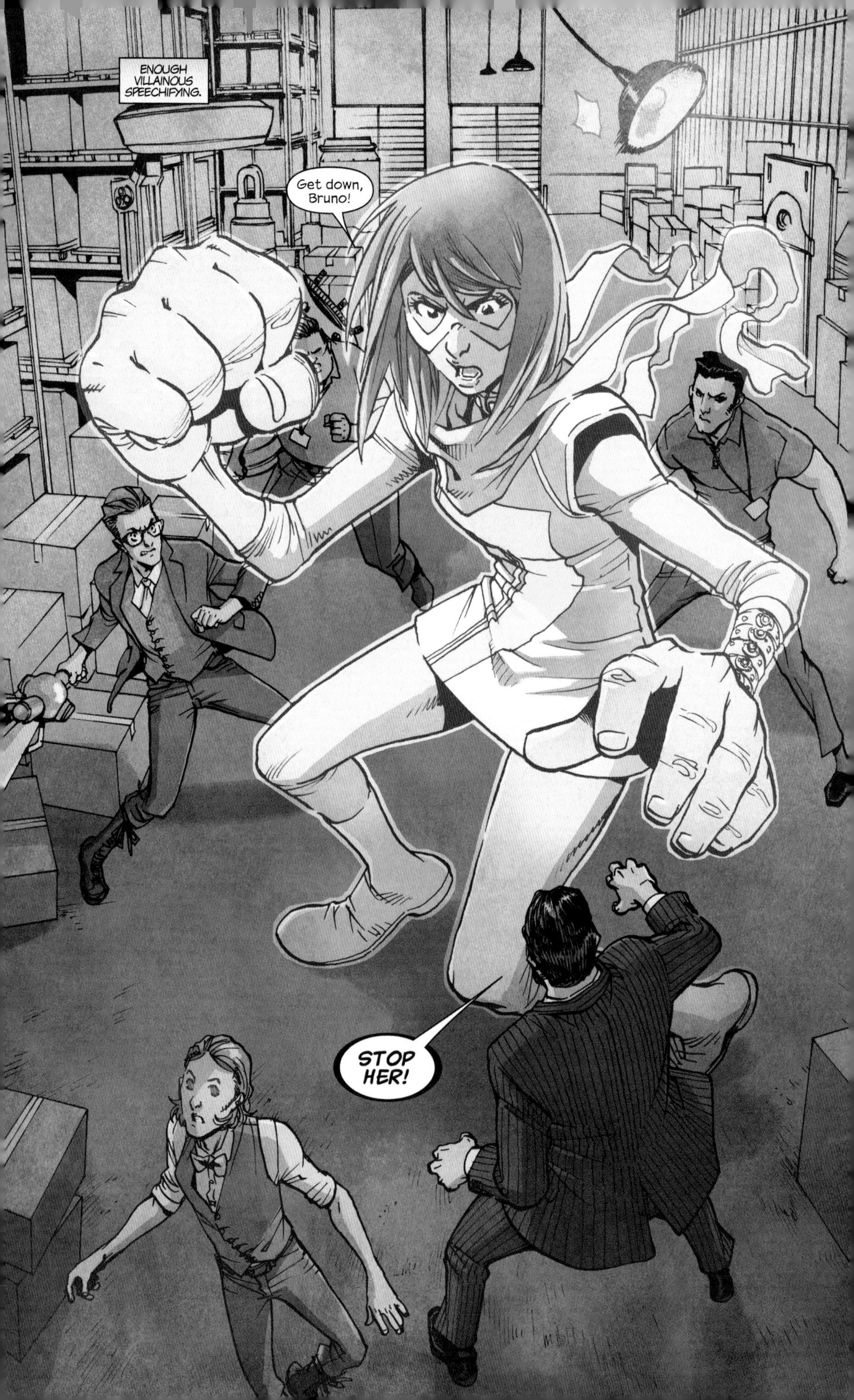
ENOUGH VILLAINOUS SPEECHIFYING.
Get down, Bruno!
STOP HER!

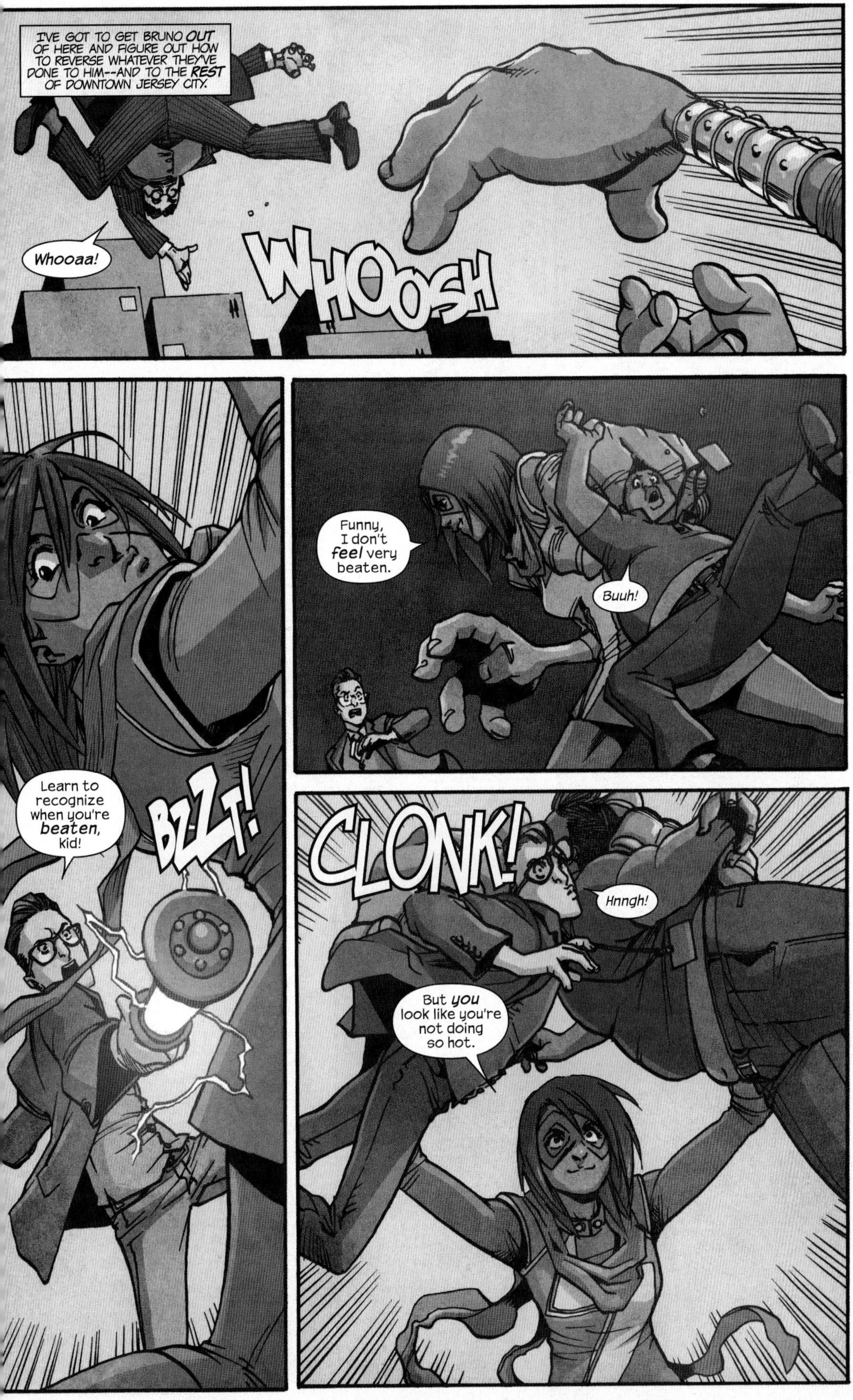

I'VE GOT TO GET BRUNO OUT OF HERE AND FIGURE OUT HOW TO REVERSE WHATEVER THEY'VE DONE TO HIM--AND TO THE REST OF DOWNTOWN JERSEY CITY.
Whooaa!
WHOOSH
Learn to recognize when you're beaten, kid!
BZZT!
Funny, I don't feel very beaten.
Buuh!
CLONK!
Hnngh!
But you look like you're not doing so hot.

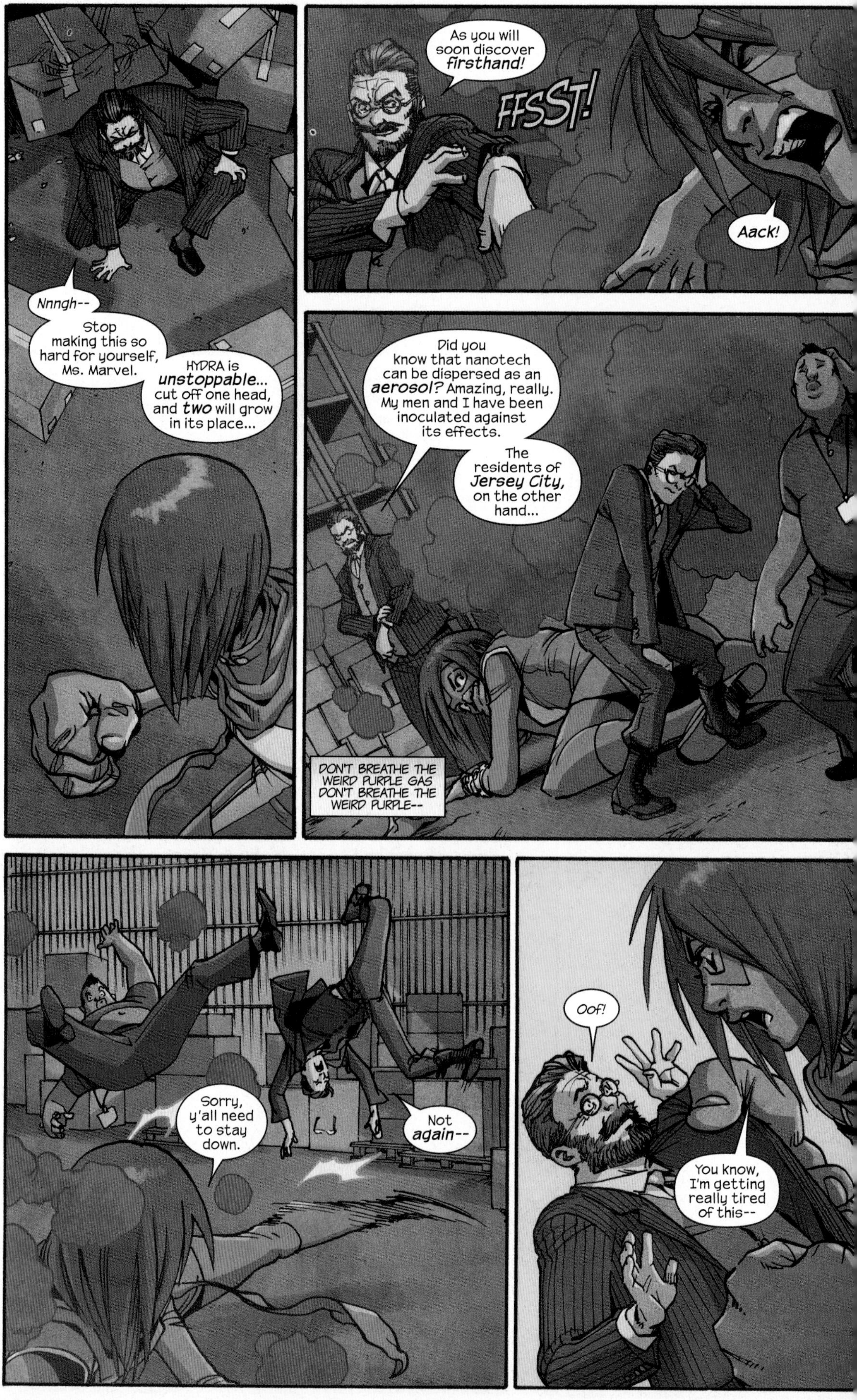

Nnngh--
Stop making this so hard for yourself, Ms. Marvel.
HYDRA is unstoppable... cut off one head, and two will grow in its place...
As you will soon discover firsthand!
FFSST!
Aack!
Did you know that nanotech can be dispersed as an aerosol? Amazing, really. My men and I have been inoculated against its effects.
The residents of Jersey City, on the other hand...
DON'T BREATHE THE WEIRD PURPLE GAS DON'T BREATHE THE WEIRD PURPLE--
Sorry, y'all need to stay down.
Not again--
Oof!
You know, I'm getting really tired of this--

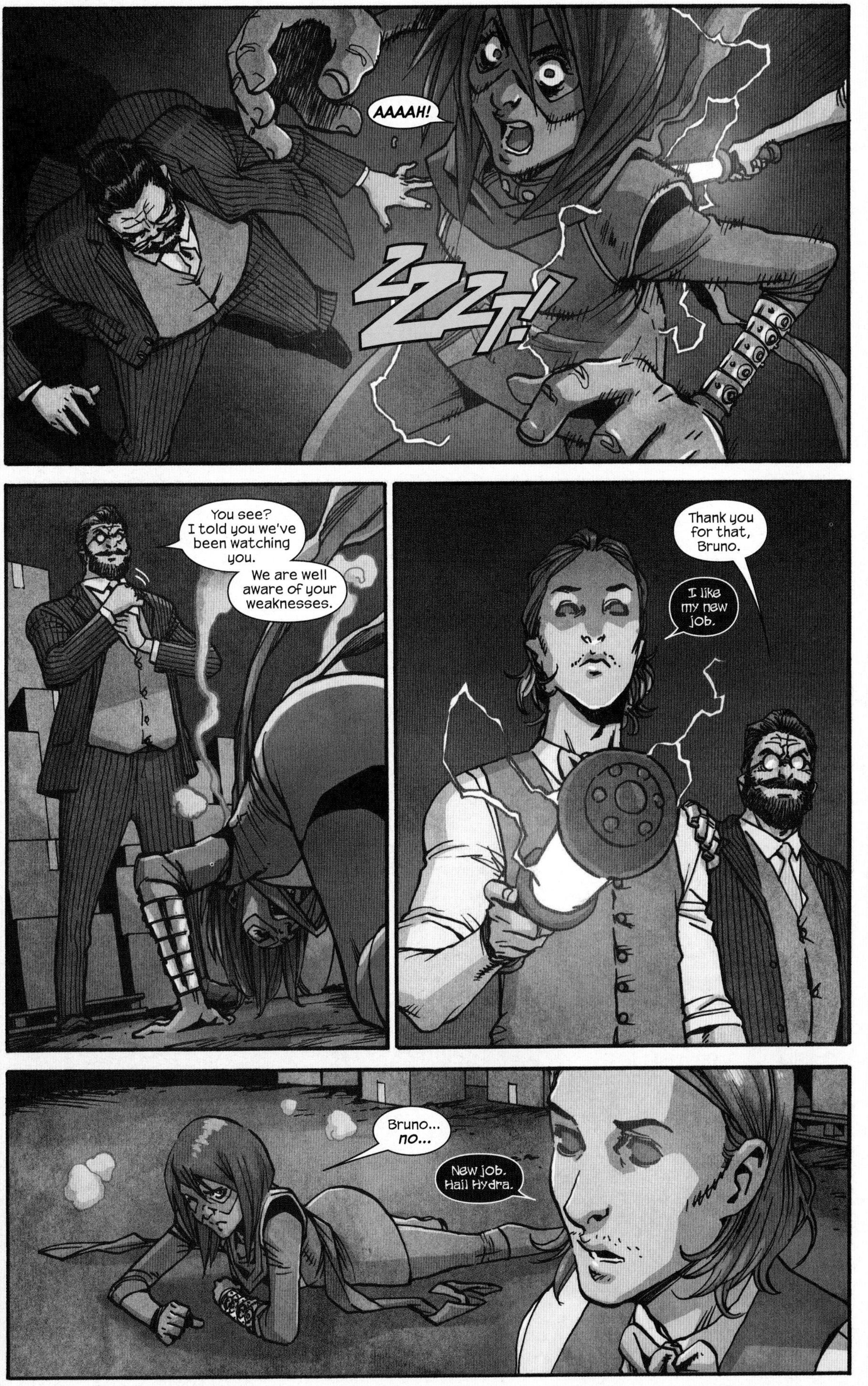
AAAAH!
ZZZT!
You see? I told you we've been watching you.
We are well aware of your weaknesses.
Thank you for that, Bruno.
I like my new job.
Bruno... no...
New job. Hail Hydra.

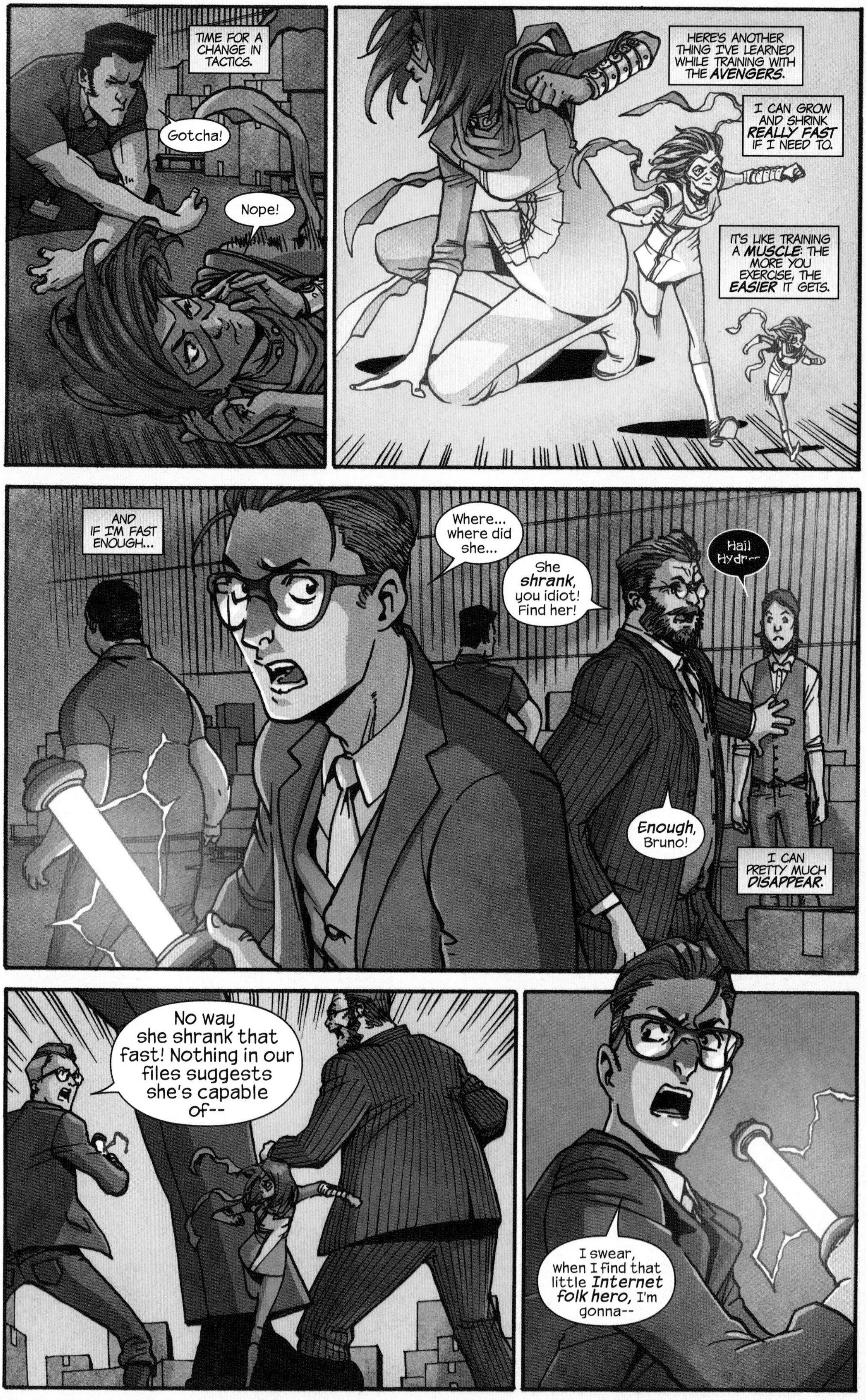

TIME FOR A CHANGE IN TACTICS.
Gotcha!
Nope!
HERE'S ANOTHER THING I'VE LEARNED WHILE TRAINING WITH THE AVENGERS.
I CAN GROW AND SHRINK REALLY FAST IF I NEED TO.
IT'S LIKE TRAINING A MUSCLE: THE MORE YOU EXERCISE, THE EASIER IT GETS.
AND IF I'M FAST ENOUGH...
Where... where did she...
She shrank, you idiot! Find her!
Hail Hydr--
Enough, Bruno!
I CAN PRETTY MUCH DISAPPEAR.
No way she shrank that fast! Nothing in our files suggests she's capable of--
I swear, when I find that little Internet folk hero, I'm gonna--

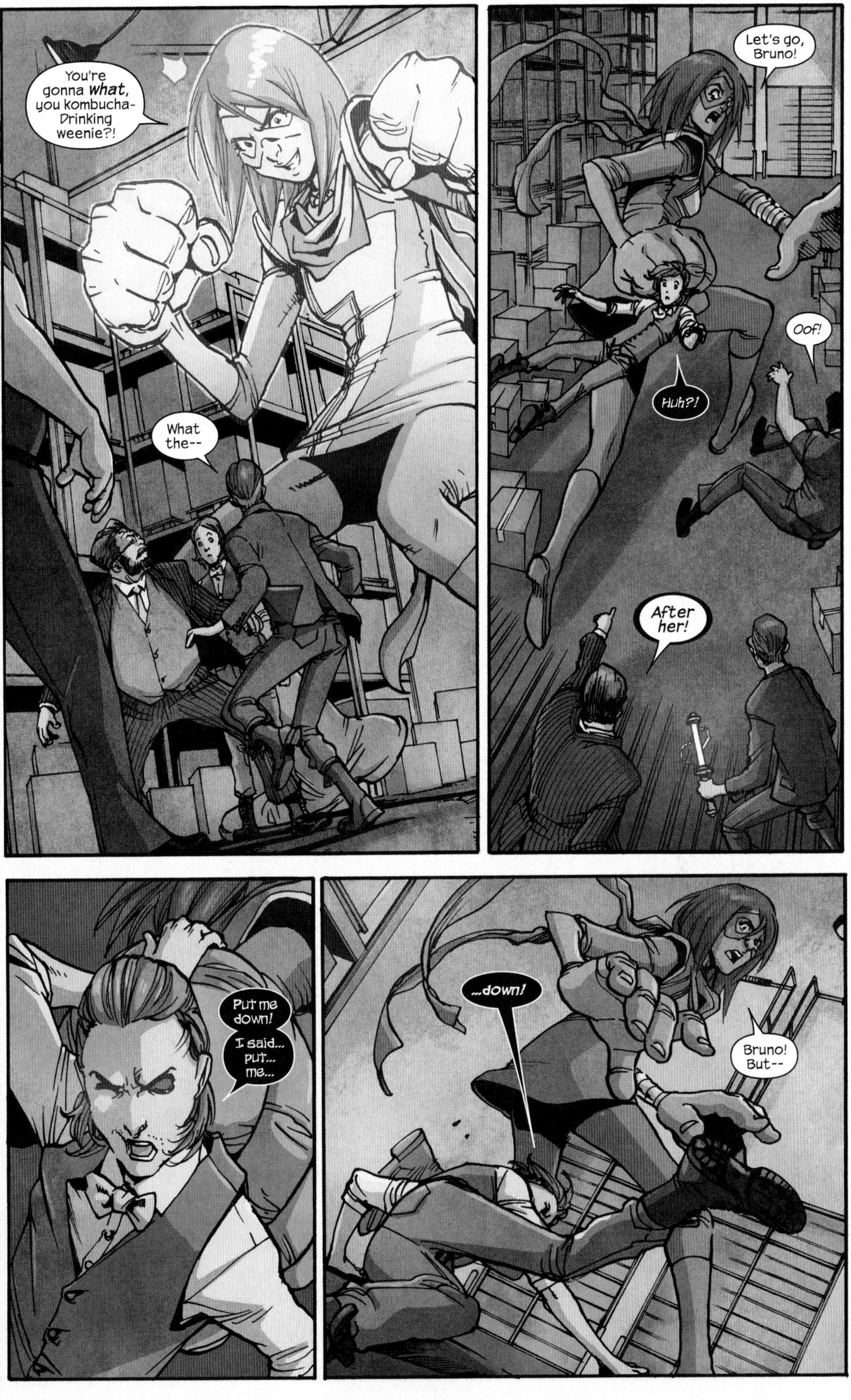
You're gonna what, you kombucha-Drinking weenie?!
What the--
Let's go, Bruno!
Oof!
Huh?!
After her!
Put me down!
I said... put... me...
...down!
Bruno! But--

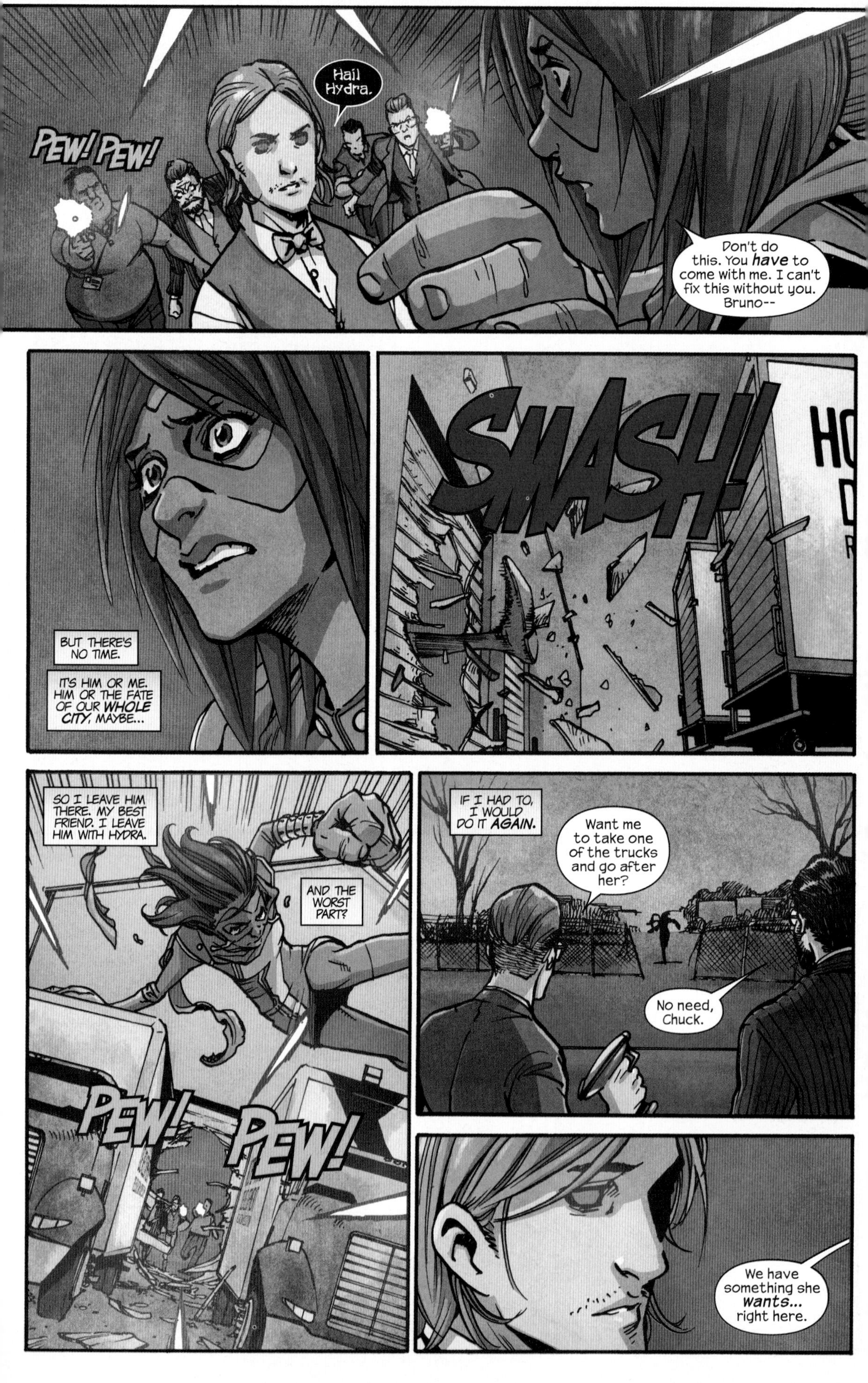
PEW! PEW!
Hail Hydra.
Don't do this. You *have* to come with me. I can't fix this without you. Bruno--
BUT THERE'S NO TIME.
IT'S HIM OR ME. HIM OR THE FATE OF OUR *WHOLE CITY,* MAYBE...
SMASH!
SO I LEAVE HIM THERE. MY BEST FRIEND. I LEAVE HIM WITH HYDRA.
AND THE WORST PART?
PEW! PEW!
IF I HAD TO, I WOULD DO IT *AGAIN.*
Want me to take one of the trucks and go after her?
No need, Chuck.
We have something she *wants...* right here.

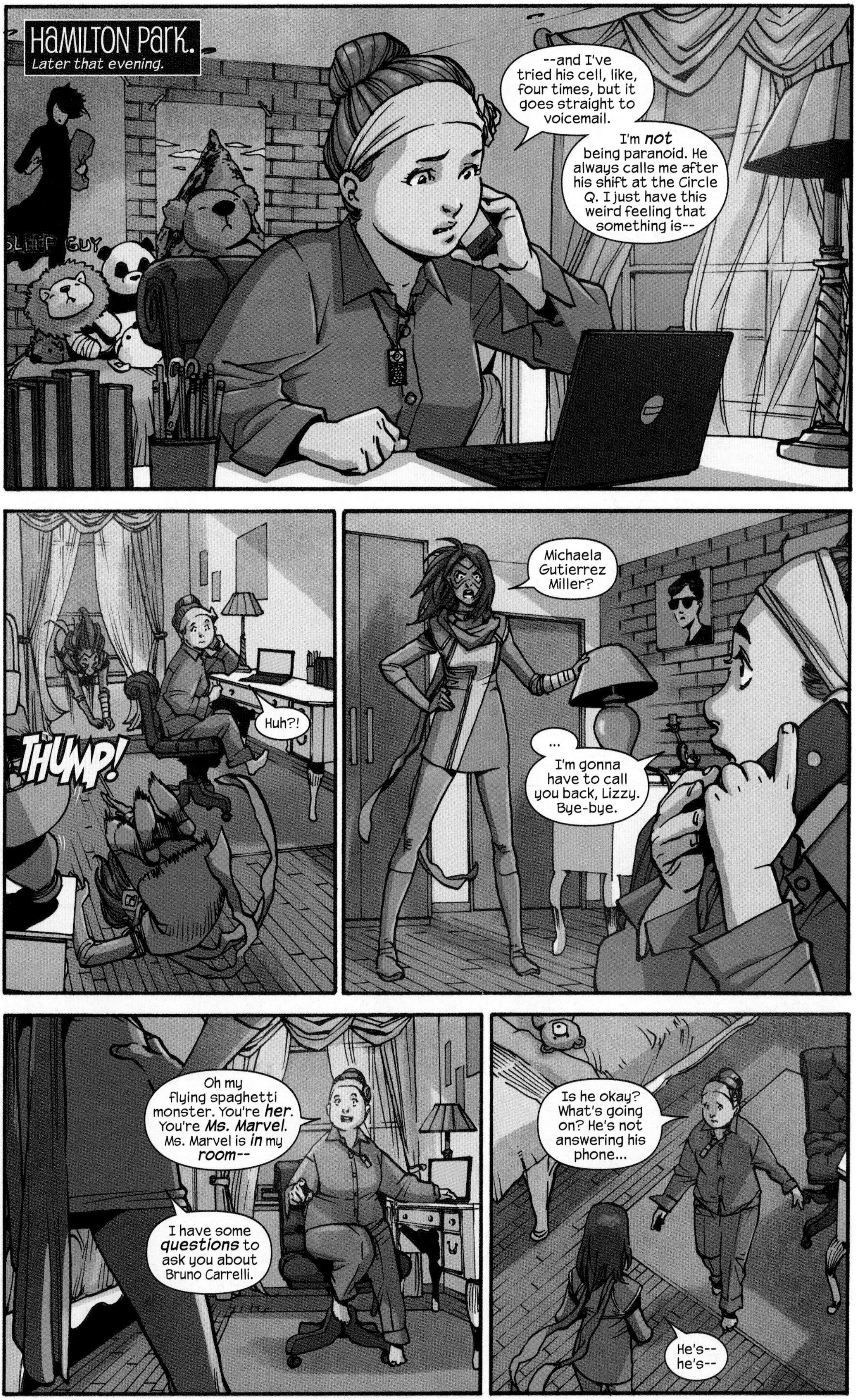
HAMILTON PARK.
Later that evening.
--and I've tried his cell, like, four times, but it goes straight to voicemail.
I'm not being paranoid. He always calls me after his shift at the Circle Q. I just have this weird feeling that something is--
SLEEP GUY
Huh?!
THUMP!
Michaela Gutierrez Miller?
... I'm gonna have to call you back, Lizzy. Bye-bye.
Oh my flying spaghetti monster. You're her. You're Ms. Marvel. Ms. Marvel is in my room--
I have some questions to ask you about Bruno Carrelli.
Is he okay? What's going on? He's not answering his phone...
He's-- he's--

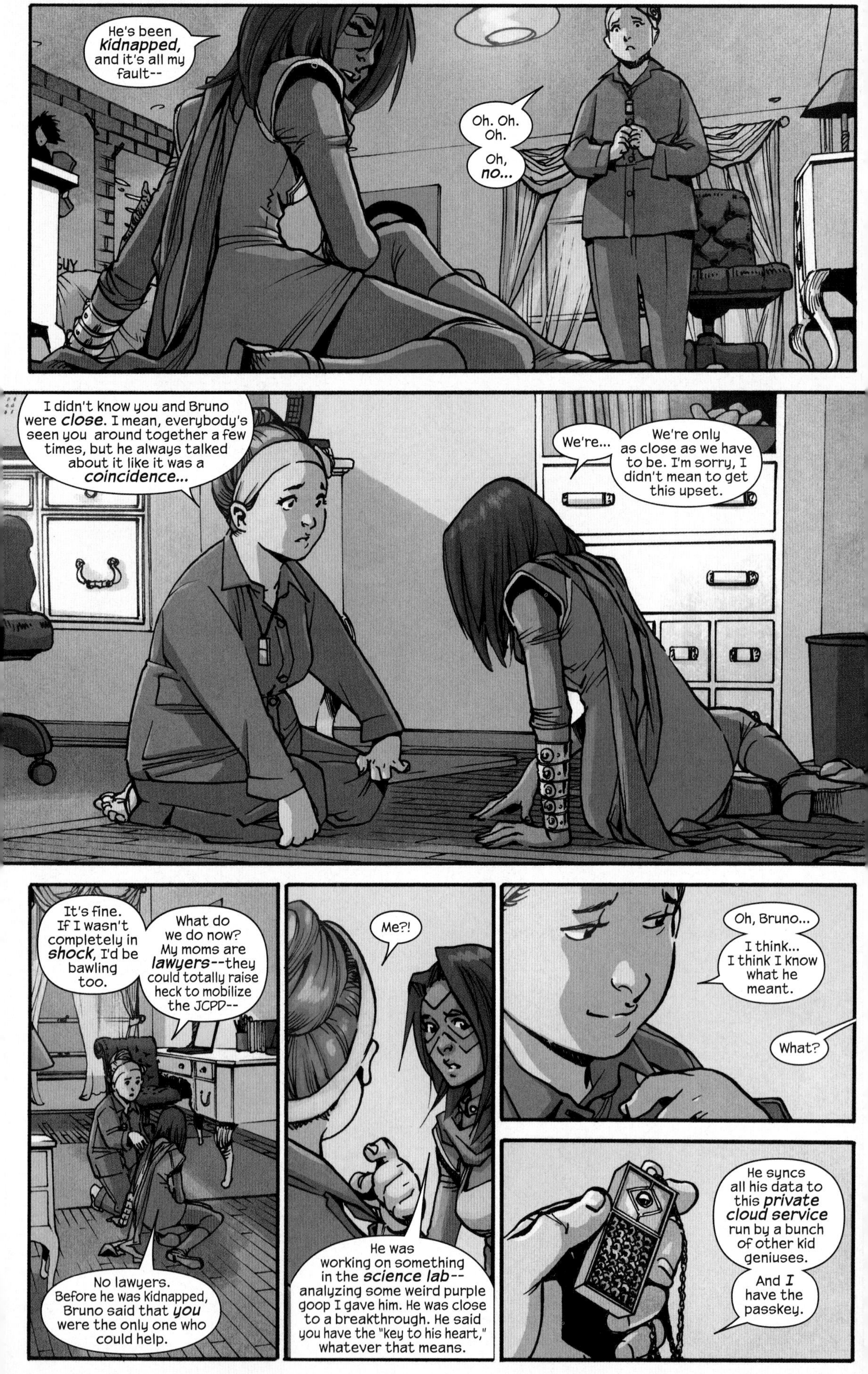
He's been kidnapped, and it's all my fault--
Oh. Oh. Oh.
Oh, no...
I didn't know you and Bruno were close. I mean, everybody's seen you around together a few times, but he always talked about it like it was a coincidence...
We're...
We're only as close as we have to be. I'm sorry, I didn't mean to get this upset.
It's fine. If I wasn't completely in shock, I'd be bawling too.
What do we do now? My moms are lawyers--they could totally raise heck to mobilize the JCPD--
No lawyers. Before he was kidnapped, Bruno said that you were the only one who could help.
Me?!
He was working on something in the science lab--analyzing some weird purple goop I gave him. He was close to a breakthrough. He said you have the "key to his heart," whatever that means.
Oh, Bruno...
I think... I think I know what he meant.
What?
He syncs all his data to this private cloud service run by a bunch of other kid geniuses.
And I have the passkey.

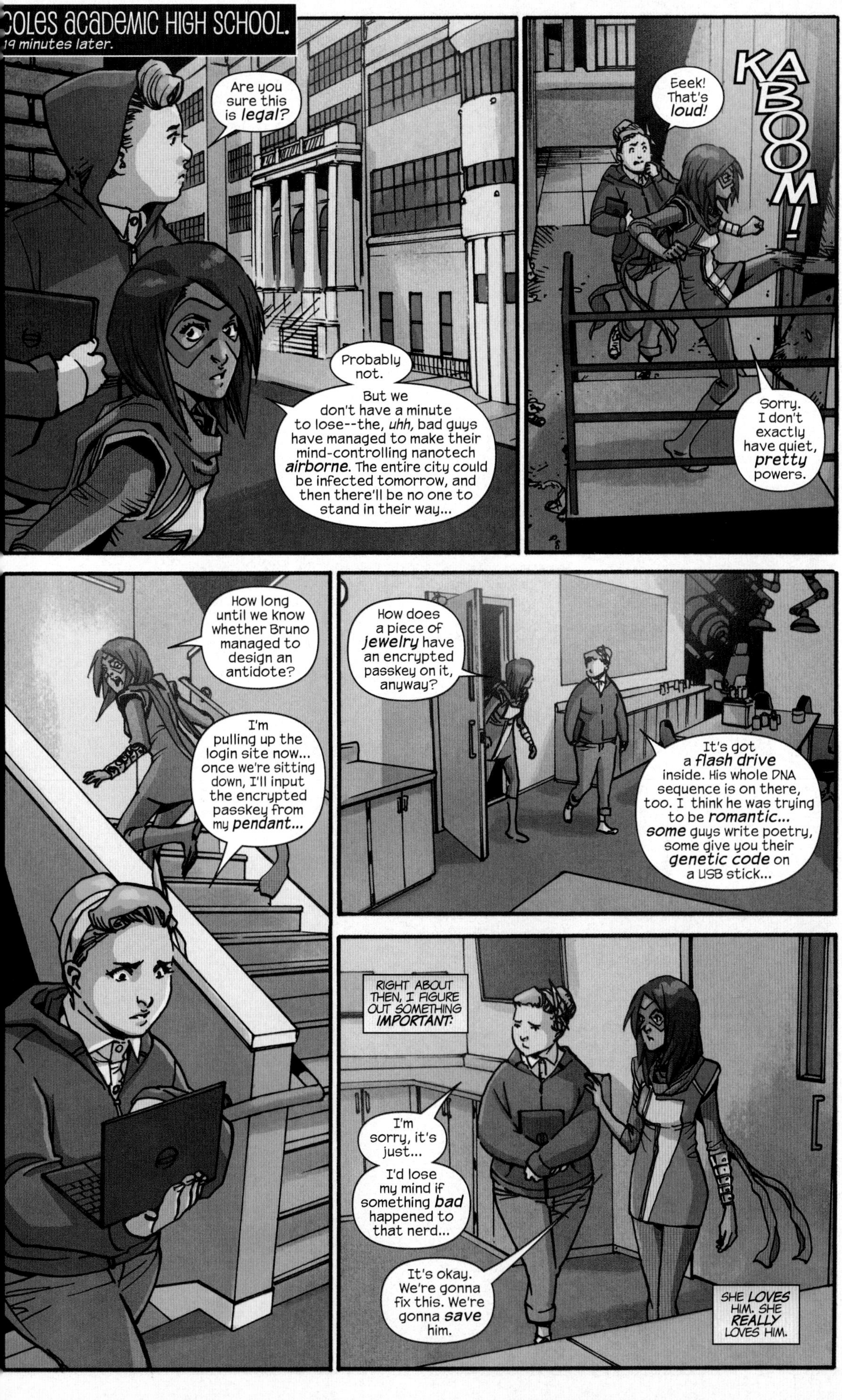
COLES ACADEMIC HIGH SCHOOL.
19 minutes later.
Are you sure this is *legal?*
Probably not.
But we don't have a minute to lose--the, *uhh,* bad guys have managed to make their mind-controlling nanotech **airborne**. The entire city could be infected tomorrow, and then there'll be no one to stand in their way...
KABOOM!
Eeek! That's *loud!*
Sorry. I don't exactly have quiet, **pretty** powers.
How long until we know whether Bruno managed to design an antidote?
I'm pulling up the login site now... once we're sitting down, I'll input the encrypted passkey from my *pendant...*
How does a piece of **jewelry** have an encrypted passkey on it, anyway?
It's got a **flash drive** inside. His whole DNA sequence is on there, too. I think he was trying to be **romantic... some** guys write poetry, some give you their **genetic code** on a USB stick...
RIGHT ABOUT THEN, I FIGURE OUT SOMETHING *IMPORTANT:*
I'm sorry, it's just...
I'd lose my mind if something **bad** happened to that nerd...
It's okay. We're gonna fix this. We're gonna **save** him.
SHE *LOVES* HIM. SHE *REALLY* LOVES HIM.

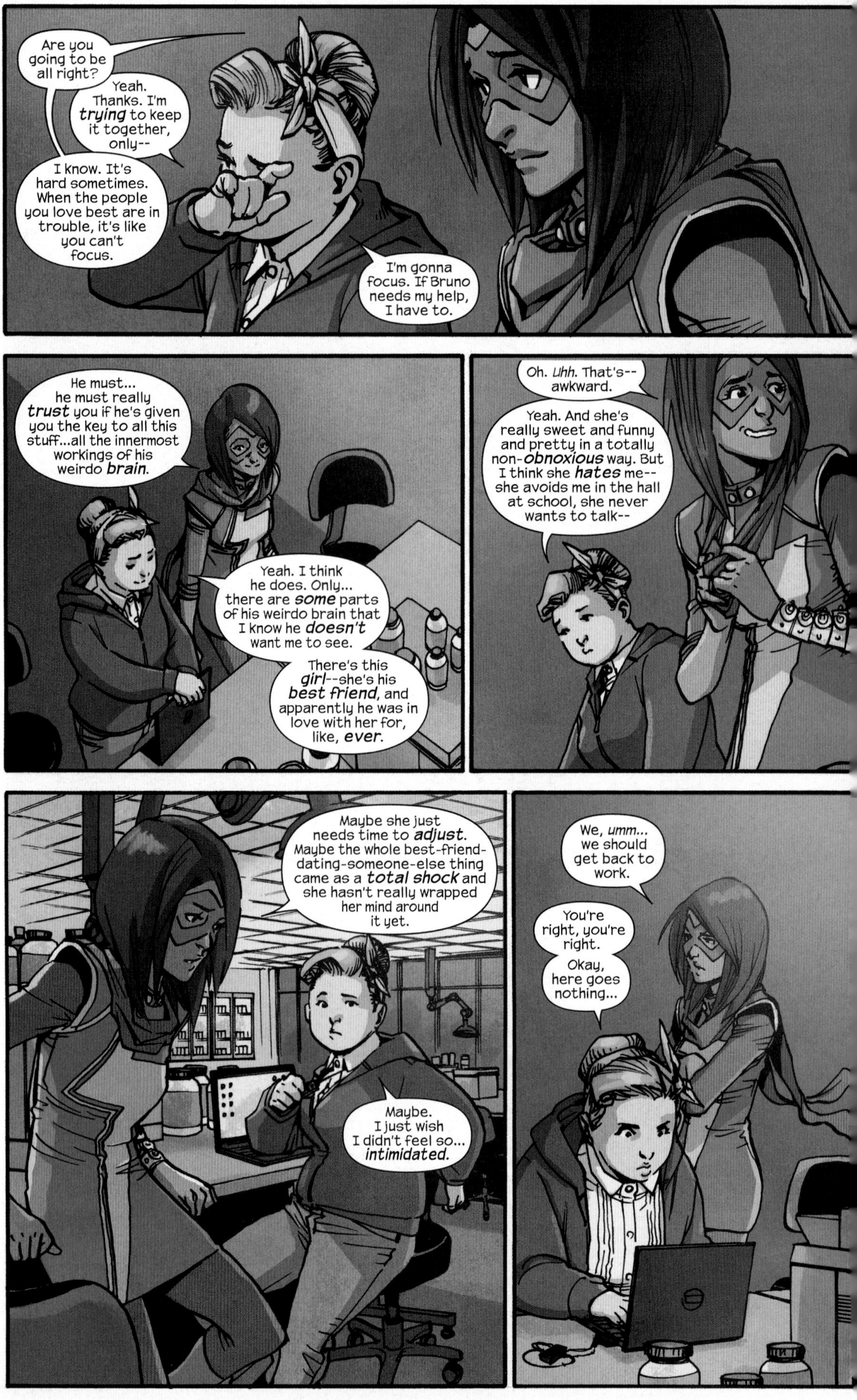
Are you going to be all right?
Yeah. Thanks. I'm *trying* to keep it together, only--
I know. It's hard sometimes. When the people you love best are in trouble, it's like you can't focus.
I'm gonna focus. If Bruno needs my help, I have to.
He must... he must really *trust* you if he's given you the key to all this stuff...all the innermost workings of his weirdo *brain*.
Yeah. I think he does. Only... there are *some* parts of his weirdo brain that I know he *doesn't* want me to see.
There's this *girl*--she's his *best friend*, and apparently he was in love with her for, like, *ever*.
Oh. *Uhh*. That's--awkward.
Yeah. And she's really sweet and funny and pretty in a totally non-*obnoxious* way. But I think she *hates* me--she avoids me in the hall at school, she never wants to talk--
Maybe she just needs time to *adjust*. Maybe the whole best-friend-dating-someone-else thing came as a *total shock* and she hasn't really wrapped her mind around it yet.
Maybe. I just wish I didn't feel so... *intimidated*.
We, *umm*... we should get back to work.
You're right, you're right.
Okay, here goes nothing...

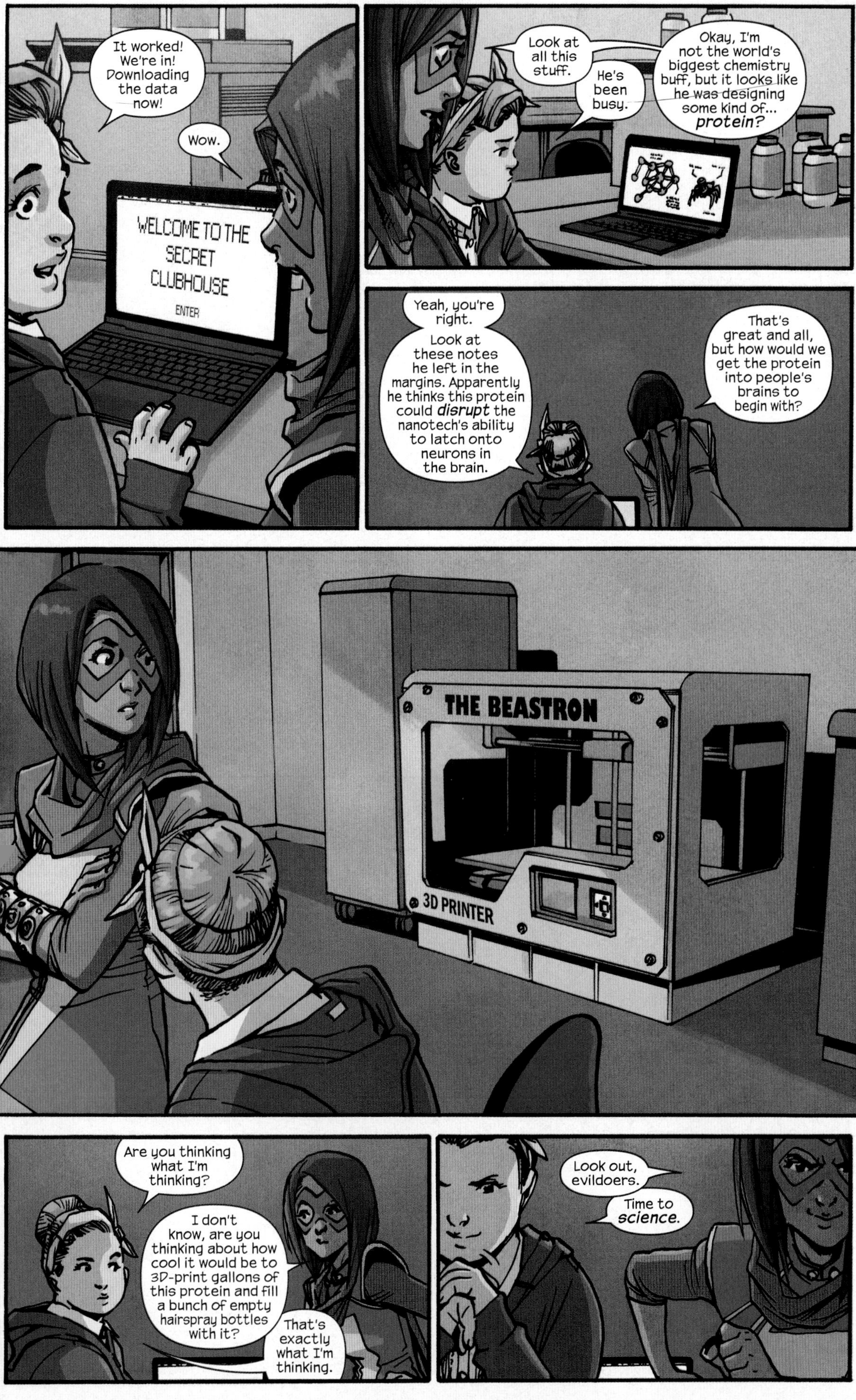

It worked! We're in! Downloading the data now!
Wow.
WELCOME TO THE SECRET CLUBHOUSE
ENTER
Look at all this stuff.
He's been busy.
Okay, I'm not the world's biggest chemistry buff, but it looks like he was designing some kind of... *protein?*
Yeah, you're right.
Look at these notes he left in the margins. Apparently he thinks this protein could ***disrupt*** the nanotech's ability to latch onto neurons in the brain.
That's great and all, but how would we get the protein into people's brains to begin with?
THE BEASTRON
3D PRINTER
Are you thinking what I'm thinking?
I don't know, are you thinking about how cool it would be to 3D-print gallons of this protein and fill a bunch of empty hairspray bottles with it?
That's exactly what I'm thinking.
Look out, evildoers.
Time to *science*.

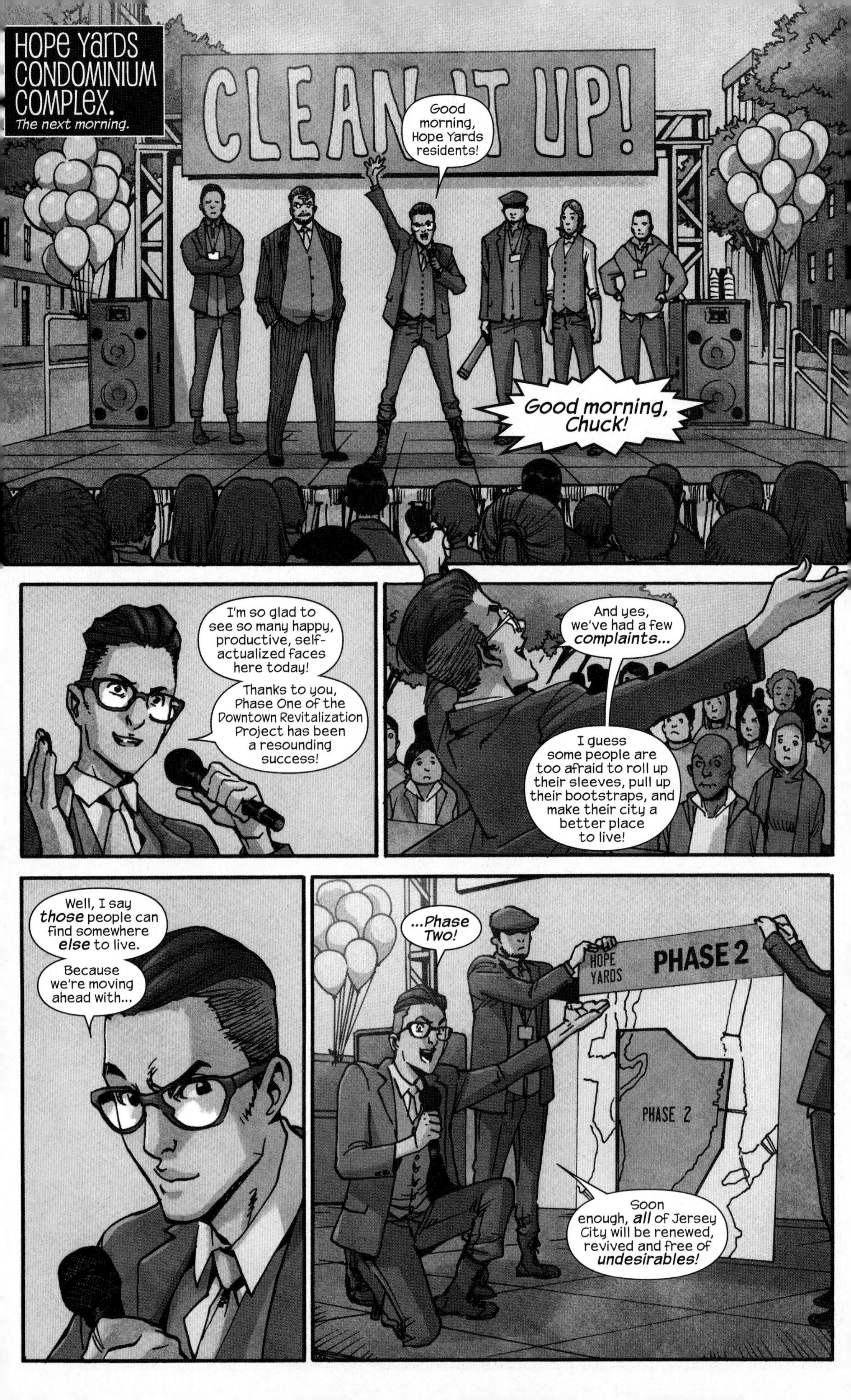

HOPE YARDS CONDOMINIUM COMPLEX.
The next morning.
CLEAN IT UP!
Good morning, Hope Yards residents!
Good morning, Chuck!
I'm so glad to see so many happy, productive, self-actualized faces here today!
Thanks to you, Phase One of the Downtown Revitalization Project has been a resounding success!
And yes, we've had a few *complaints...*
I guess some people are too afraid to roll up their sleeves, pull up their bootstraps, and make their city a better place to live!
Well, I say *those* people can find somewhere *else* to live.
Because we're moving ahead with...
...Phase Two!
HOPE YARDS
PHASE 2
PHASE 2
Soon enough, *all* of Jersey City will be renewed, revived and free of *undesirables!*

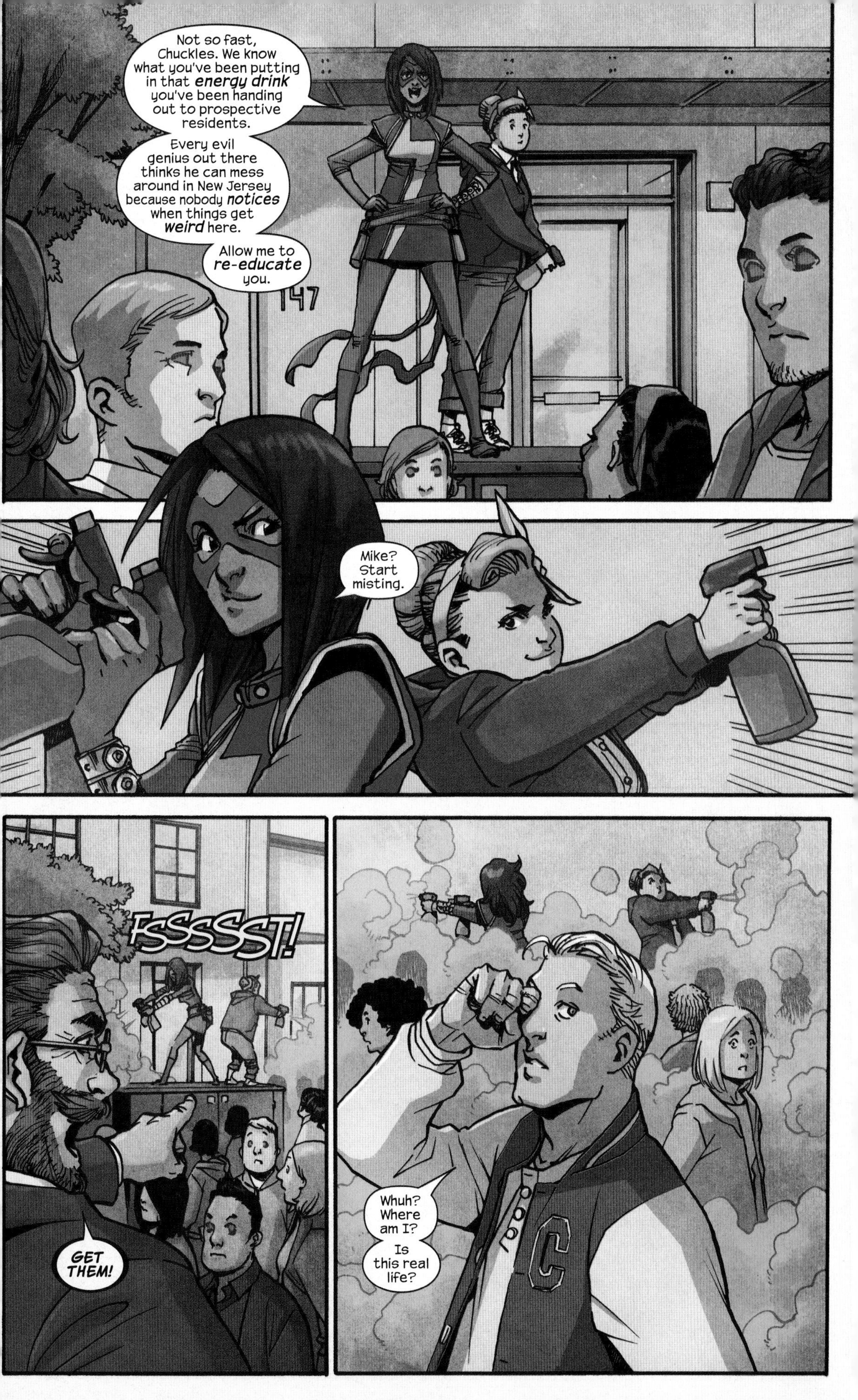

Not so fast, Chuckles. We know what you've been putting in that ***energy drink*** you've been handing out to prospective residents.
Every evil genius out there thinks he can mess around in New Jersey because nobody ***notices*** when things get ***weird*** here.
Allow me to ***re-educate*** you.
147
Mike? Start misting.
FSSSSST!
GET THEM!
Whuh? Where am I?
Is this real life?

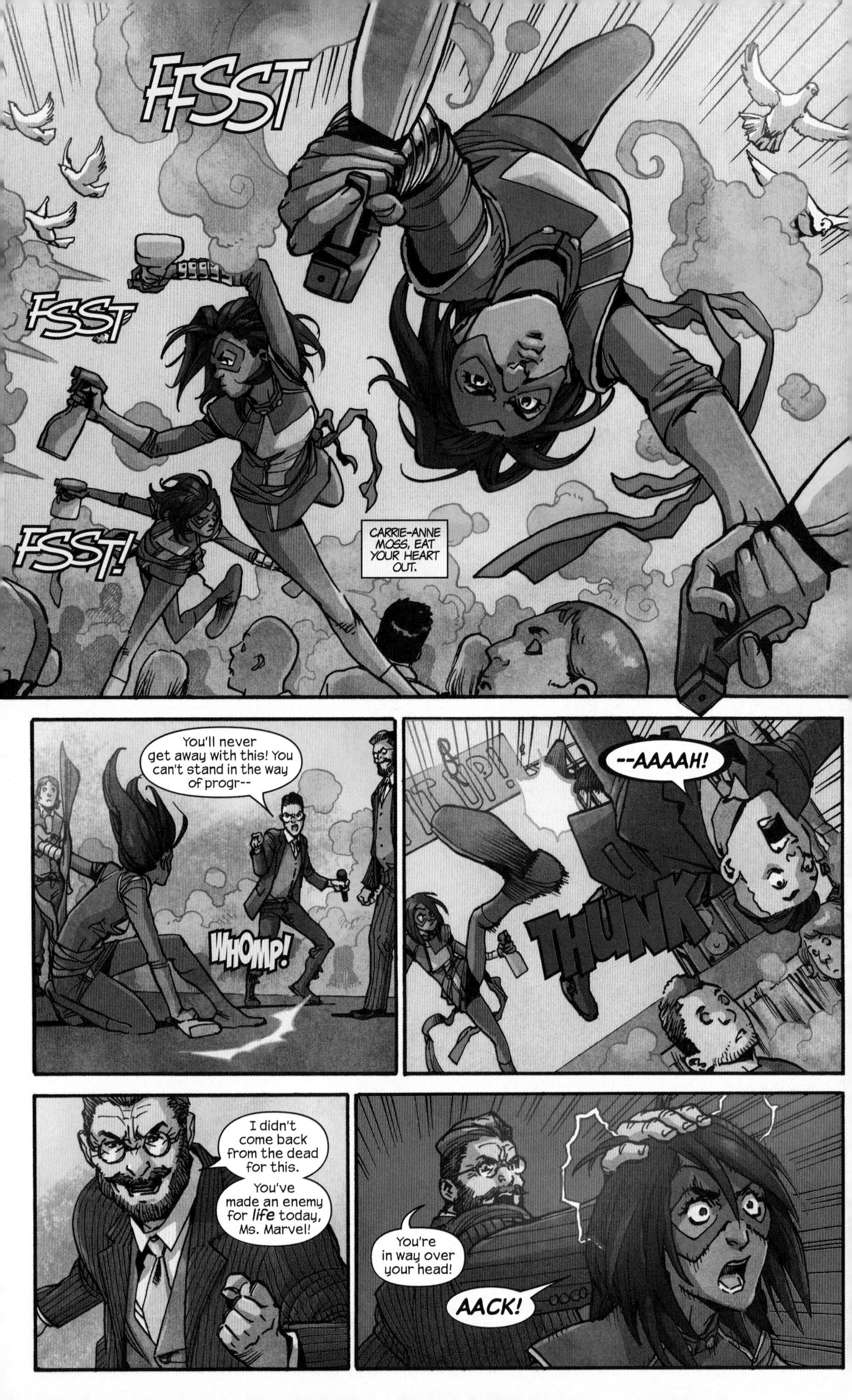
FFSST
FSST
FSST!
CARRIE-ANNE MOSS, EAT YOUR HEART OUT.
You'll never get away with this! You can't stand in the way of progr--
WHOMP!
--AAAAH!
THUNK
I didn't come back from the dead for this.
You've made an enemy for *life* today, Ms. Marvel!
You're in way over your head!
AACK!

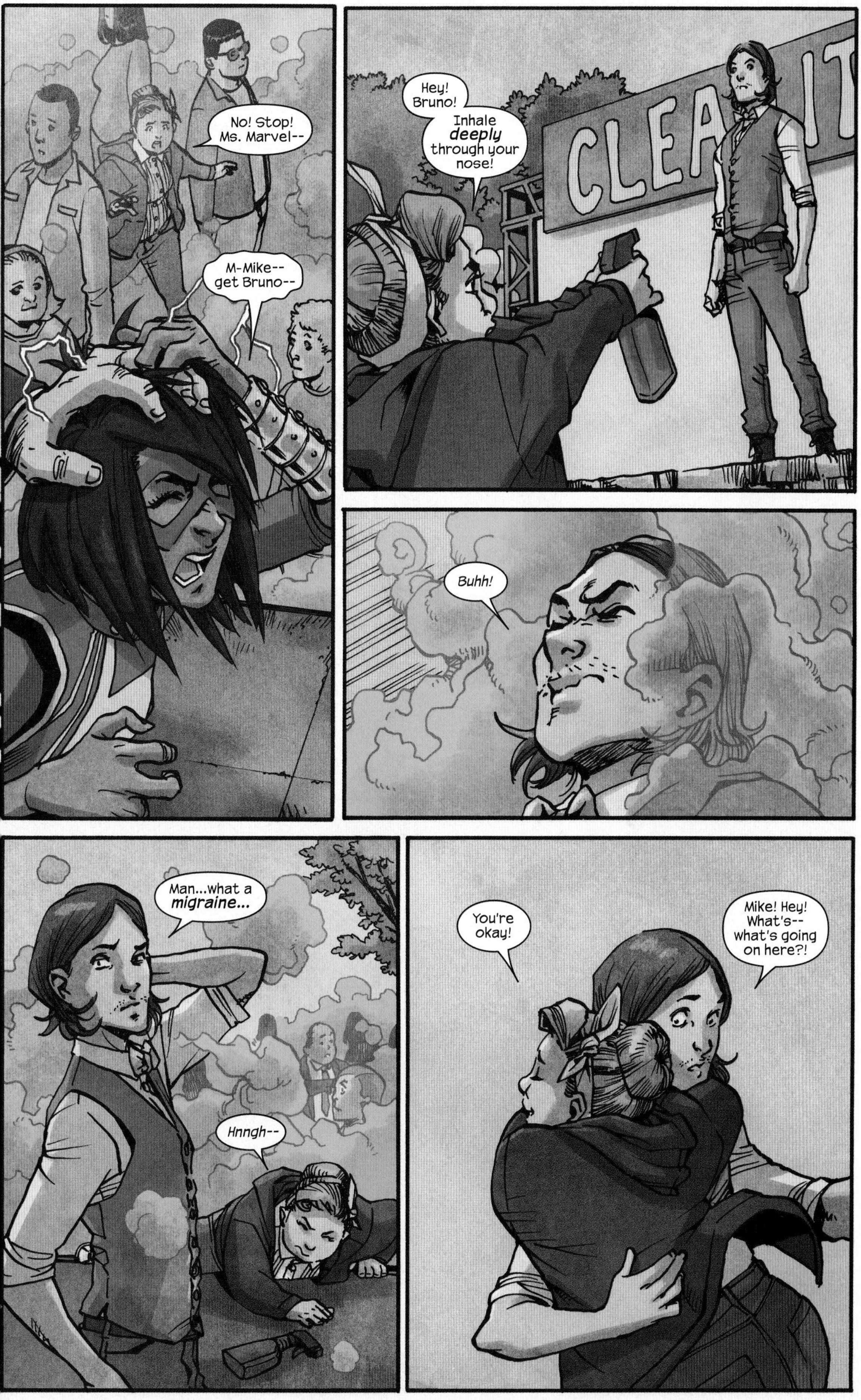
No! Stop! Ms. Marvel--
M-Mike-- get Bruno--
Hey! Bruno!
Inhale *deeply* through your nose!
CLEA
Buhh!
Man...what a *migraine*...
Hnngh--
You're okay!
Mike! Hey! What's-- what's going on here?!

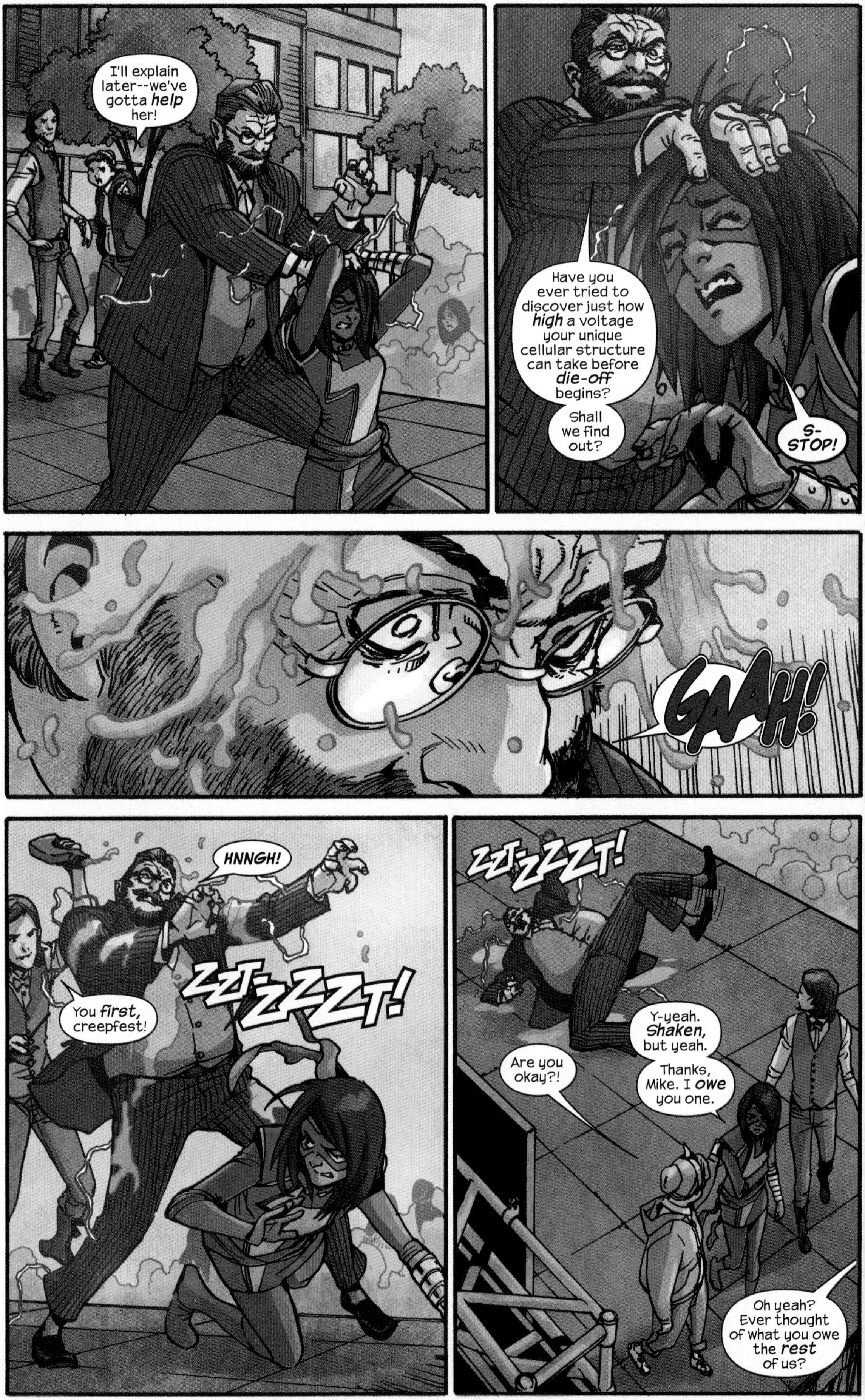

I'll explain later--we've gotta help her!
Have you ever tried to discover just how high a voltage your unique cellular structure can take before die-off begins?
Shall we find out?
S-STOP!
GAAH!
HNNGH!
You first, creepfest!
ZZT-ZZZZT!
ZZT-ZZZZT!
Are you okay?!
Y-yeah. Shaken, but yeah.
Thanks, Mike. I owe you one.
Oh yeah? Ever thought of what you owe the rest of us?

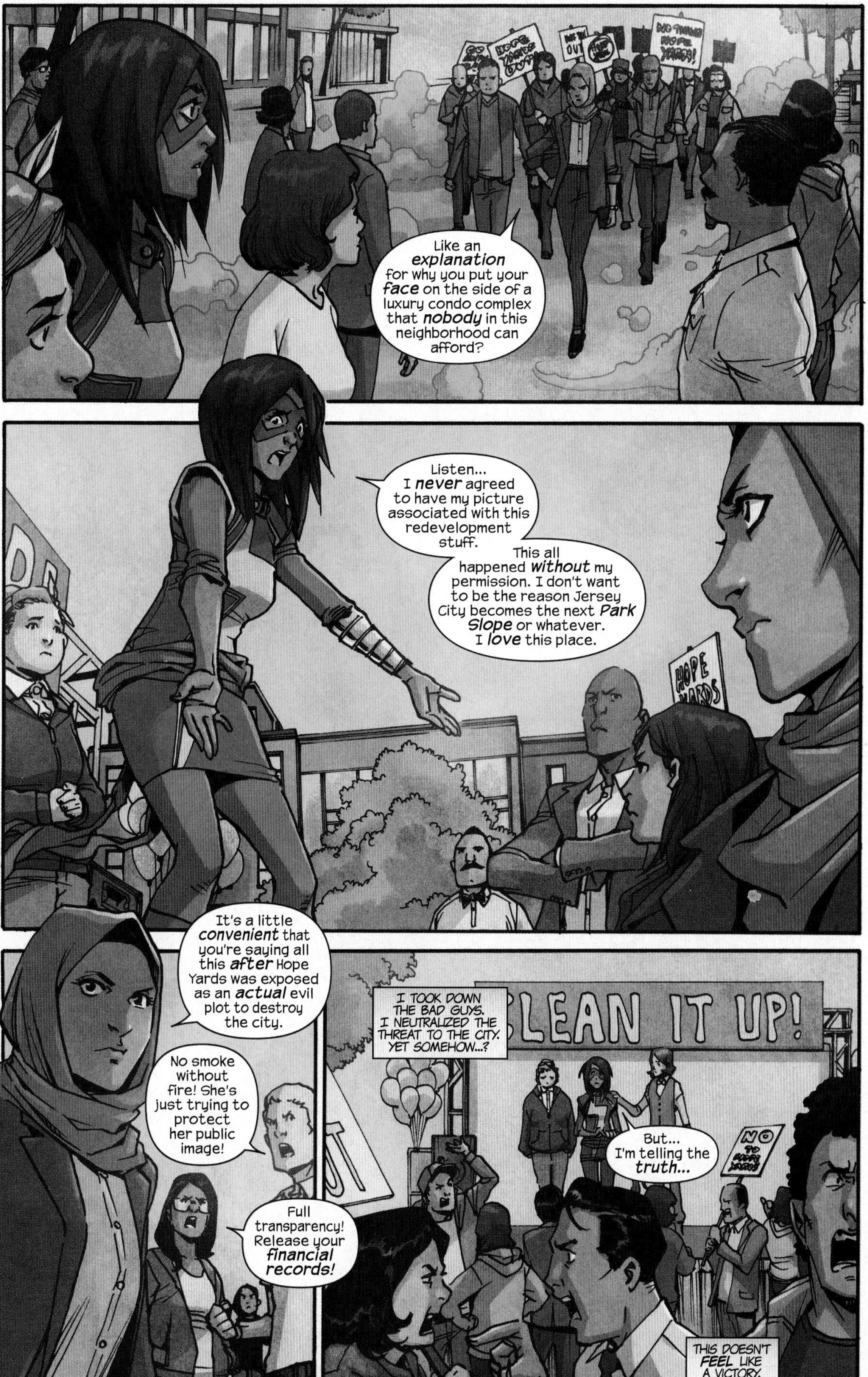

Like an explanation for why you put your face on the side of a luxury condo complex that nobody in this neighborhood can afford?
Listen... I never agreed to have my picture associated with this redevelopment stuff.
This all happened without my permission. I don't want to be the reason Jersey City becomes the next Park Slope or whatever. I love this place.
HOPE YARDS
It's a little convenient that you're saying all this after Hope Yards was exposed as an actual evil plot to destroy the city.
No smoke without fire! She's just trying to protect her public image!
Full transparency! Release your financial records!
I TOOK DOWN THE BAD GUYS. I NEUTRALIZED THE THREAT TO THE CITY. YET SOMEHOW...?
LEAN IT UP!
But... I'm telling the truth...
THIS DOESN'T FEEL LIKE A VICTORY.

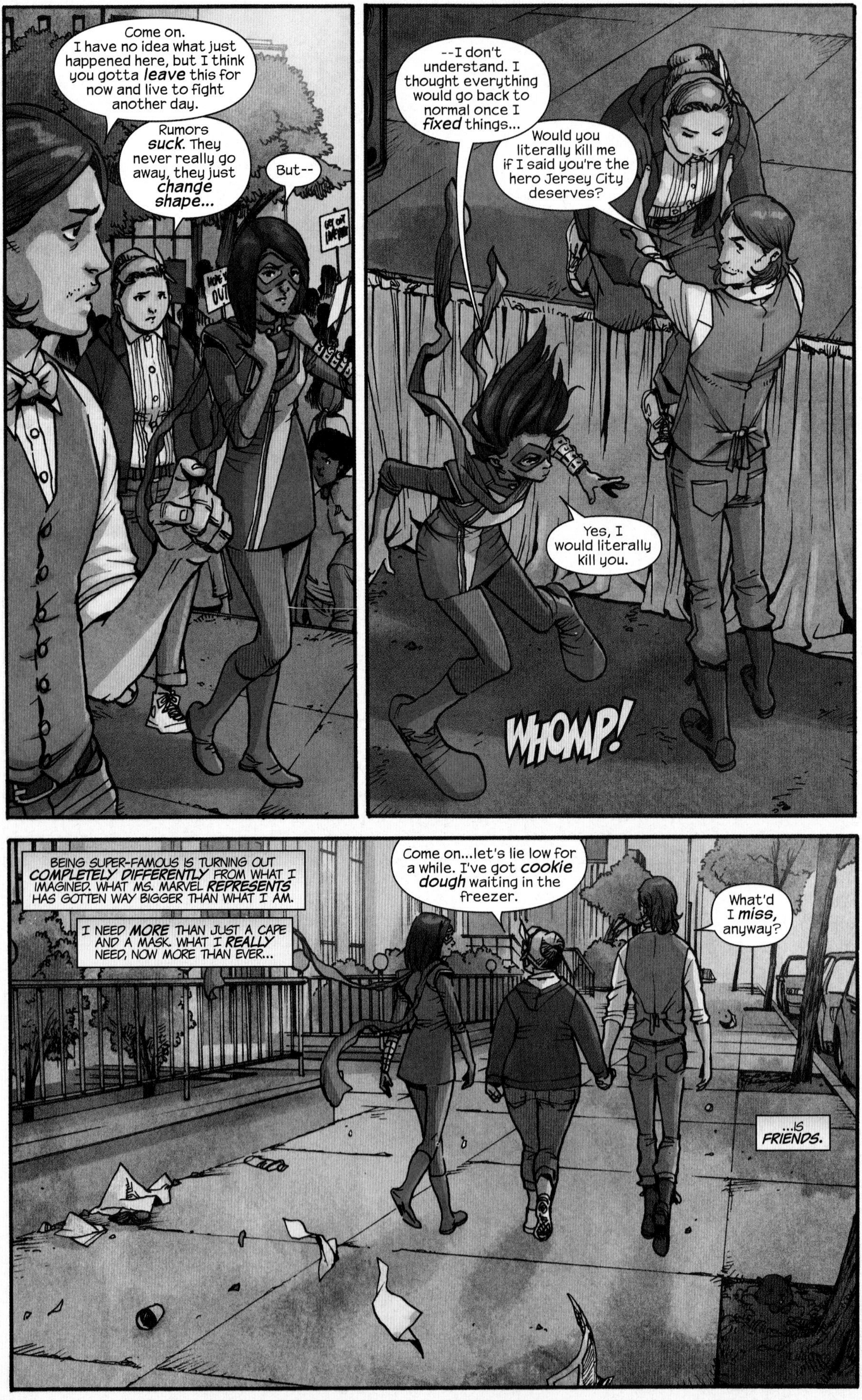

Come on. I have no idea what just happened here, but I think you gotta *leave* this for now and live to fight another day.
Rumors **suck**. They never really go away, they just ***change shape...***
But--
--I don't understand. I thought everything would go back to normal once I ***fixed*** things...
Would you literally kill me if I said you're the hero Jersey City deserves?
Yes, I would literally kill you.
WHOMP!
BEING SUPER-FAMOUS IS TURNING OUT ***COMPLETELY DIFFERENTLY*** FROM WHAT I IMAGINED. WHAT MS. MARVEL ***REPRESENTS*** HAS GOTTEN WAY BIGGER THAN WHAT I AM.
I NEED ***MORE*** THAN JUST A CAPE AND A MASK. WHAT I ***REALLY*** NEED, NOW MORE THAN EVER...
Come on...let's lie low for a while. I've got ***cookie dough*** waiting in the freezer.
What'd I ***miss,*** anyway?
...IS ***FRIENDS.***

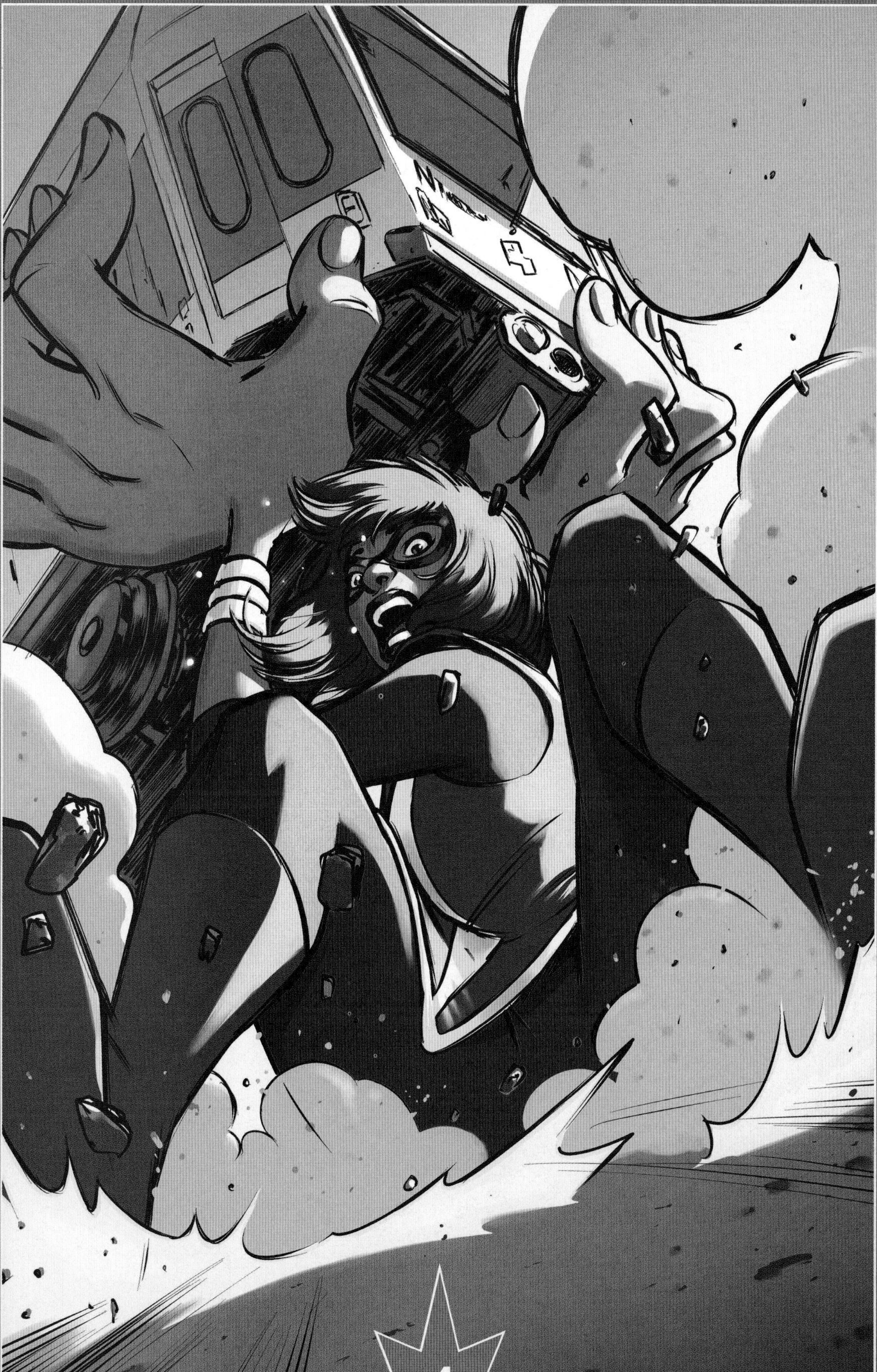
4

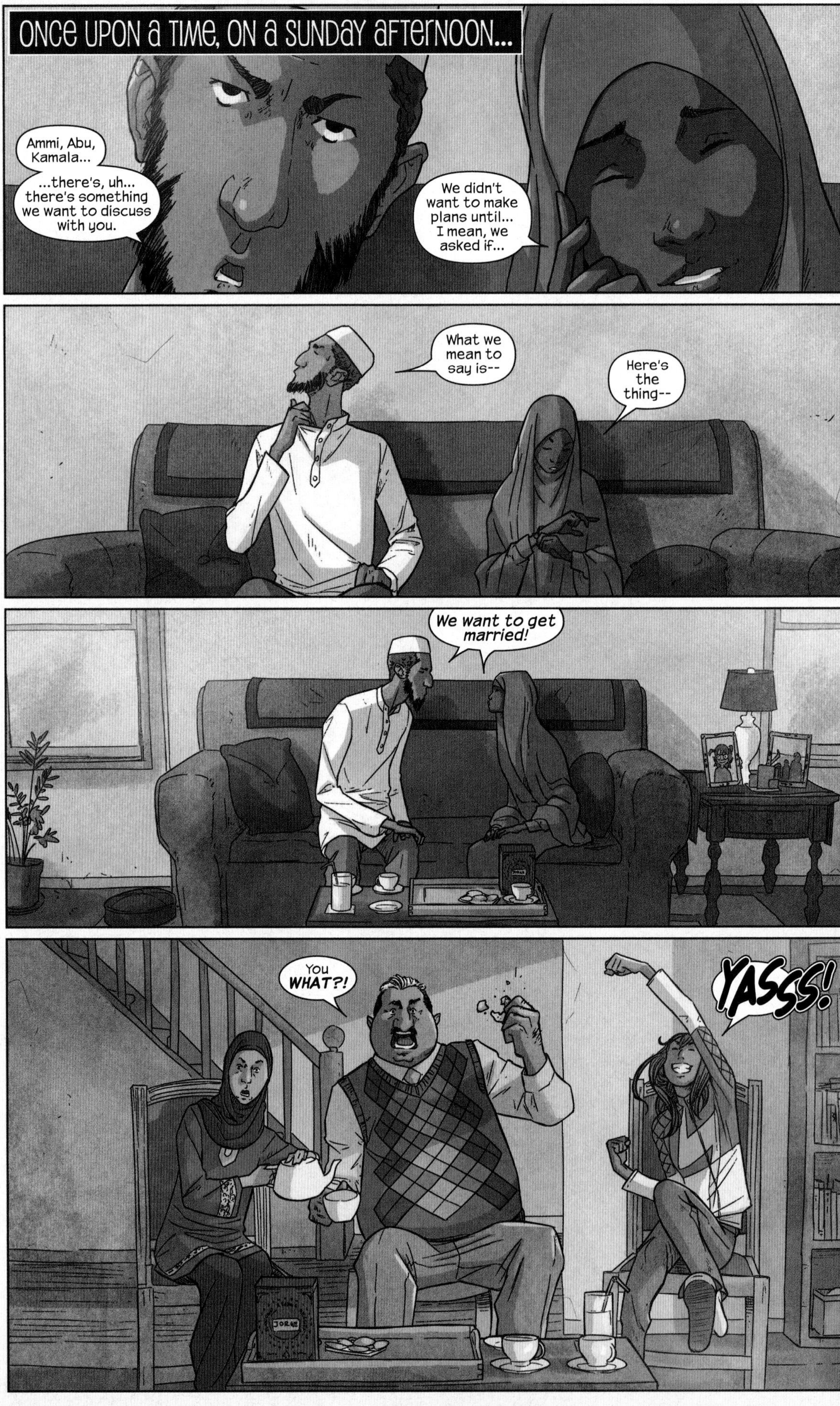
ONCE UPON A TIME, ON A SUNDAY AFTERNOON...
Ammi, Abu, Kamala...
...there's, uh... there's something we want to discuss with you.
We didn't want to make plans until... I mean, we asked if...
What we mean to say is--
Here's the thing--
We want to get married!
You WHAT?!
YASSS!

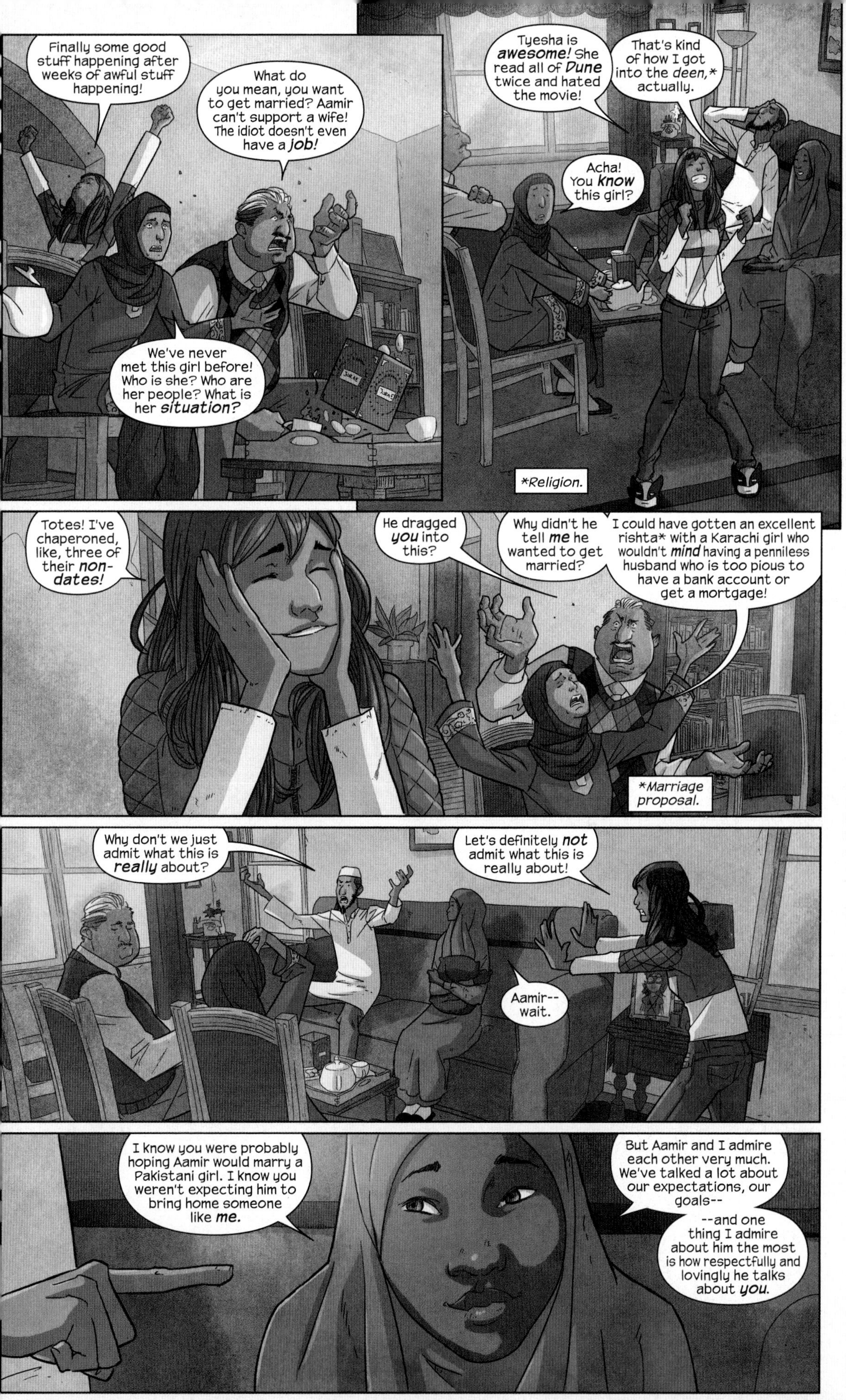
Finally some good stuff happening after weeks of awful stuff happening!
What do you mean, you want to get married? Aamir can't support a wife! The idiot doesn't even have a *job!*
We've never met this girl before! Who is she? Who are her people? What is her *situation?*
Tyesha is *awesome!* She read all of *Dune* twice and hated the movie!
That's kind of how I got into the *deen,** actually.
Acha! You *know* this girl?
*Religion.
Totes! I've chaperoned, like, three of their *non-dates!*
He dragged *you* into this?
Why didn't he tell *me* he wanted to get married?
I could have gotten an excellent rishta* with a Karachi girl who wouldn't *mind* having a penniless husband who is too pious to have a bank account or get a mortgage!
*Marriage proposal.
Why don't we just admit what this is *really* about?
Let's definitely *not* admit what this is really about!
Aamir-- wait.
I know you were probably hoping Aamir would marry a Pakistani girl. I know you weren't expecting him to bring home someone like *me.*
But Aamir and I admire each other very much. We've talked a lot about our expectations, our goals--
--and one thing I admire about him the most is how respectfully and lovingly he talks about *you.*

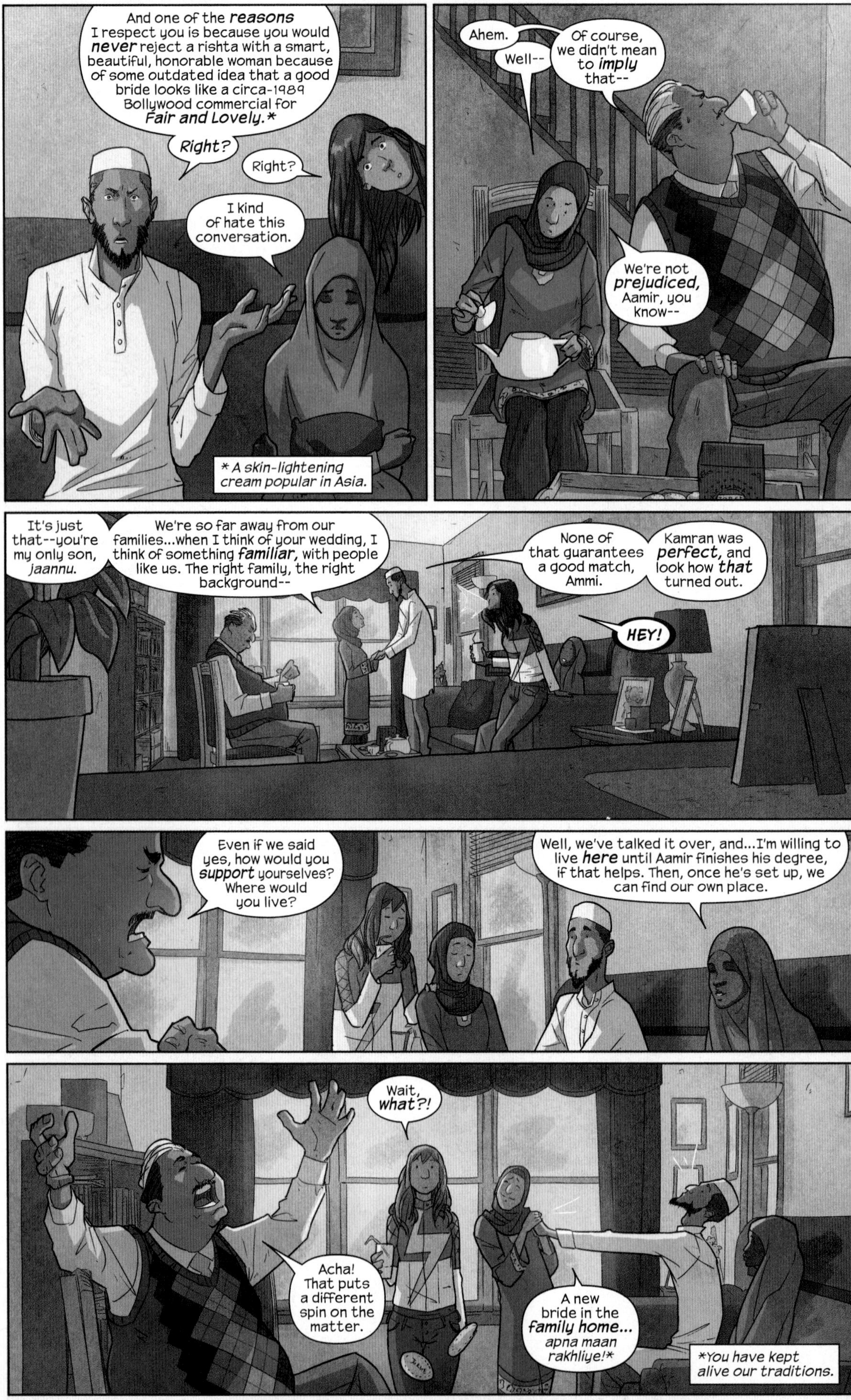

And one of the reasons I respect you is because you would never reject a rishta with a smart, beautiful, honorable woman because of some outdated idea that a good bride looks like a circa-1989 Bollywood commercial for Fair and Lovely.*
Right?
Right?
I kind of hate this conversation.
* A skin-lightening cream popular in Asia.
Ahem.
Well--
Of course, we didn't mean to imply that--
We're not prejudiced, Aamir, you know--
It's just that--you're my only son, jaannu.
We're so far away from our families...when I think of your wedding, I think of something familiar, with people like us. The right family, the right background--
None of that guarantees a good match, Ammi.
Kamran was perfect, and look how that turned out.
HEY!
Even if we said yes, how would you support yourselves? Where would you live?
Well, we've talked it over, and...I'm willing to live here until Aamir finishes his degree, if that helps. Then, once he's set up, we can find our own place.
Wait, what?!
Acha! That puts a different spin on the matter.
A new bride in the family home... apna maan rakhliye!*
*You have kept alive our traditions.

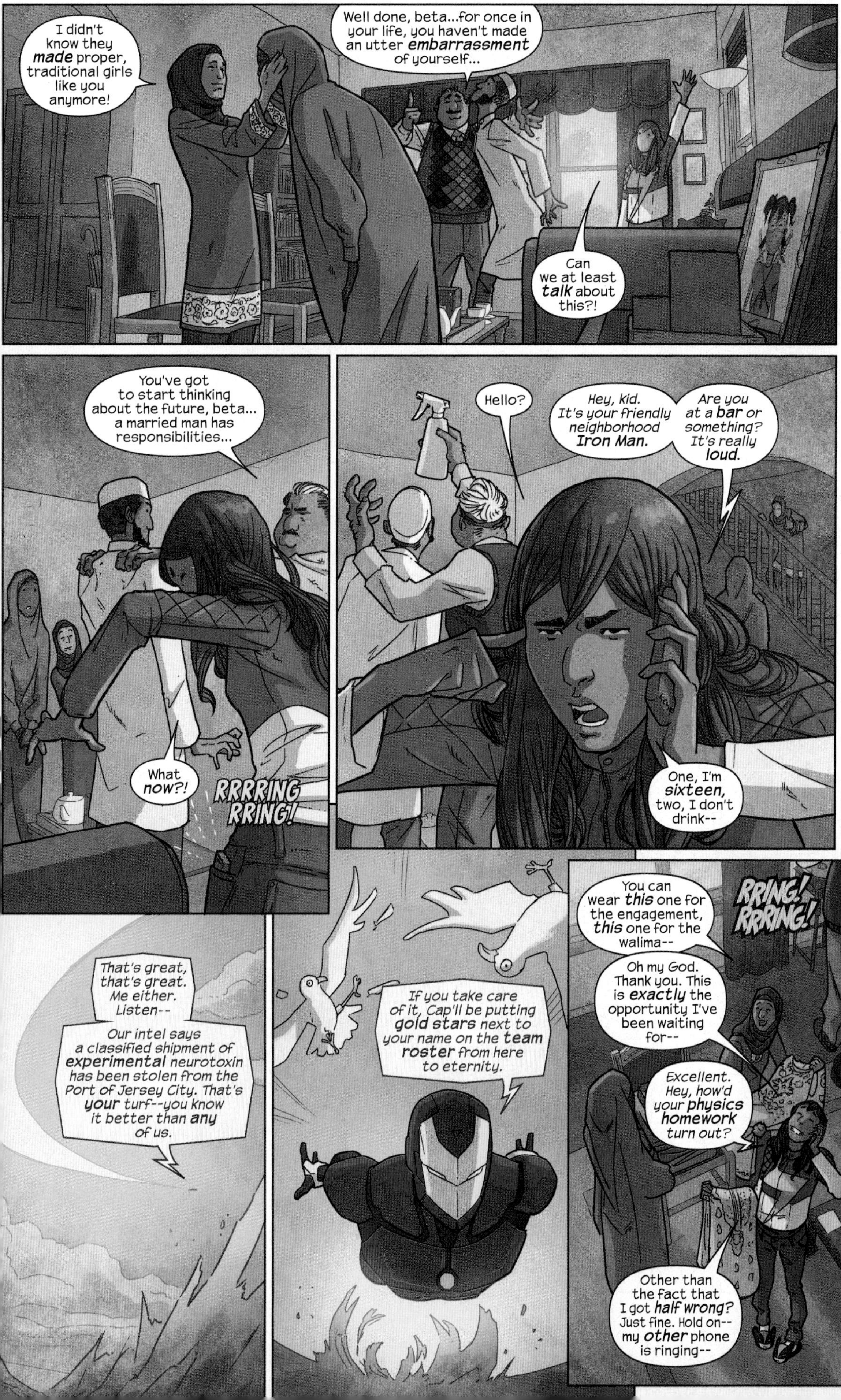

I didn't know they made proper, traditional girls like you anymore!
Well done, beta...for once in your life, you haven't made an utter embarrassment of yourself...
Can we at least talk about this?!
You've got to start thinking about the future, beta... a married man has responsibilities...
What now?!
RRRRING RRING!
Hello?
Hey, kid. It's your friendly neighborhood Iron Man.
Are you at a bar or something? It's really loud.
One, I'm sixteen, two, I don't drink--
That's great, that's great. Me either. Listen--
Our intel says a classified shipment of experimental neurotoxin has been stolen from the Port of Jersey City. That's your turf--you know it better than any of us.
If you take care of it, Cap'll be putting gold stars next to your name on the team roster from here to eternity.
You can wear this one for the engagement, this one for the walima--
RRING! RRRING!
Oh my God. Thank you. This is exactly the opportunity I've been waiting for--
Excellent. Hey, how'd your physics homework turn out?
Other than the fact that I got half wrong? Just fine. Hold on-- my other phone is ringing--

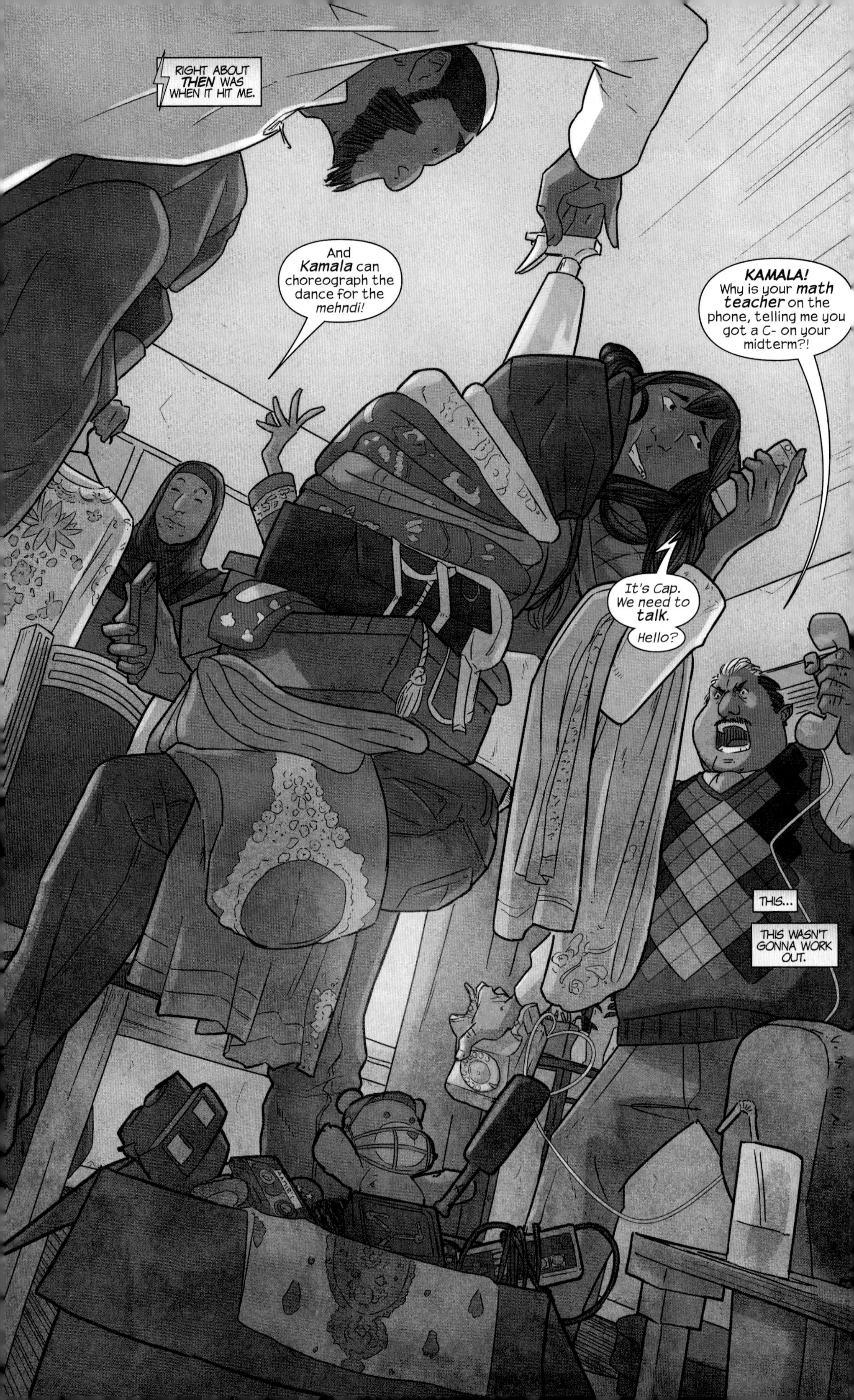
RIGHT ABOUT THEN WAS WHEN IT HIT ME.
And Kamala can choreograph the dance for the mehndi!
KAMALA! Why is your math teacher on the phone, telling me you got a C- on your midterm?!
It's Cap. We need to talk.
Hello?
THIS...
THIS WASN'T GONNA WORK OUT.

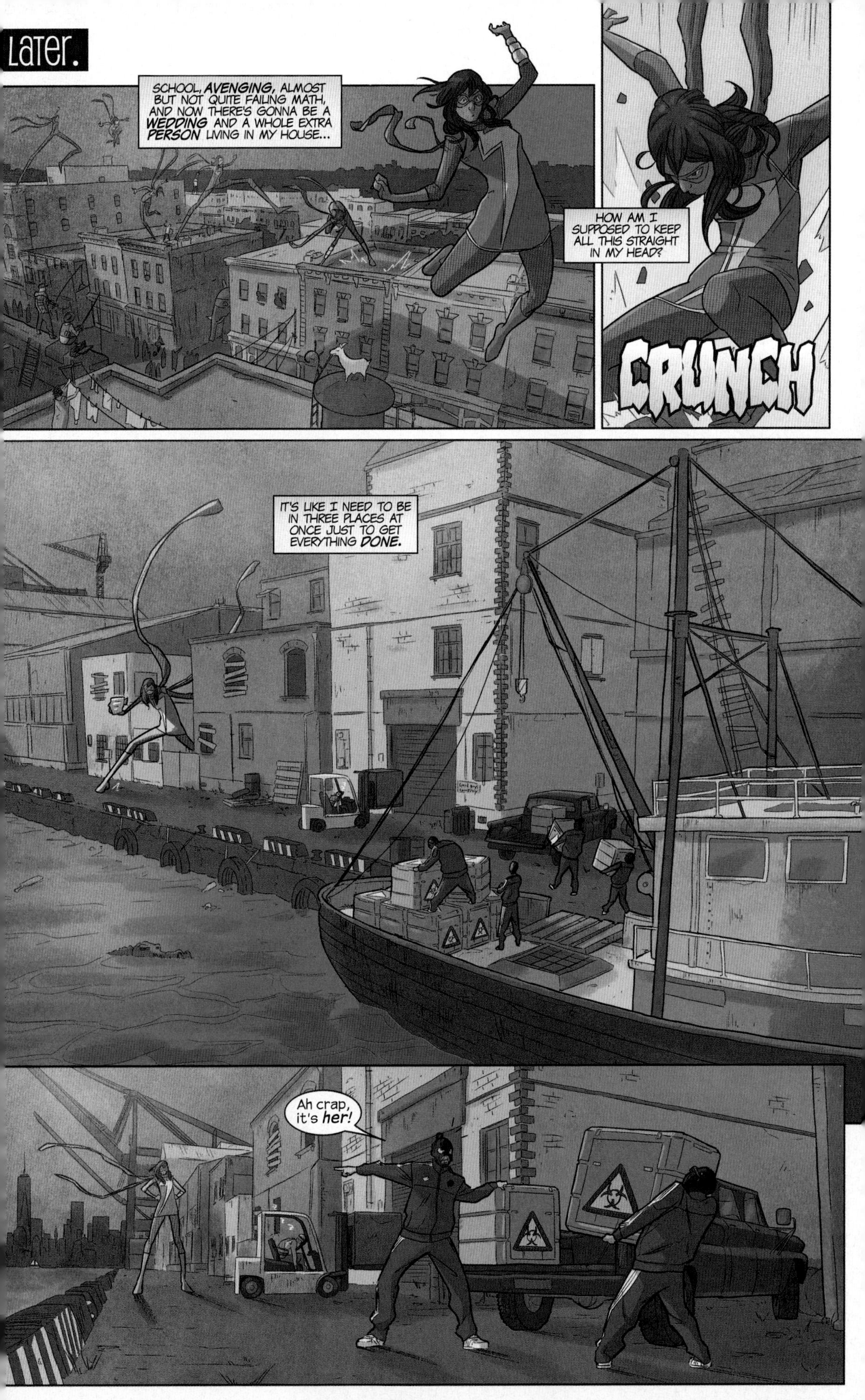
LATER.
SCHOOL, AVENGING, ALMOST BUT NOT QUITE FAILING MATH, AND NOW THERE'S GONNA BE A WEDDING AND A WHOLE EXTRA PERSON LIVING IN MY HOUSE...
HOW AM I SUPPOSED TO KEEP ALL THIS STRAIGHT IN MY HEAD?
CRUNCH
IT'S LIKE I NEED TO BE IN THREE PLACES AT ONCE JUST TO GET EVERYTHING DONE.
Ah crap, it's her!

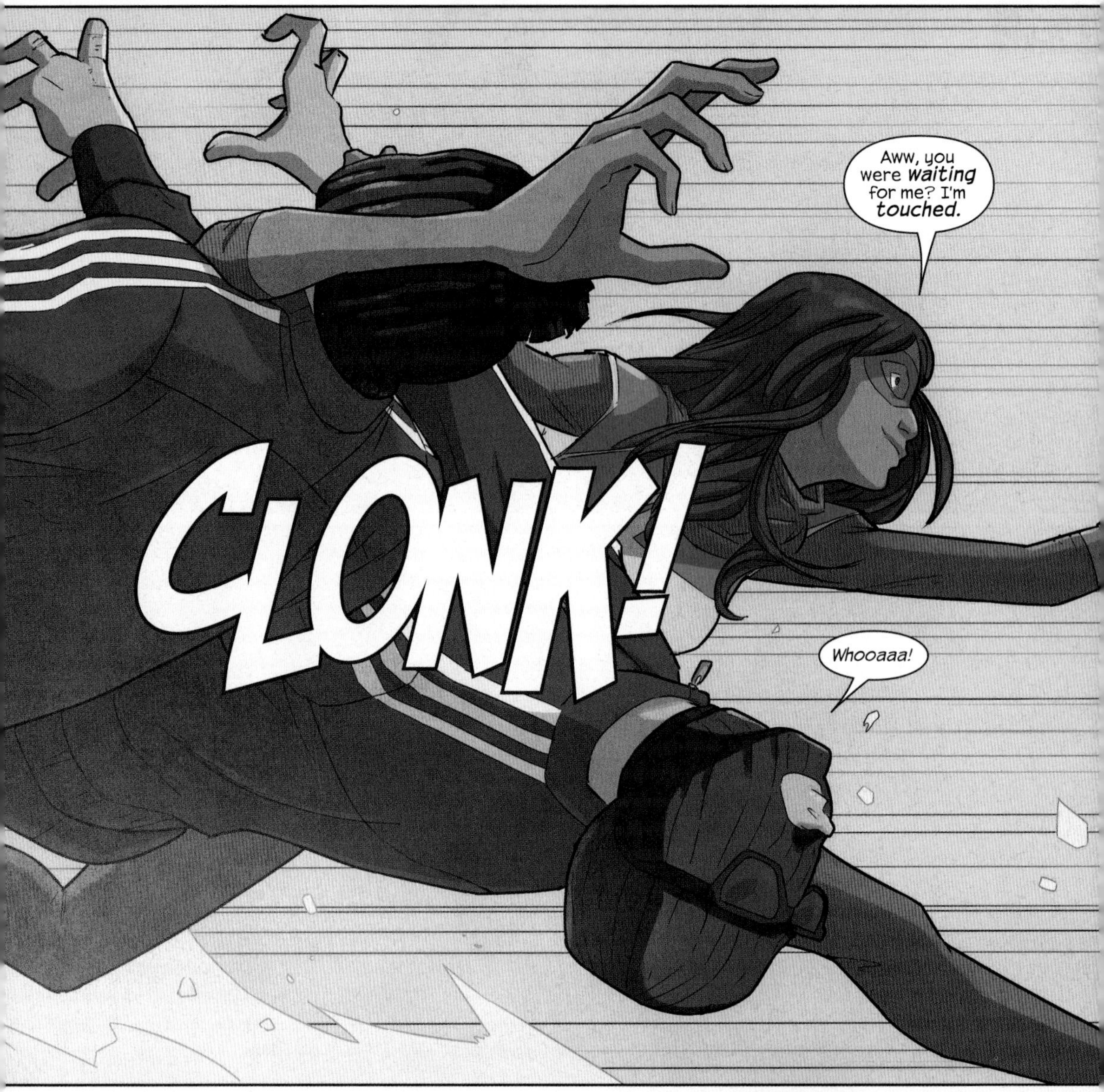
Aww, you were waiting for me? I'm touched.
CLONK!
Whooaaa!

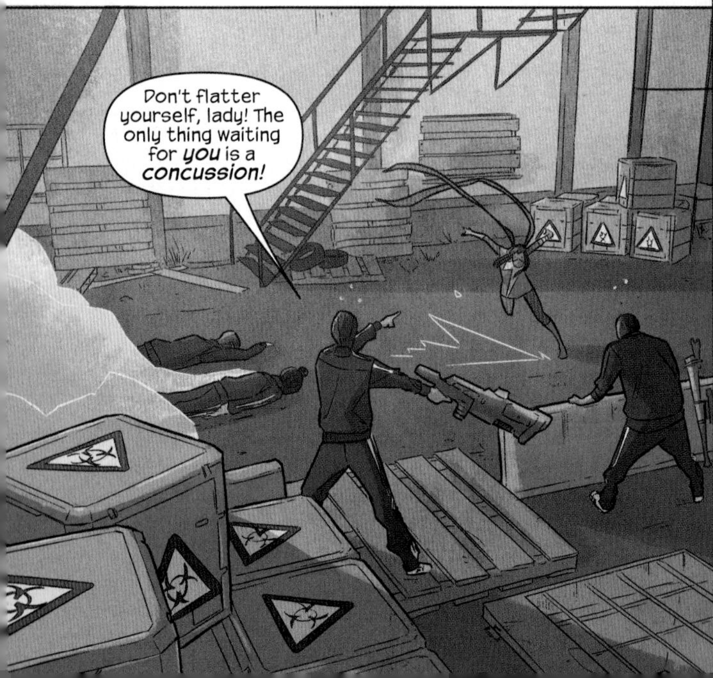
Don't flatter yourself, lady! The only thing waiting for you is a concussion!

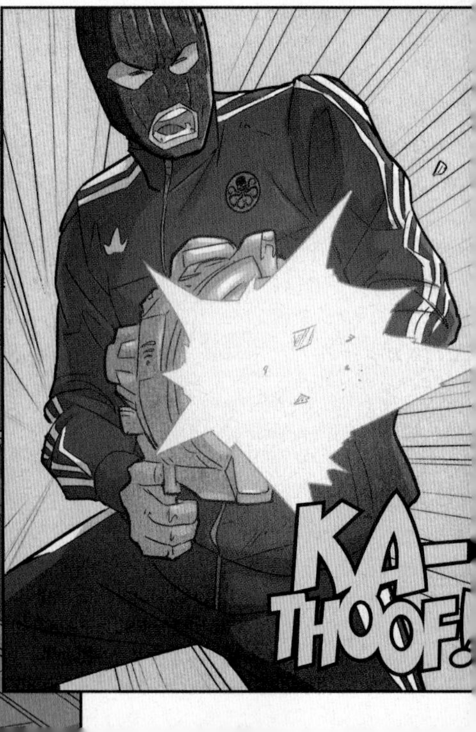
KA-THOOF!

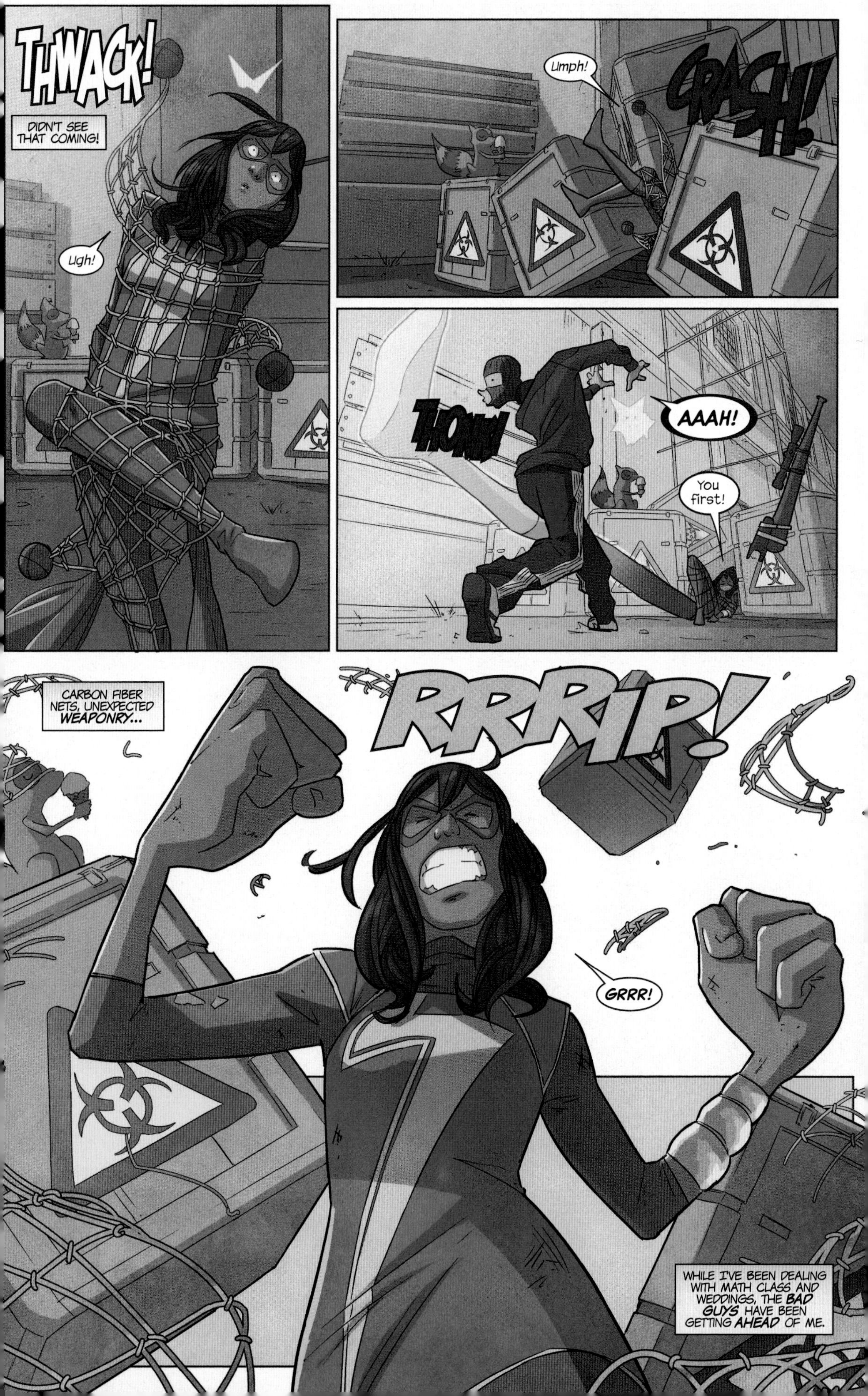
THWACK!
DIDN'T SEE THAT COMING!
Ugh!
Umph!
CRASH!
THONK!
AAAH!
You first!
CARBON FIBER NETS, UNEXPECTED WEAPONRY...
RRRIP!
GRRR!
WHILE I'VE BEEN DEALING WITH MATH CLASS AND WEDDINGS, THE BAD GUYS HAVE BEEN GETTING AHEAD OF ME.

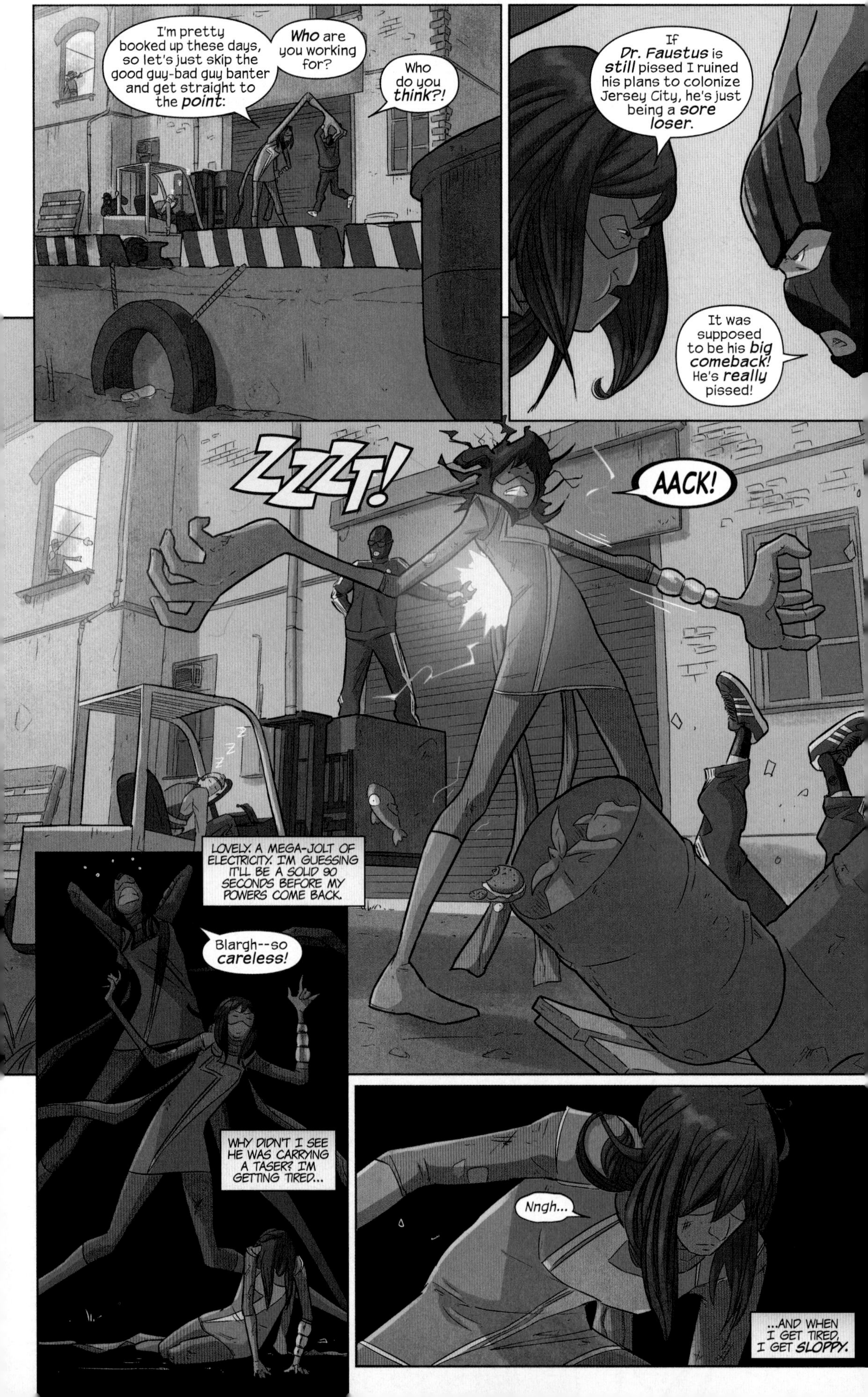
I'm pretty booked up these days, so let's just skip the good guy-bad guy banter and get straight to the point:
Who are you working for?
Who do you think?!
If Dr. Faustus is still pissed I ruined his plans to colonize Jersey City, he's just being a sore loser.
It was supposed to be his big comeback! He's really pissed!
ZZZZT!
AACK!
LOVELY. A MEGA-JOLT OF ELECTRICITY. I'M GUESSING IT'LL BE A SOLID 90 SECONDS BEFORE MY POWERS COME BACK.
Blargh--so careless!
WHY DIDN'T I SEE HE WAS CARRYING A TASER? I'M GETTING TIRED...
Nngh...
...AND WHEN I GET TIRED, I GET SLOPPY.

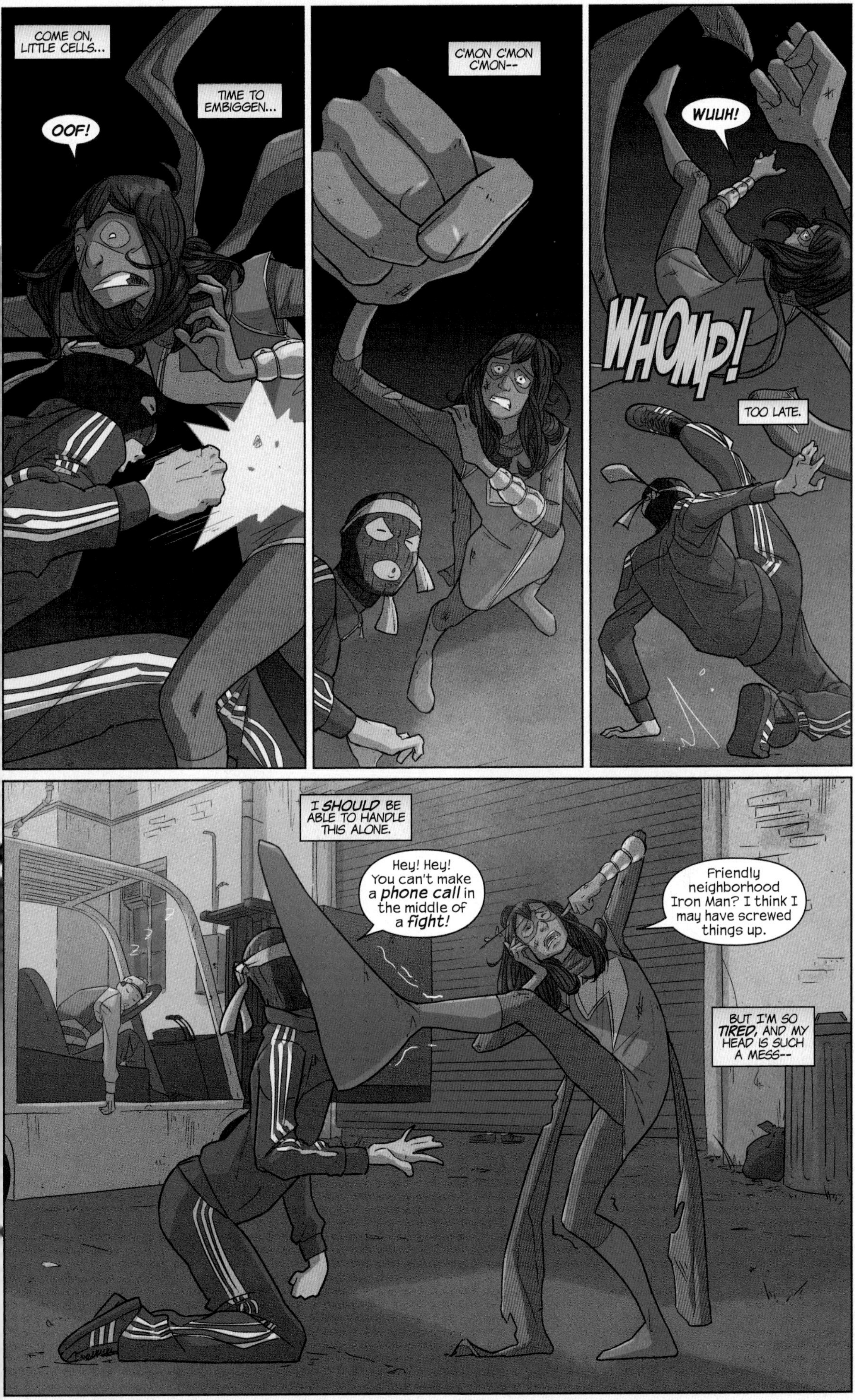
COME ON, LITTLE CELLS...
TIME TO EMBIGGEN...
OOF!
C'MON C'MON C'MON--
WUUH!
WHOMP!
TOO LATE.
I SHOULD BE ABLE TO HANDLE THIS ALONE.
Hey! Hey! You can't make a phone call in the middle of a fight!
Friendly neighborhood Iron Man? I think I may have screwed things up.
BUT I'M SO TIRED, AND MY HEAD IS SUCH A MESS--

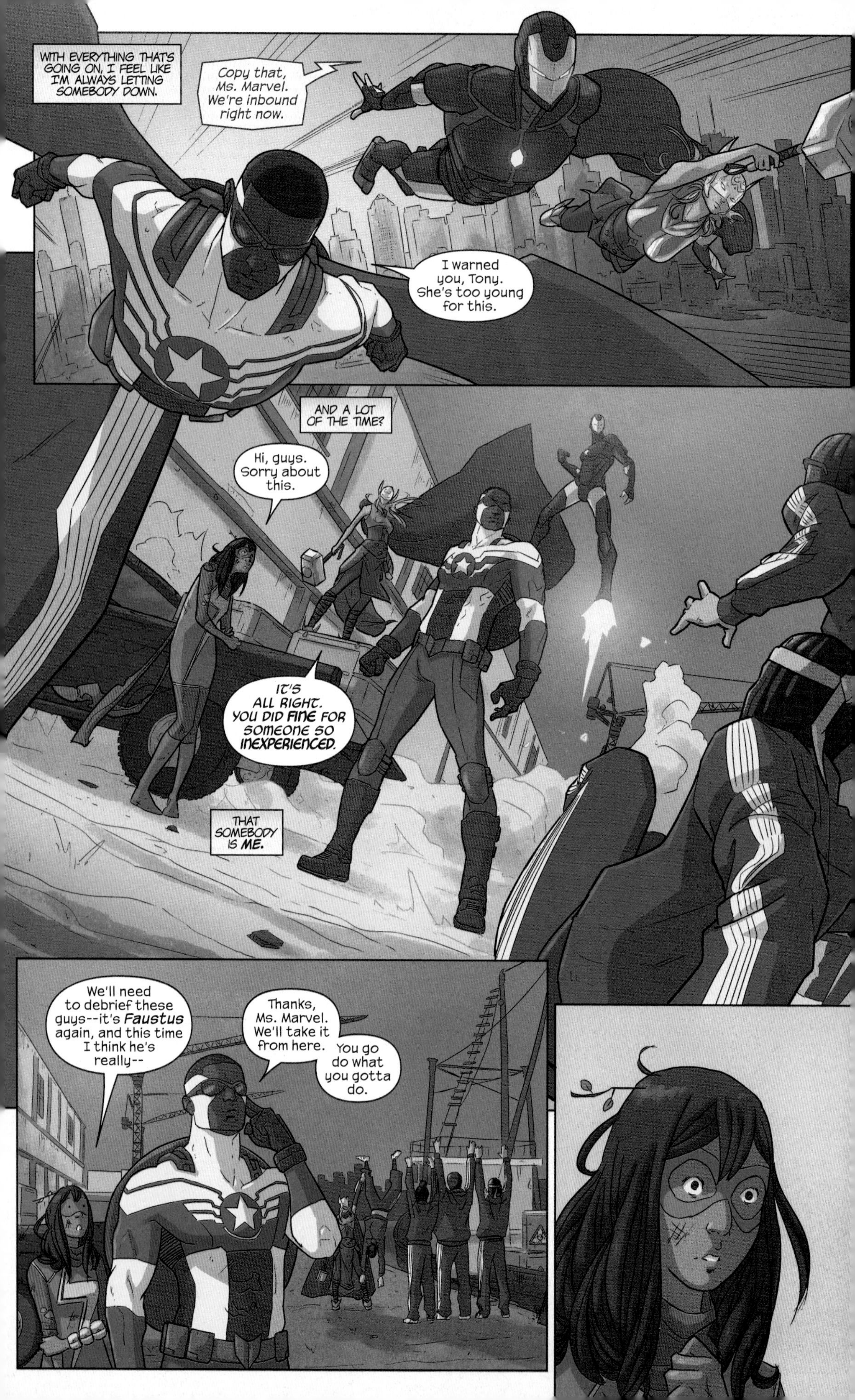

WITH EVERYTHING THAT'S GOING ON, I FEEL LIKE I'M ALWAYS LETTING SOMEBODY DOWN.
Copy that, Ms. Marvel. We're inbound right now.
I warned you, Tony. She's too young for this.
AND A LOT OF THE TIME?
Hi, guys. Sorry about this.
IT'S ALL RIGHT. YOU DID FINE FOR SOMEONE SO INEXPERIENCED.
THAT SOMEBODY IS ME.
We'll need to debrief these guys--it's Faustus again, and this time I think he's really--
Thanks, Ms. Marvel. We'll take it from here.
You go do what you gotta do.

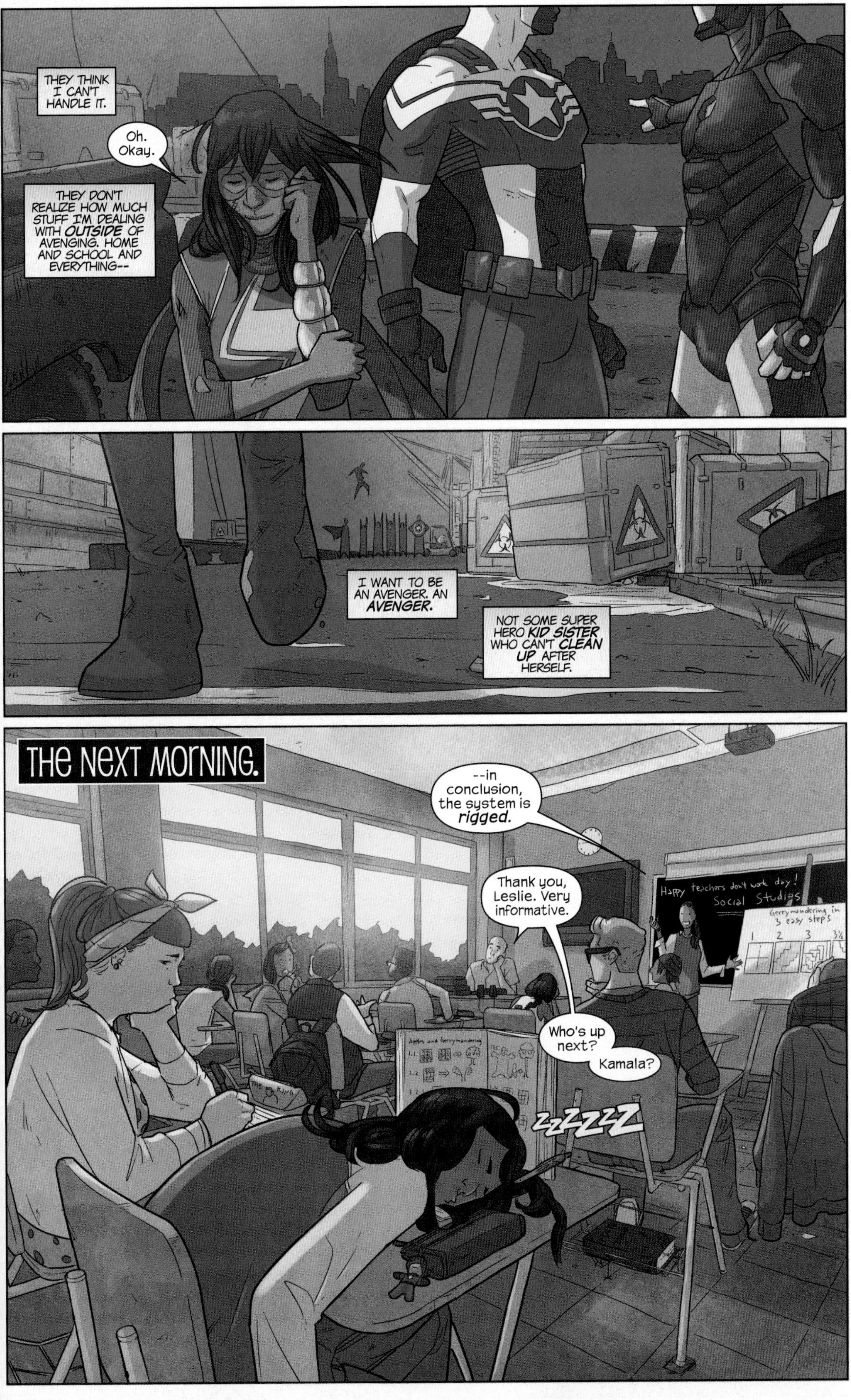
THEY THINK I CAN'T HANDLE IT.
Oh. Okay.
THEY DON'T REALIZE HOW MUCH STUFF I'M DEALING WITH **OUTSIDE** OF AVENGING. HOME AND SCHOOL AND EVERYTHING--
I WANT TO BE AN AVENGER. AN ***AVENGER.***
NOT SOME SUPER HERO ***KID SISTER*** WHO CAN'T ***CLEAN UP*** AFTER HERSELF.
THE NEXT MORNING.
--in conclusion, the system is ***rigged.***
Happy teachers don't work day!
Social Studies
Gerrymandering in 3 easy steps
Thank you, Leslie. Very informative.
Who's up next?
Kamala?
ZZZZZZ

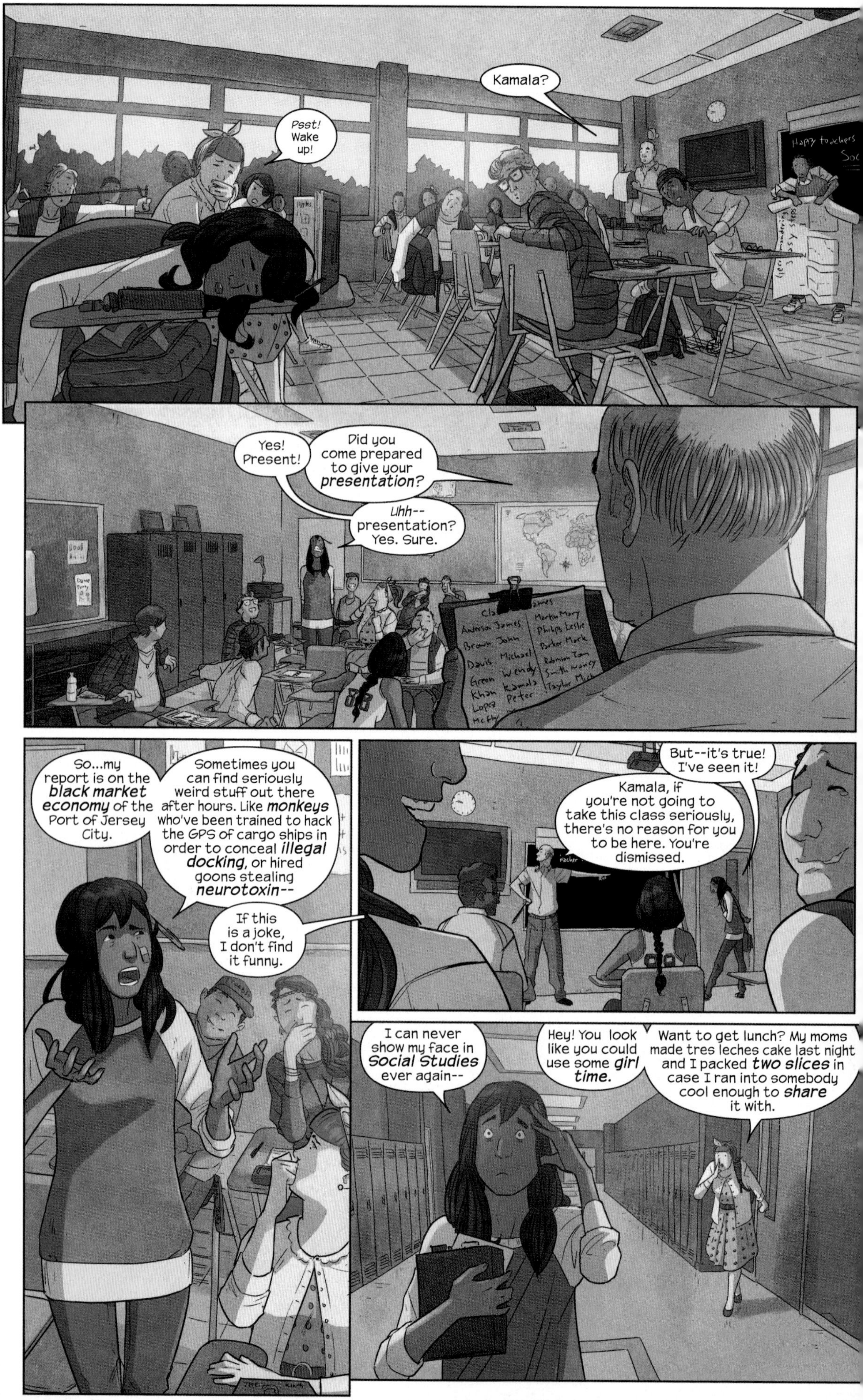
Psst! Wake up!
Kamala?
Yes! Present!
Did you come prepared to give your *presentation*?
Uhh-- presentation? Yes. Sure.
So...my report is on the *black market economy* of the Port of Jersey City.
Sometimes you can find seriously weird stuff out there after hours. Like *monkeys* who've been trained to hack the GPS of cargo ships in order to conceal *illegal docking*, or hired goons stealing *neurotoxin*--
If this is a joke, I don't find it funny.
Kamala, if you're not going to take this class seriously, there's no reason for you to be here. You're dismissed.
But--it's true! I've seen it!
I can never show my face in *Social Studies* ever again--
Hey! You look like you could use some *girl time.*
Want to get lunch? My moms made tres leches cake last night and I packed *two slices* in case I ran into somebody cool enough to *share* it with.

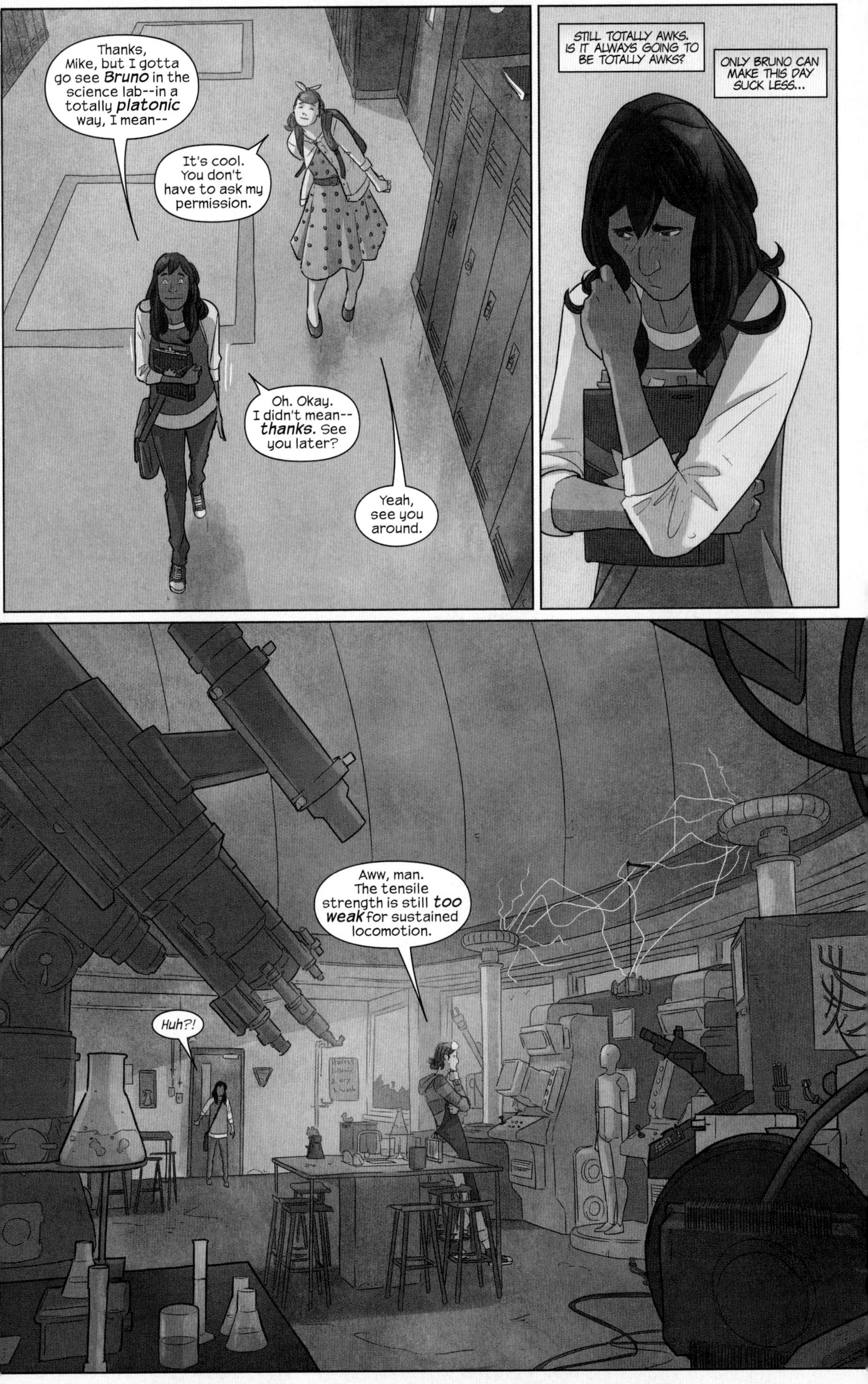

Thanks, Mike, but I gotta go see Bruno in the science lab--in a totally platonic way, I mean--
It's cool. You don't have to ask my permission.
Oh. Okay. I didn't mean-- thanks. See you later?
Yeah, see you around.
STILL TOTALLY AWKS. IS IT ALWAYS GOING TO BE TOTALLY AWKS?
ONLY BRUNO CAN MAKE THIS DAY SUCK LESS...
Aww, man. The tensile strength is still too weak for sustained locomotion.
Huh?!

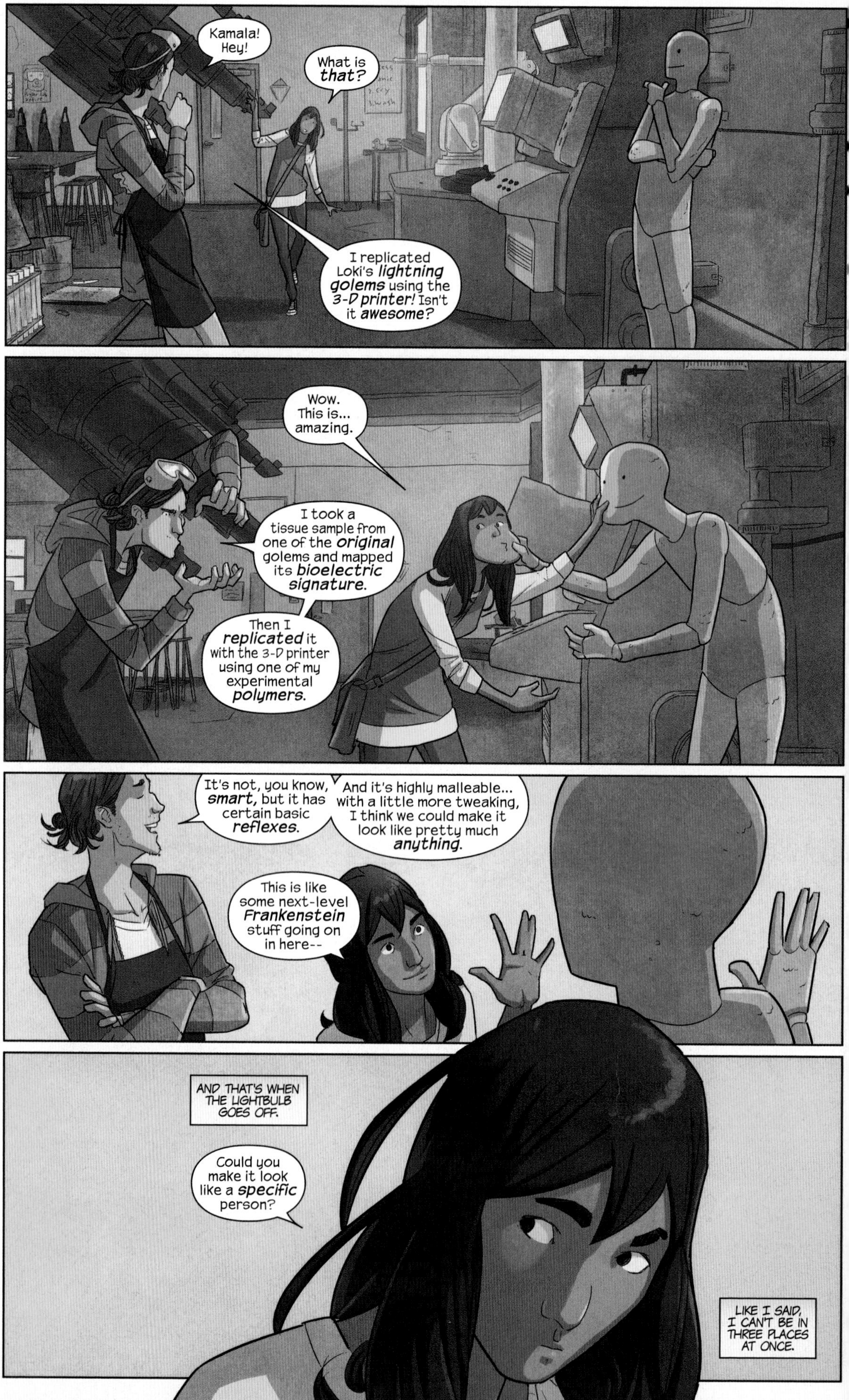
Kamala! Hey!
What is that?
I replicated Loki's lightning golems using the 3-D printer! Isn't it awesome?
Wow. This is... amazing.
I took a tissue sample from one of the original golems and mapped its bioelectric signature.
Then I replicated it with the 3-D printer using one of my experimental polymers.
It's not, you know, smart, but it has certain basic reflexes.
And it's highly malleable... with a little more tweaking, I think we could make it look like pretty much anything.
This is like some next-level Frankenstein stuff going on in here--
AND THAT'S WHEN THE LIGHTBULB GOES OFF.
Could you make it look like a specific person?
LIKE I SAID, I CAN'T BE IN THREE PLACES AT ONCE.

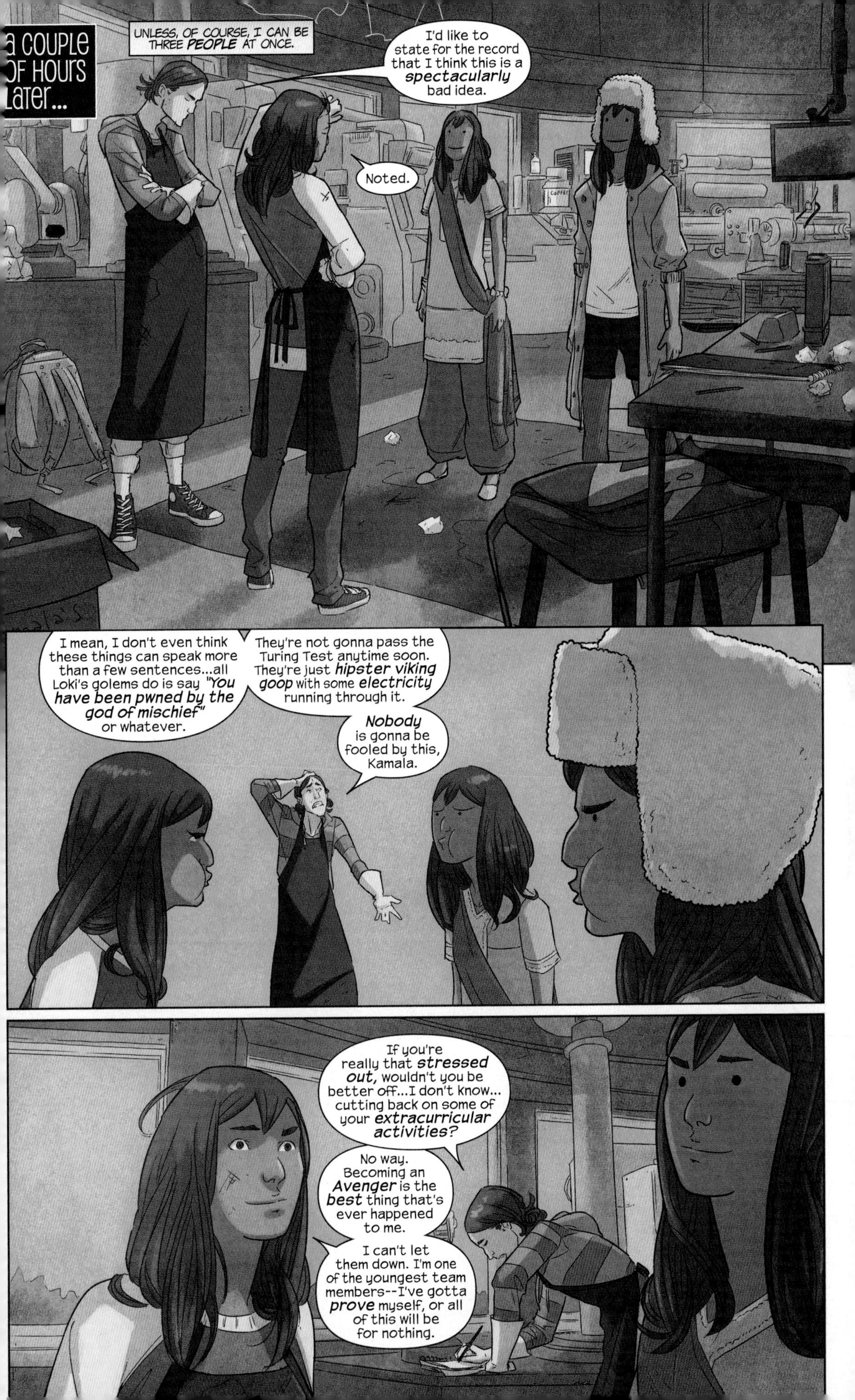
A COUPLE OF HOURS LATER...
UNLESS, OF COURSE, I CAN BE THREE PEOPLE AT ONCE.
I'd like to state for the record that I think this is a spectacularly bad idea.
Noted.
I mean, I don't even think these things can speak more than a few sentences...all Loki's golems do is say "You have been pwned by the god of mischief" or whatever.
They're not gonna pass the Turing Test anytime soon. They're just hipster viking goop with some electricity running through it.
Nobody is gonna be fooled by this, Kamala.
If you're really that stressed out, wouldn't you be better off...I don't know... cutting back on some of your extracurricular activities?
No way. Becoming an Avenger is the best thing that's ever happened to me.
I can't let them down. I'm one of the youngest team members--I've gotta prove myself, or all of this will be for nothing.

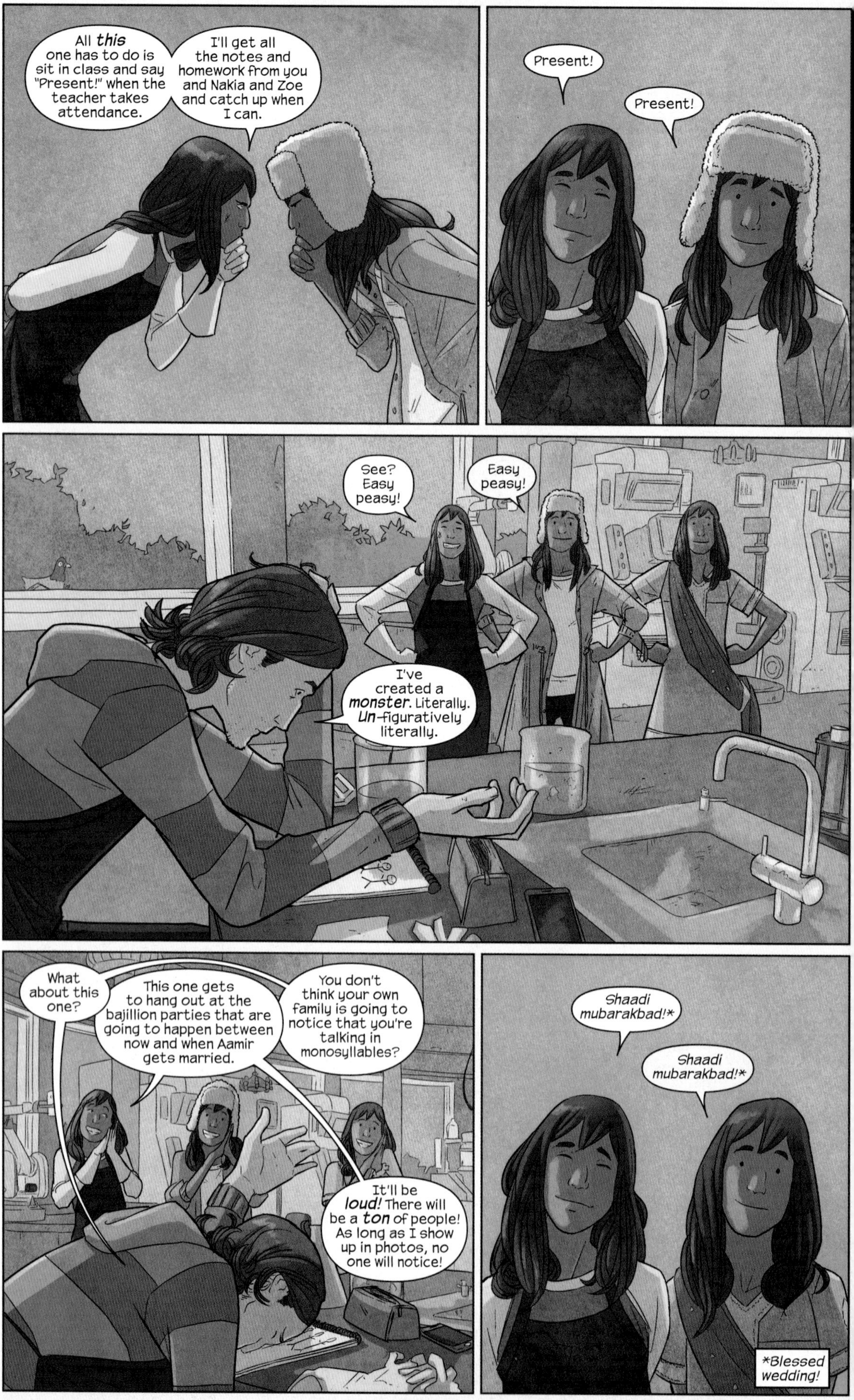
All this one has to do is sit in class and say "Present!" when the teacher takes attendance.
I'll get all the notes and homework from you and Nakia and Zoe and catch up when I can.
Present!
Present!
See? Easy peasy!
Easy peasy!
I've created a monster. Literally. Un-figuratively literally.
What about this one?
This one gets to hang out at the bajillion parties that are going to happen between now and when Aamir gets married.
You don't think your own family is going to notice that you're talking in monosyllables?
It'll be loud! There will be a ton of people! As long as I show up in photos, no one will notice!
Shaadi mubarakbad!*
Shaadi mubarakbad!*
*Blessed wedding!

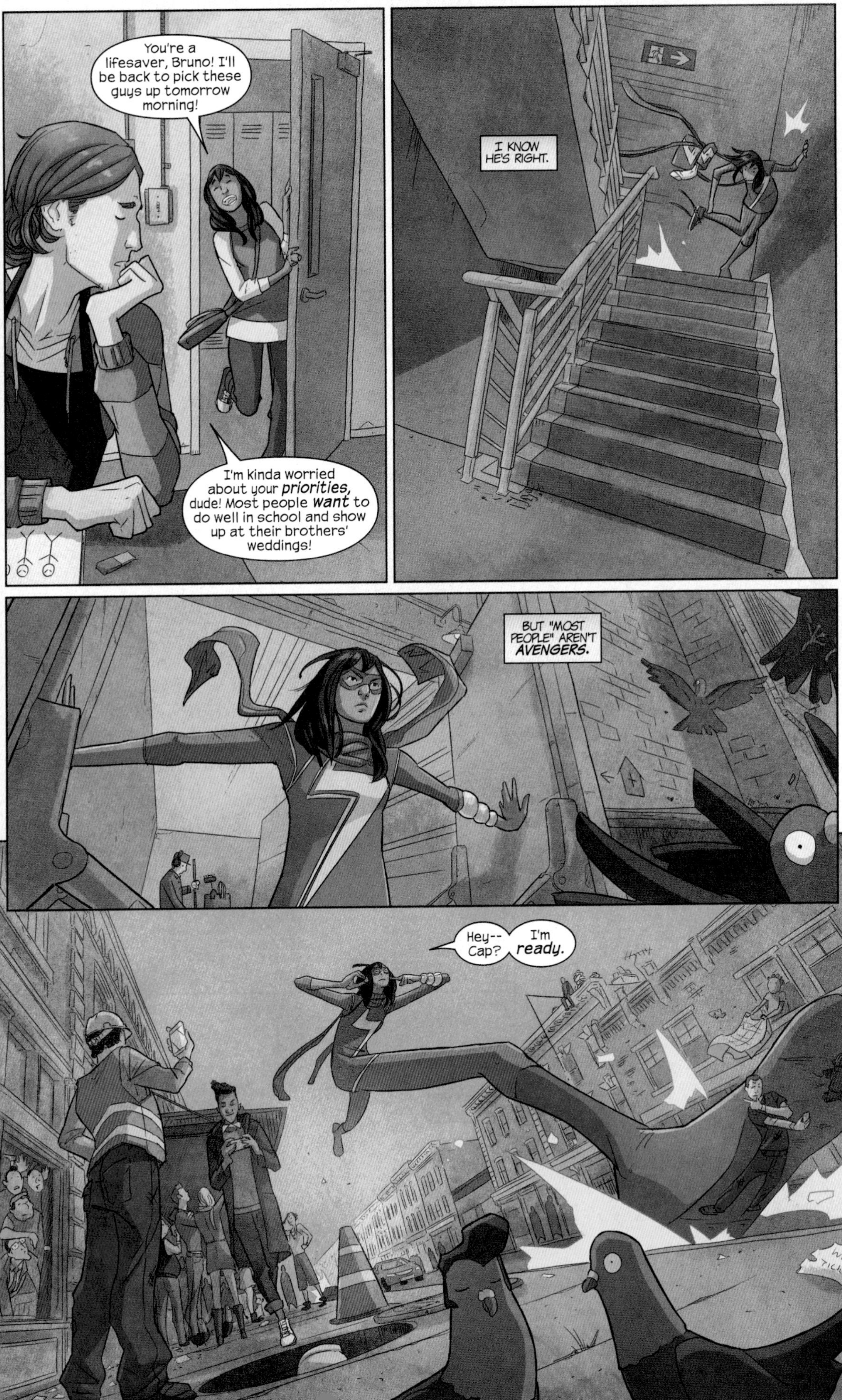
You're a lifesaver, Bruno! I'll be back to pick these guys up tomorrow morning!
I'm kinda worried about your *priorities,* dude! Most people *want* to do well in school and show up at their brothers' weddings!
I KNOW HE'S RIGHT.
BUT "MOST PEOPLE" AREN'T *AVENGERS.*
Hey-- Cap?
I'm *ready.*

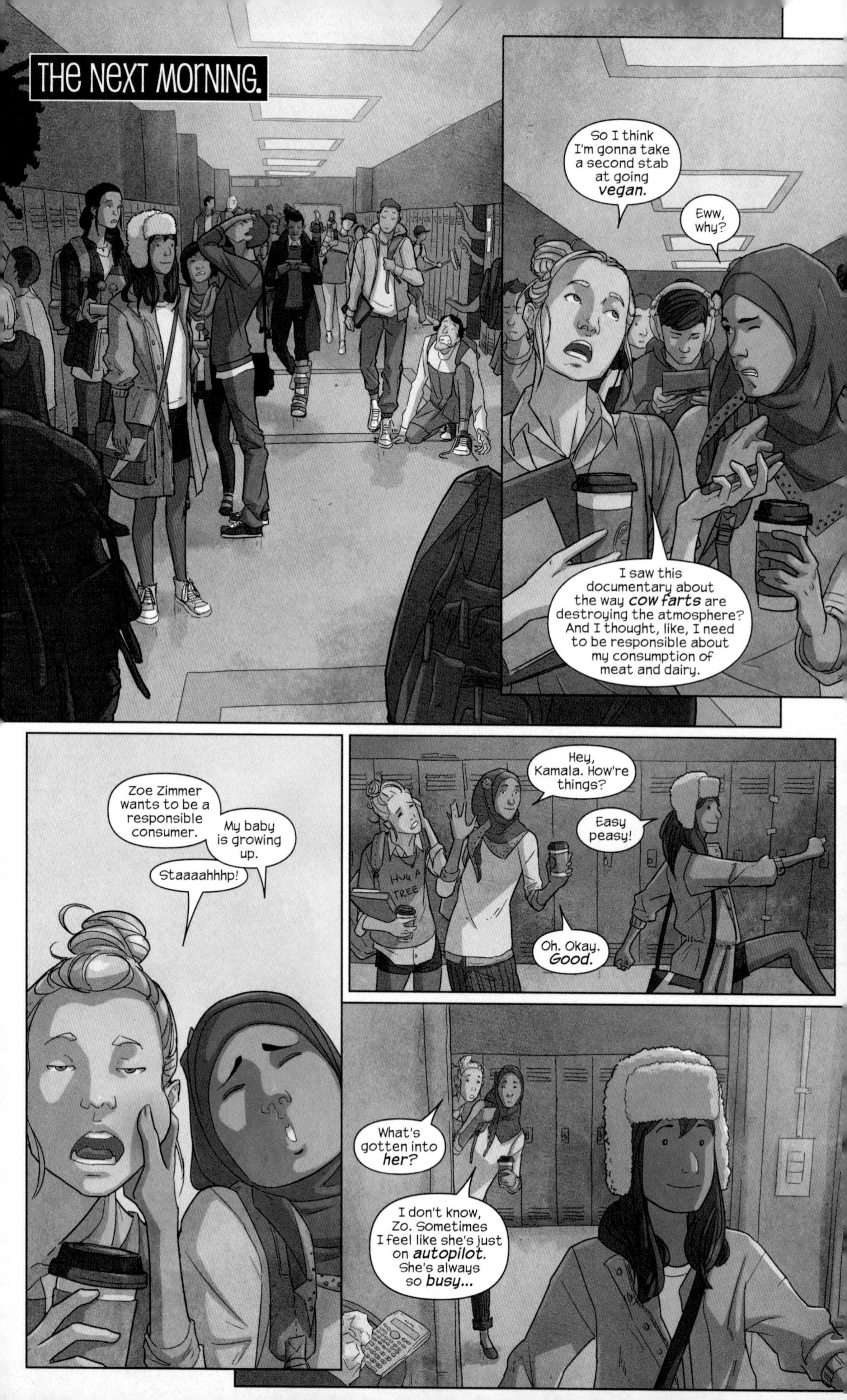
THE NEXT MORNING.
So I think I'm gonna take a second stab at going vegan.
Eww, why?
I saw this documentary about the way cow farts are destroying the atmosphere? And I thought, like, I need to be responsible about my consumption of meat and dairy.
Zoe Zimmer wants to be a responsible consumer.
My baby is growing up.
Staaaahhhp!
Hey, Kamala. How're things?
Easy peasy!
Oh. Okay. Good.
What's gotten into her?
I don't know, Zo. Sometimes I feel like she's just on autopilot. She's always so busy...
HUG A TREE

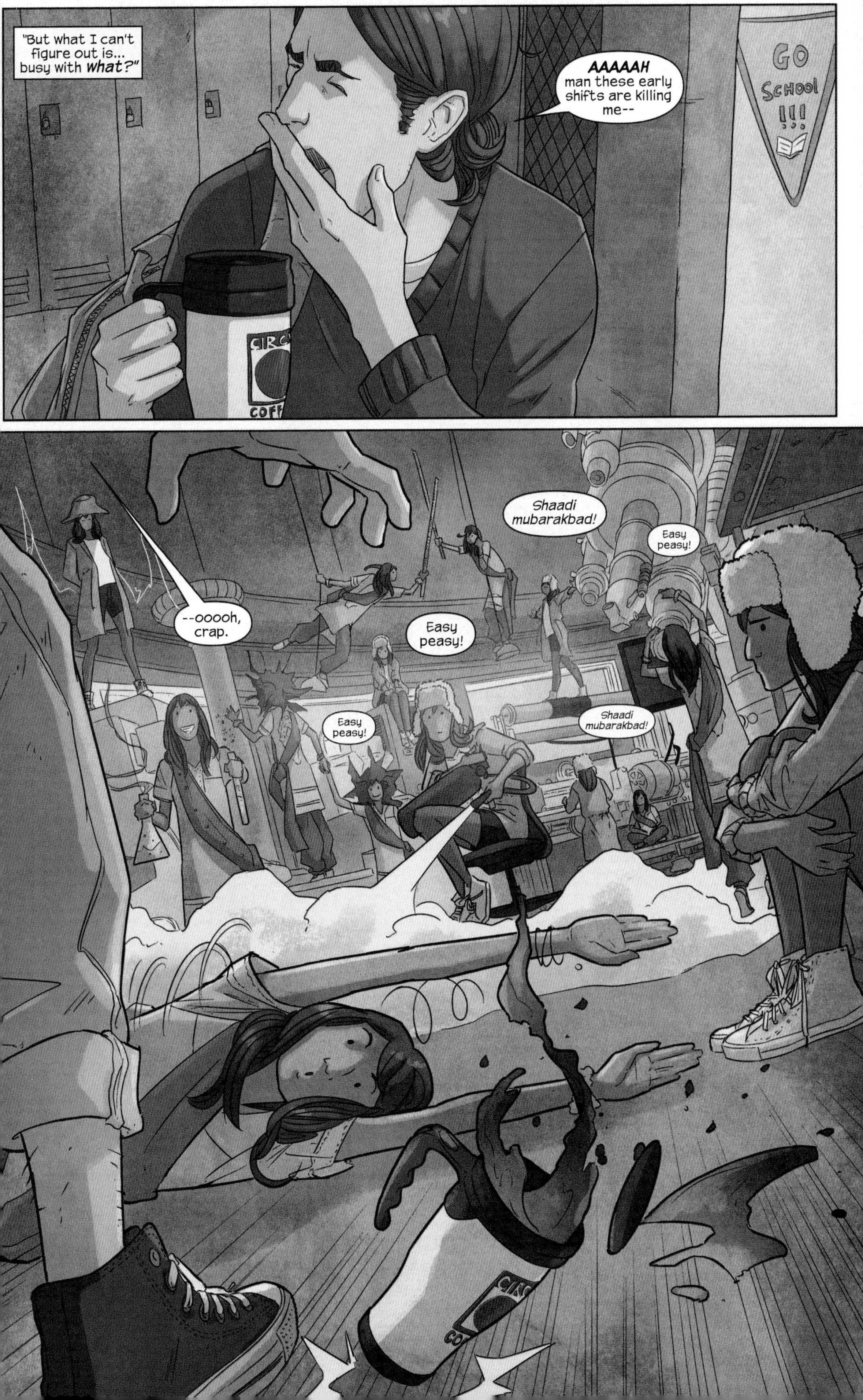
"But what I can't figure out is... busy with *what?*"
AAAAAH man these early shifts are killing me--
GO SCHOOL !!!
CIRC COFF
--ooooh, crap.
Shaadi mubarakbad!
Easy peasy!
Easy peasy!
Easy peasy!
Shaadi mubarakbad!
CIRC CO

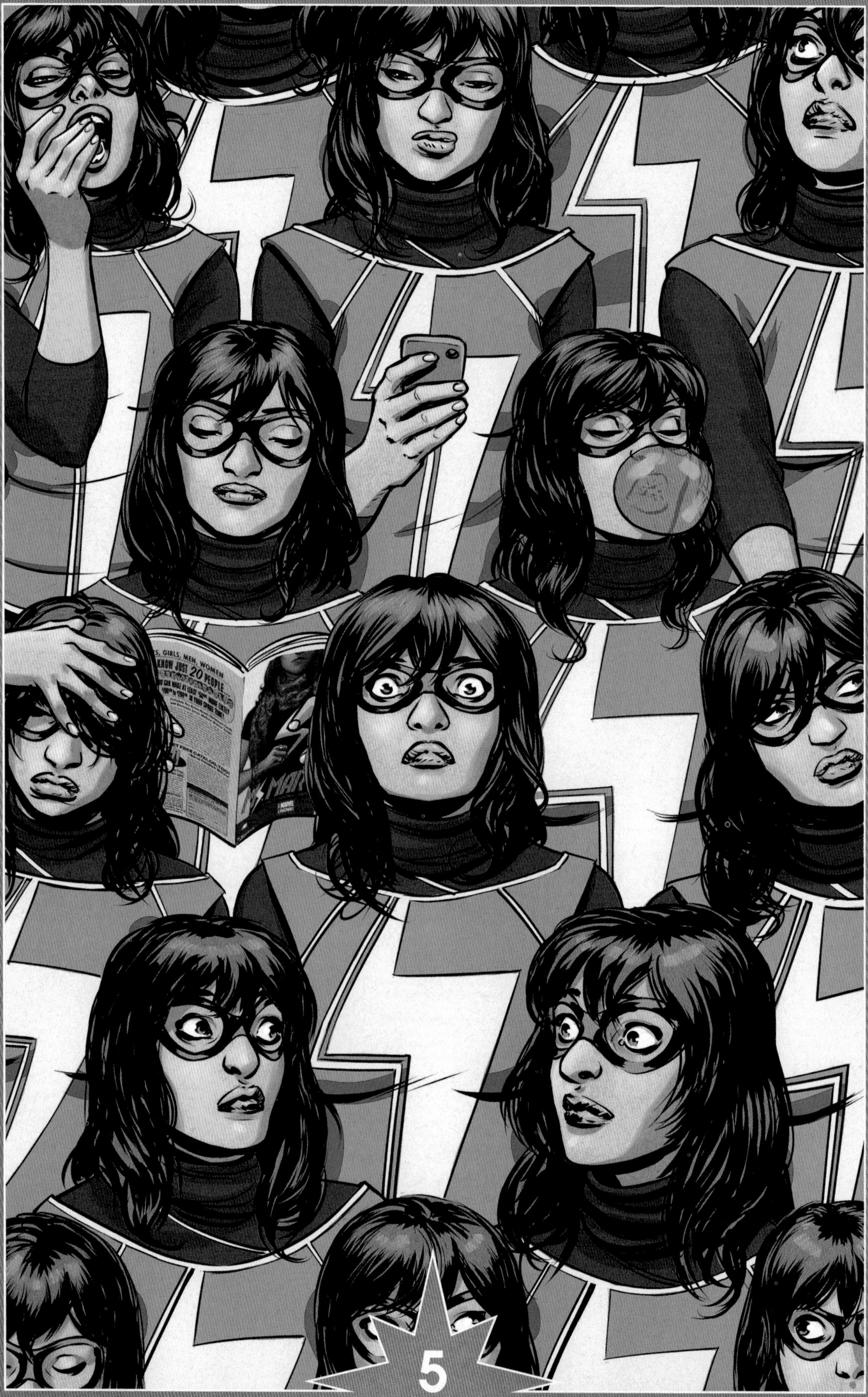
GIRLS, MEN, WOMEN
KNOW JUST 20 PEOPLE
MARVEL NOW
5

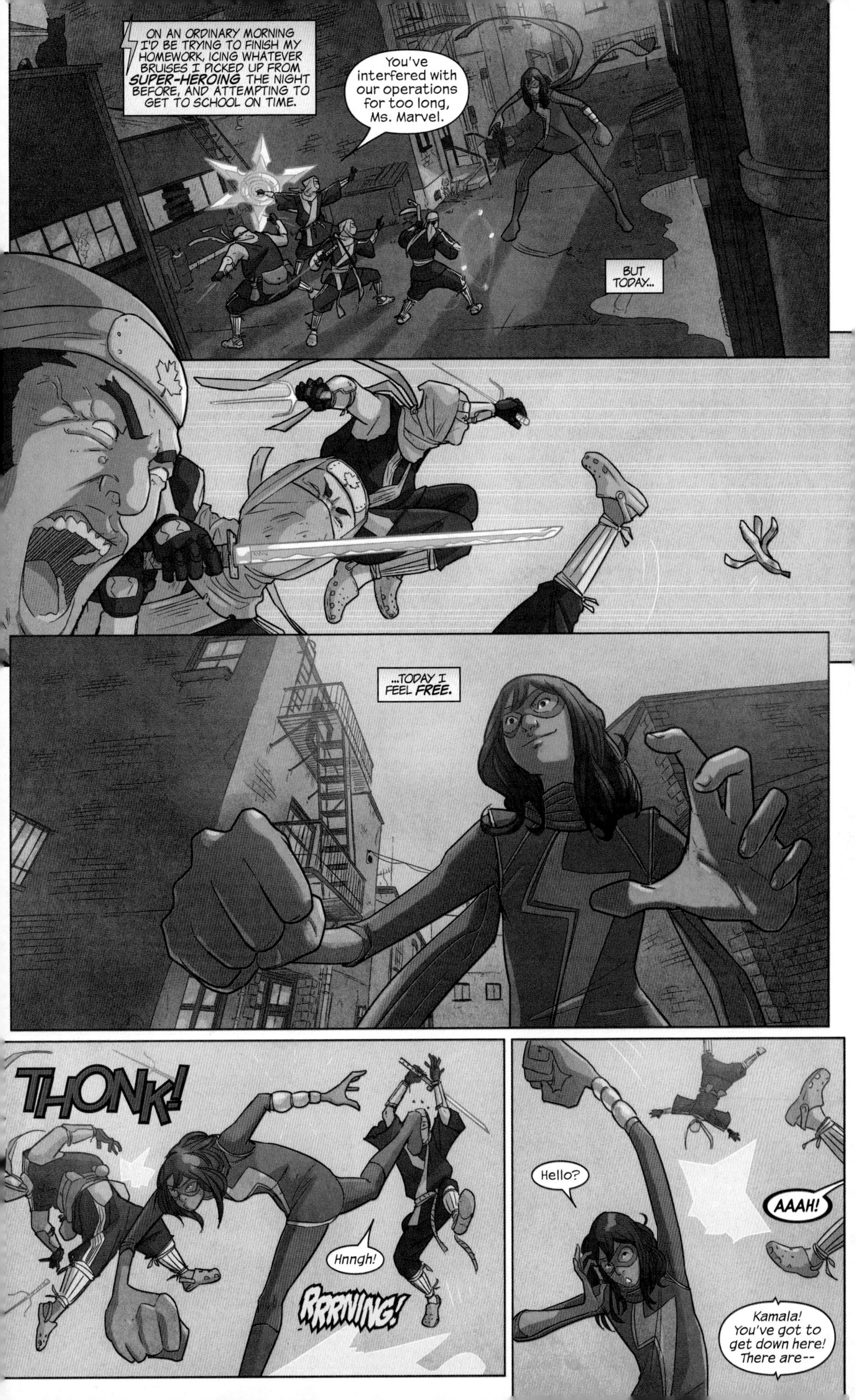
ON AN ORDINARY MORNING I'D BE TRYING TO FINISH MY HOMEWORK, ICING WHATEVER BRUISES I PICKED UP FROM SUPER-HEROING THE NIGHT BEFORE, AND ATTEMPTING TO GET TO SCHOOL ON TIME.
You've interfered with our operations for too long, Ms. Marvel.
BUT TODAY...
...TODAY I FEEL FREE.
THONK!
Hnngh!
RRRNING!
Hello?
AAAH!
Kamala! You've got to get down here! There are--

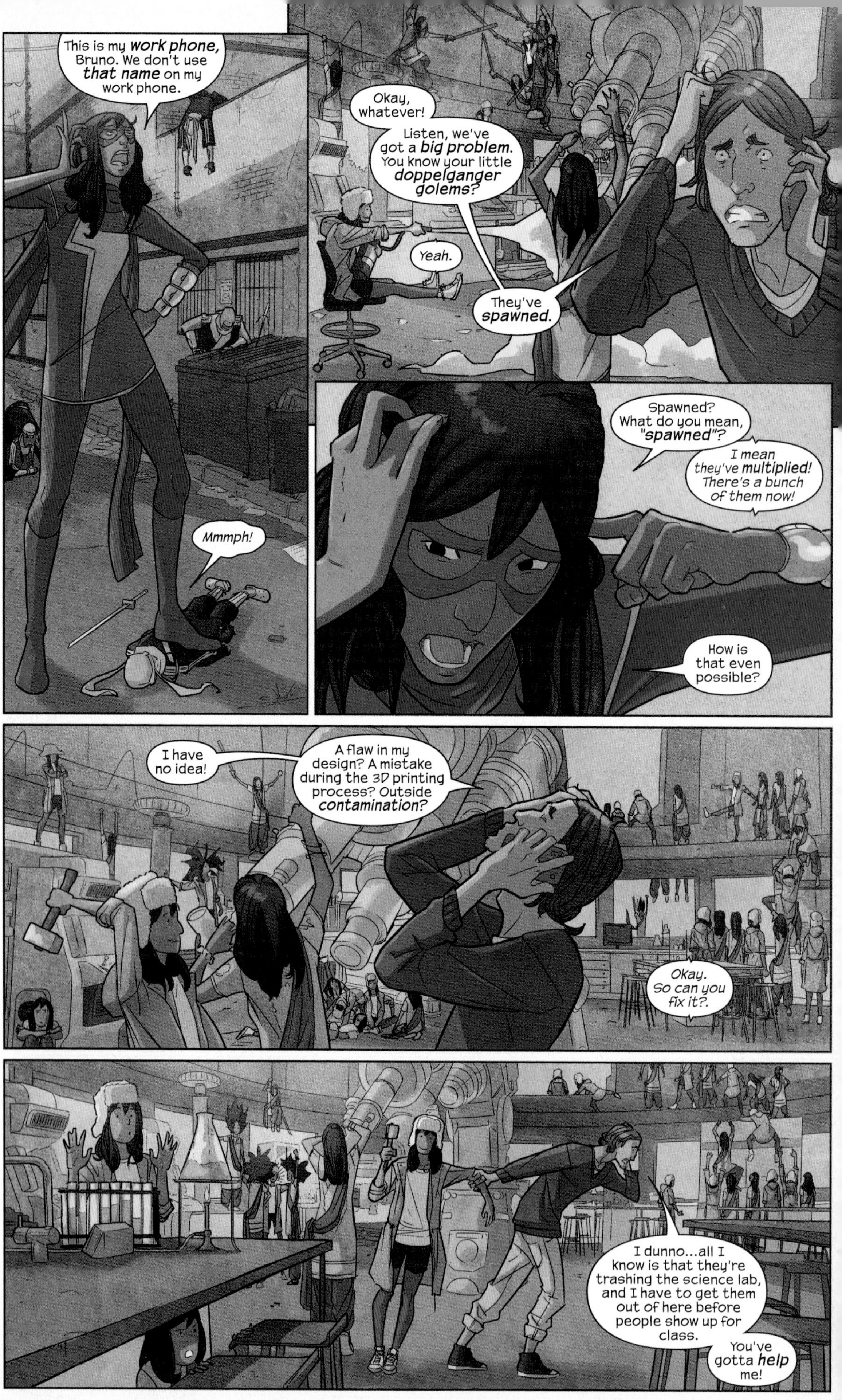
This is my work phone, Bruno. We don't use that name on my work phone.
Okay, whatever!
Listen, we've got a big problem. You know your little doppelganger golems?
Yeah.
They've spawned.
Mmmph!
Spawned? What do you mean, "spawned"?
I mean they've multiplied! There's a bunch of them now!
How is that even possible?
I have no idea!
A flaw in my design? A mistake during the 3D printing process? Outside contamination?
Okay. So can you fix it?.
I dunno...all I know is that they're trashing the science lab, and I have to get them out of here before people show up for class.
You've gotta help me!

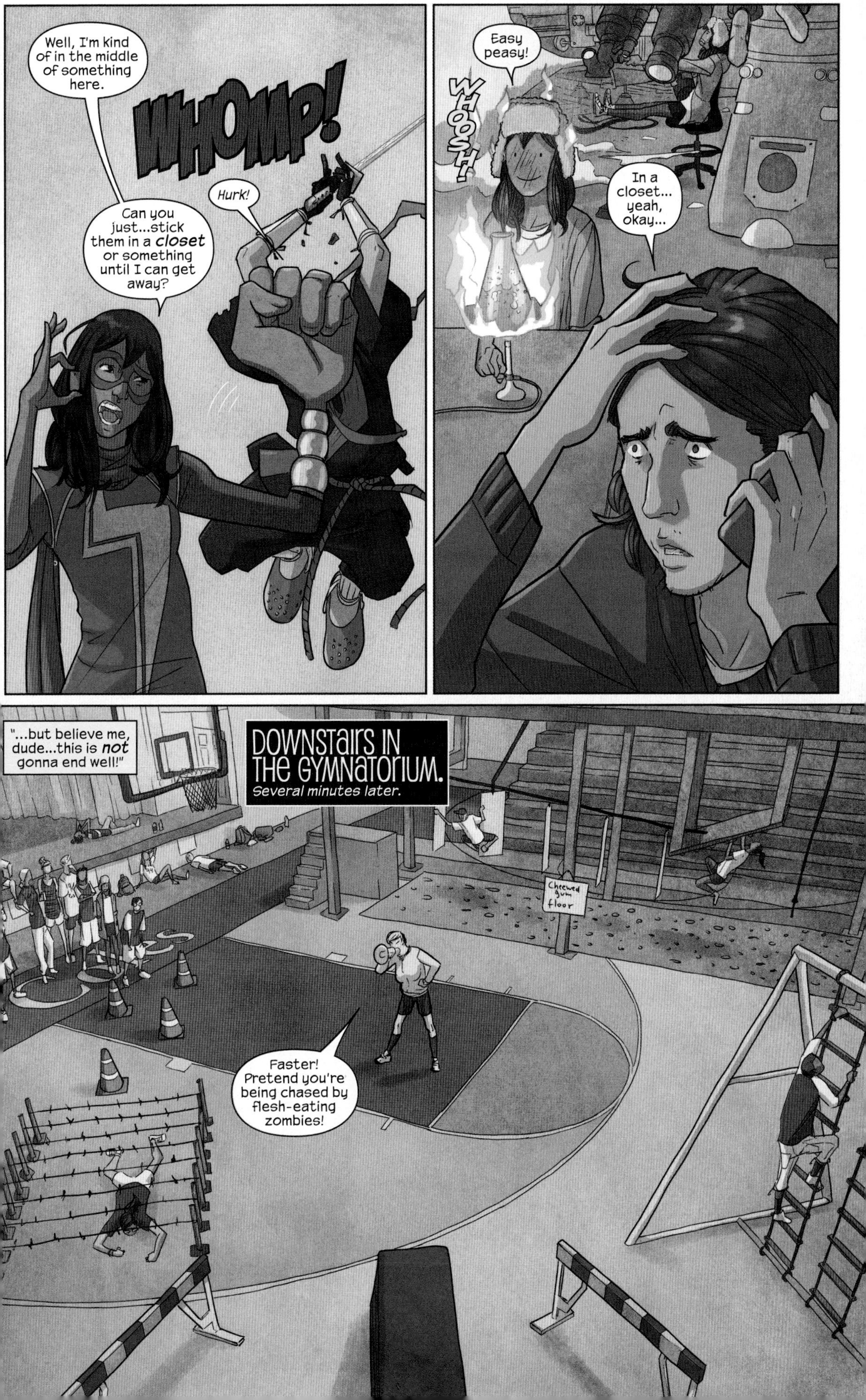
Well, I'm kind of in the middle of something here.
WHOMP!
Hurk!
Can you just...stick them in a *closet* or something until I can get away?
Easy peasy!
WHOOSH!
In a closet... yeah, okay...
"...but believe me, dude...this is *not* gonna end well!"
DOWNSTAIRS IN THE GYMNATORIUM.
Several minutes later.
Cheewed gum floor
Faster! Pretend you're being chased by flesh-eating zombies!

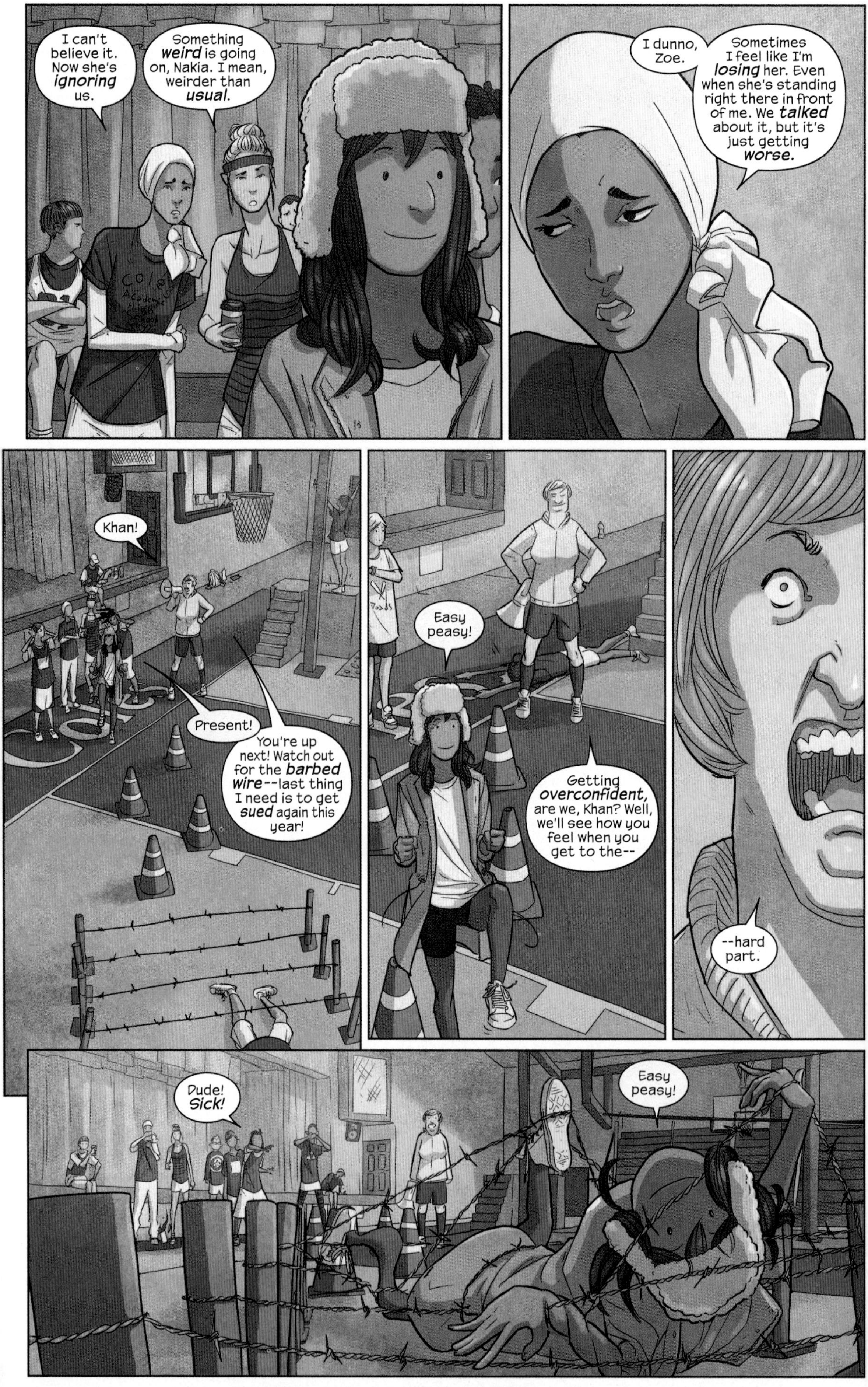
I can't believe it. Now she's *ignoring* us.
Something *weird* is going on, Nakia. I mean, weirder than *usual*.
I dunno, Zoe.
Sometimes I feel like I'm *losing* her. Even when she's standing right there in front of me. We *talked* about it, but it's just getting *worse*.
Khan!
Present!
You're up next! Watch out for the *barbed wire*--last thing I need is to get *sued* again this year!
Easy peasy!
Getting *overconfident*, are we, Khan? Well, we'll see how you feel when you get to the--
--hard part.
Dude! *Sick!*
Easy peasy!

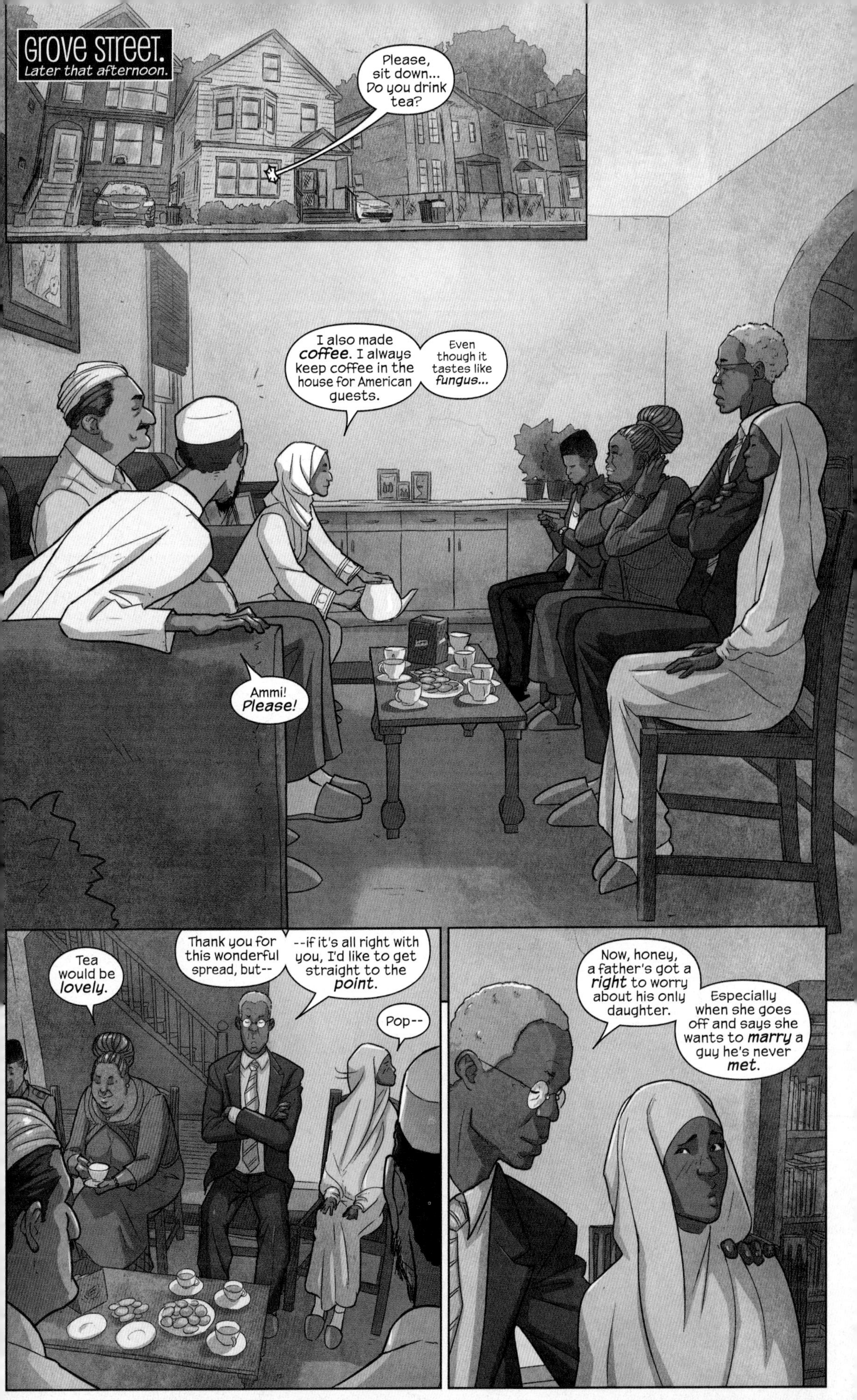
GROVE STREET.
Later that afternoon.
Please, sit down... Do you drink tea?
I also made coffee. I always keep coffee in the house for American guests.
Even though it tastes like fungus...
Ammi! Please!
Tea would be lovely.
Thank you for this wonderful spread, but--
--if it's all right with you, I'd like to get straight to the point.
Pop--
Now, honey, a father's got a right to worry about his only daughter.
Especially when she goes off and says she wants to marry a guy he's never met.

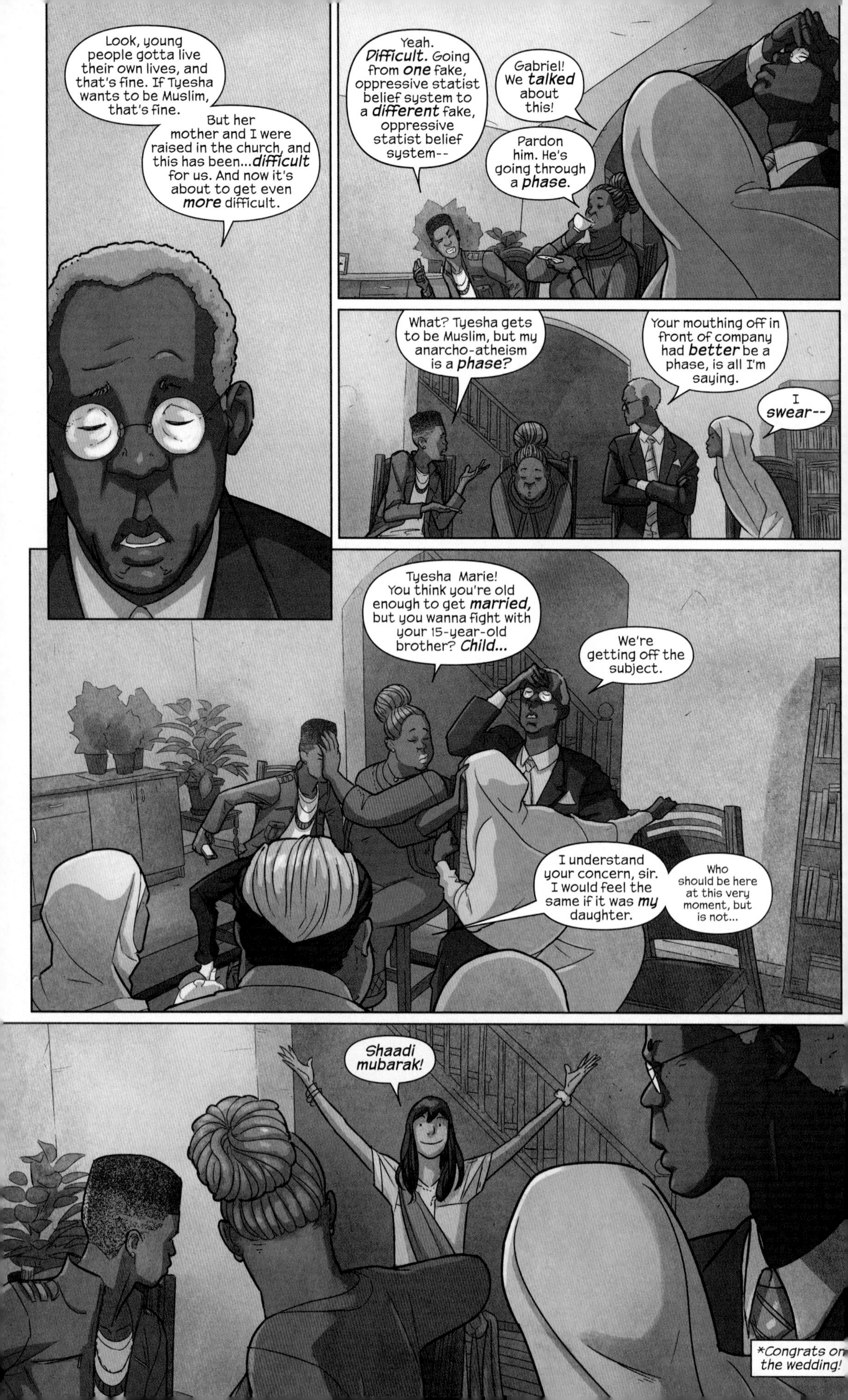

Look, young people gotta live their own lives, and that's fine. If Tyesha wants to be Muslim, that's fine.
But her mother and I were raised in the church, and this has been...*difficult* for us. And now it's about to get even *more* difficult.
Yeah. *Difficult.* Going from *one* fake, oppressive statist belief system to a *different* fake, oppressive statist belief system--
Gabriel! We *talked* about this!
Pardon him. He's going through a *phase.*
What? Tyesha gets to be Muslim, but my anarcho-atheism is a *phase?*
Your mouthing off in front of company had *better* be a phase, is all I'm saying.
I *swear--*
Tyesha Marie! You think you're old enough to get *married,* but you wanna fight with your 15-year-old brother? *Child...*
We're getting off the subject.
I understand your concern, sir. I would feel the same if it was *my* daughter.
Who should be here at this very moment, but is not...
Shaadi mubarak!
*Congrats on the wedding!

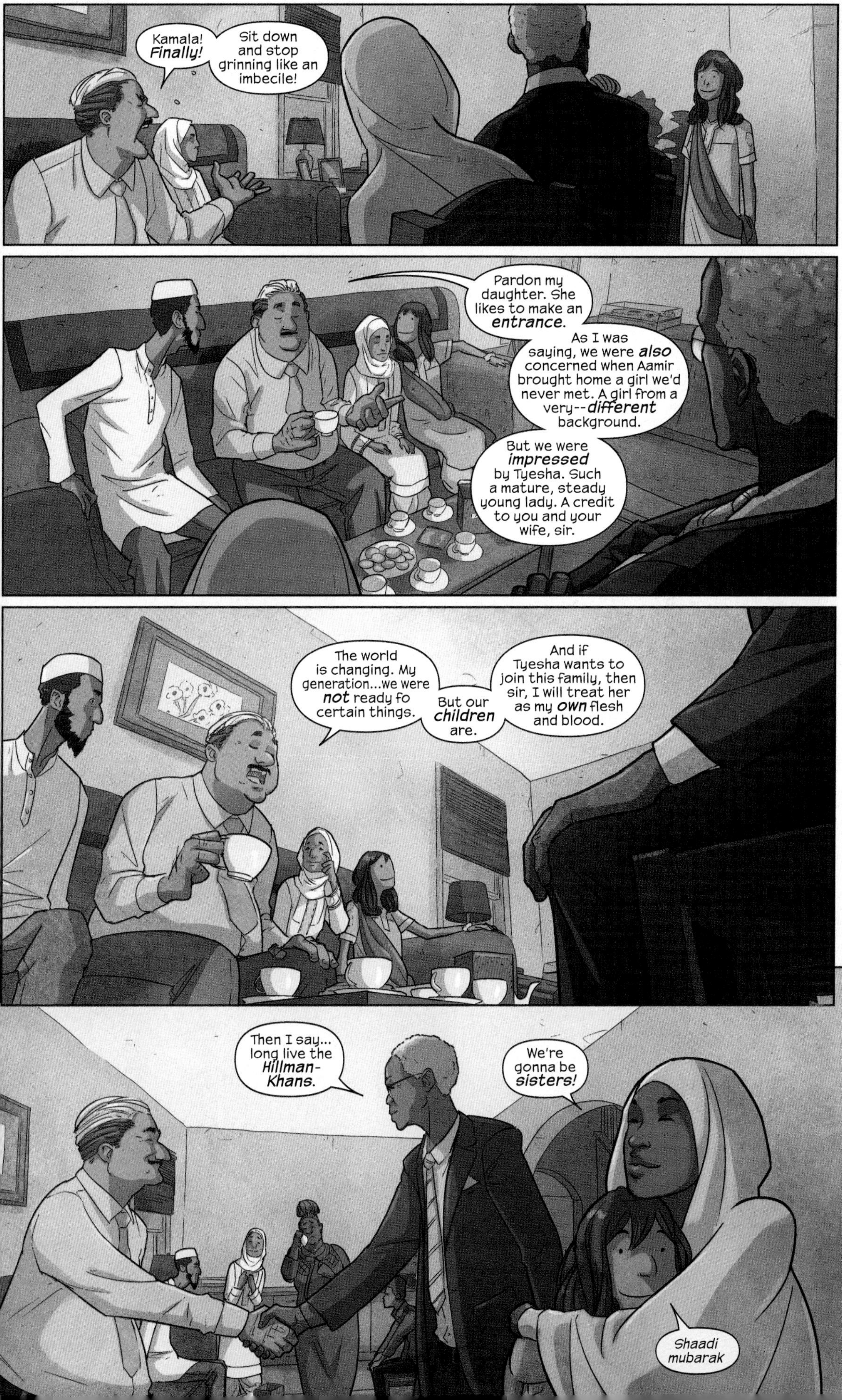
Kamala! Finally!
Sit down and stop grinning like an imbecile!
Pardon my daughter. She likes to make an entrance.
As I was saying, we were also concerned when Aamir brought home a girl we'd never met. A girl from a very--different background.
But we were impressed by Tyesha. Such a mature, steady young lady. A credit to you and your wife, sir.
The world is changing. My generation...we were not ready fo certain things.
But our children are.
And if Tyesha wants to join this family, then sir, I will treat her as my own flesh and blood.
Then I say... long live the Hillman-Khans.
We're gonna be sisters!
Shaadi mubarak

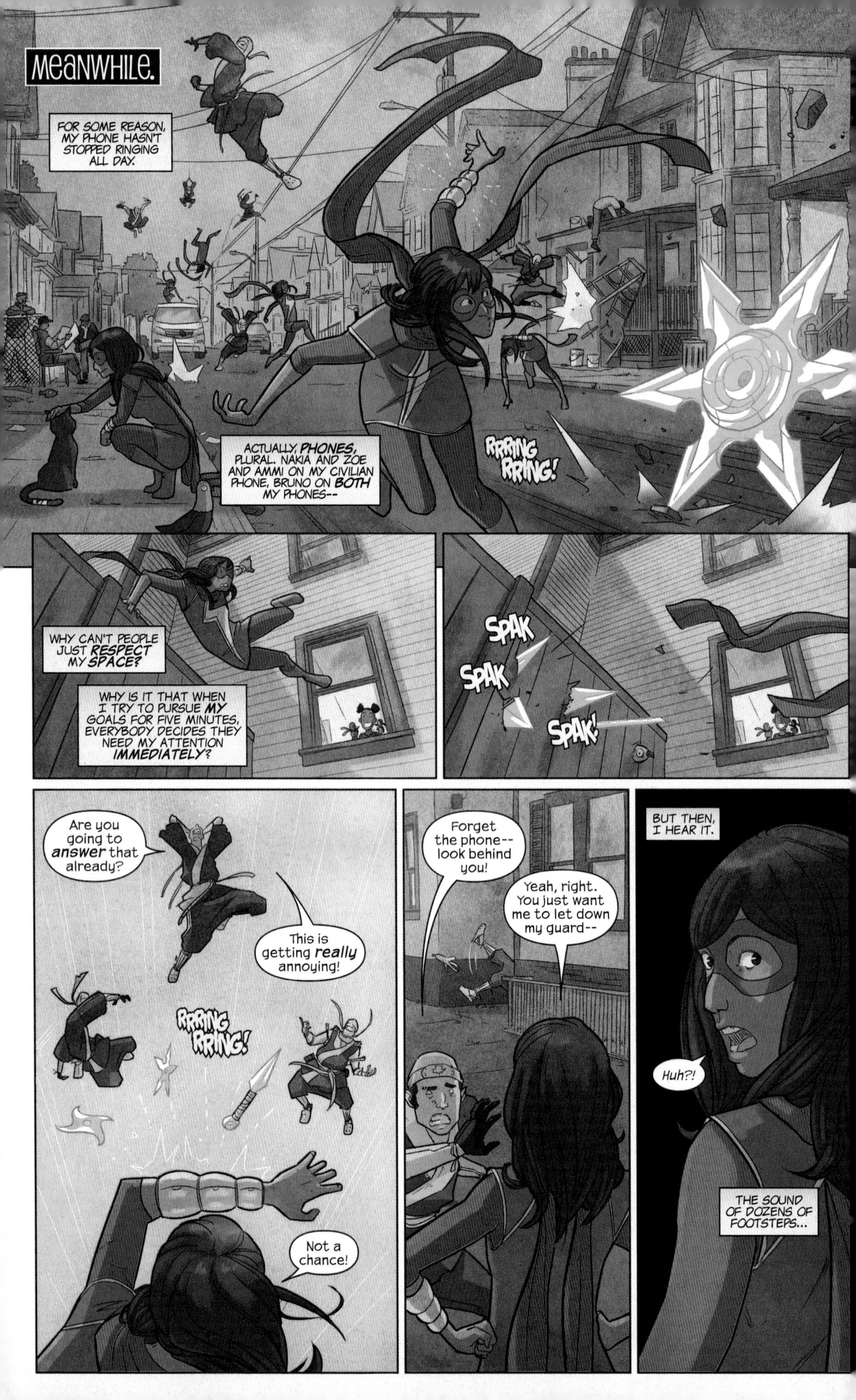
MEANWHILE.
FOR SOME REASON, MY PHONE HASN'T STOPPED RINGING ALL DAY.
ACTUALLY, PHONES, PLURAL. NAKIA AND ZOE AND AMMI ON MY CIVILIAN PHONE, BRUNO ON BOTH MY PHONES--
RRRING RRING!
WHY CAN'T PEOPLE JUST RESPECT MY SPACE?
WHY IS IT THAT WHEN I TRY TO PURSUE MY GOALS FOR FIVE MINUTES, EVERYBODY DECIDES THEY NEED MY ATTENTION IMMEDIATELY?
SPAK
SPAK
SPAK!
Are you going to answer that already?
This is getting really annoying!
RRRING RRING!
Not a chance!
Forget the phone-- look behind you!
Yeah, right. You just want me to let down my guard--
BUT THEN, I HEAR IT.
Huh?!
THE SOUND OF DOZENS OF FOOTSTEPS...

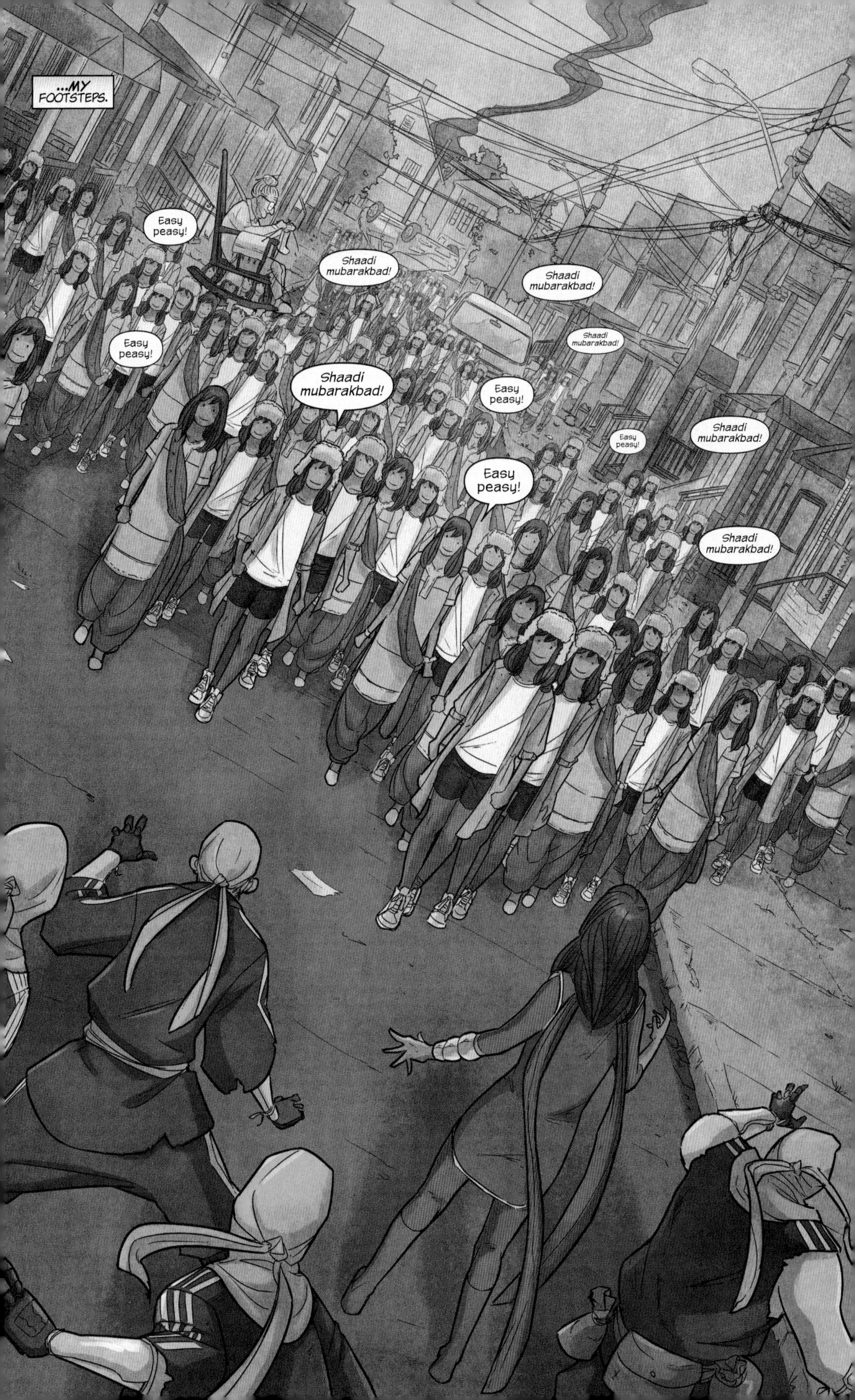
...MY FOOTSTEPS.
Easy peasy!
Shaadi mubarakbad!
Shaadi mubarakbad!
Easy peasy!
Shaadi mubarakbad!
Shaadi mubarakbad!
Easy peasy!
Easy peasy!
Shaadi mubarakbad!
Easy peasy!
Shaadi mubarakbad!

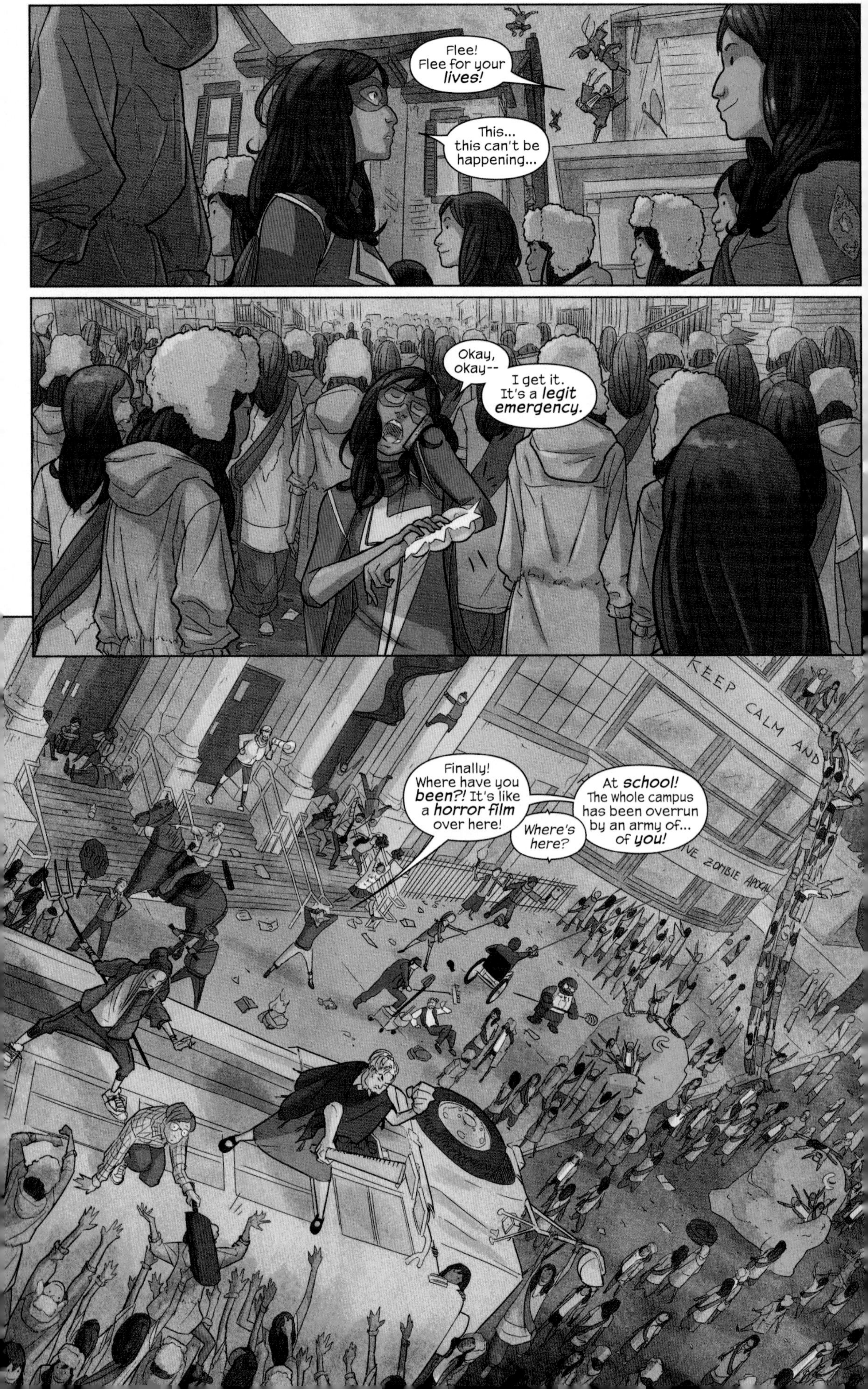
Flee! Flee for your *lives!*
This... this can't be happening...
Okay, okay--
I get it. It's a *legit emergency.*
KEEP CALM AND
STOP
Finally! Where have you *been?!* It's like a *horror film* over here!
Where's here?
At *school!* The whole campus has been overrun by an army of... of *you!*

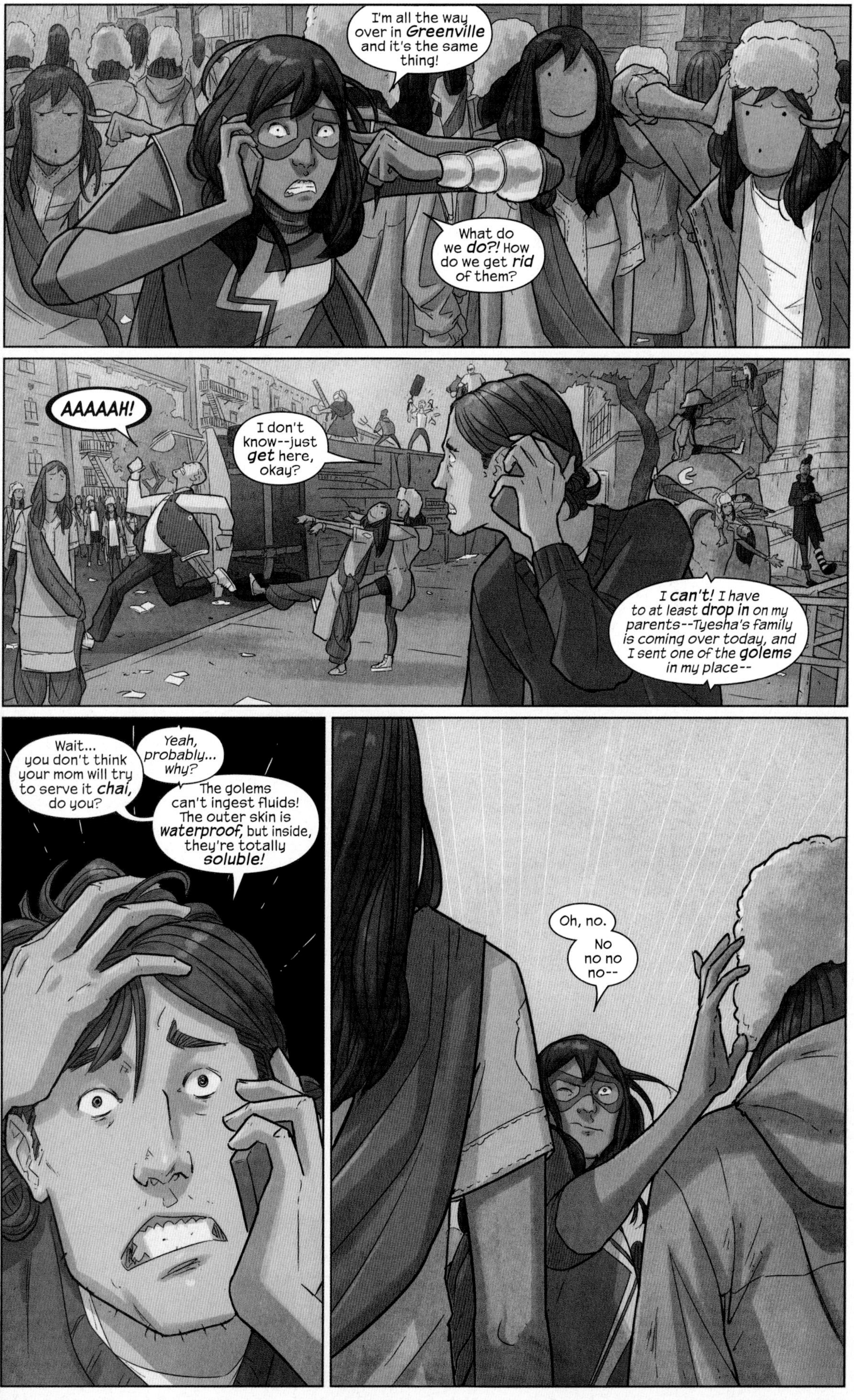

I'm all the way over in Greenville and it's the same thing!
What do we do?! How do we get rid of them?
AAAAAH!
I don't know--just get here, okay?
I can't! I have to at least drop in on my parents--Tyesha's family is coming over today, and I sent one of the golems in my place--
Wait... you don't think your mom will try to serve it chai, do you?
Yeah, probably... why?
The golems can't ingest fluids! The outer skin is waterproof, but inside, they're totally soluble!
Oh, no.
No no no no--

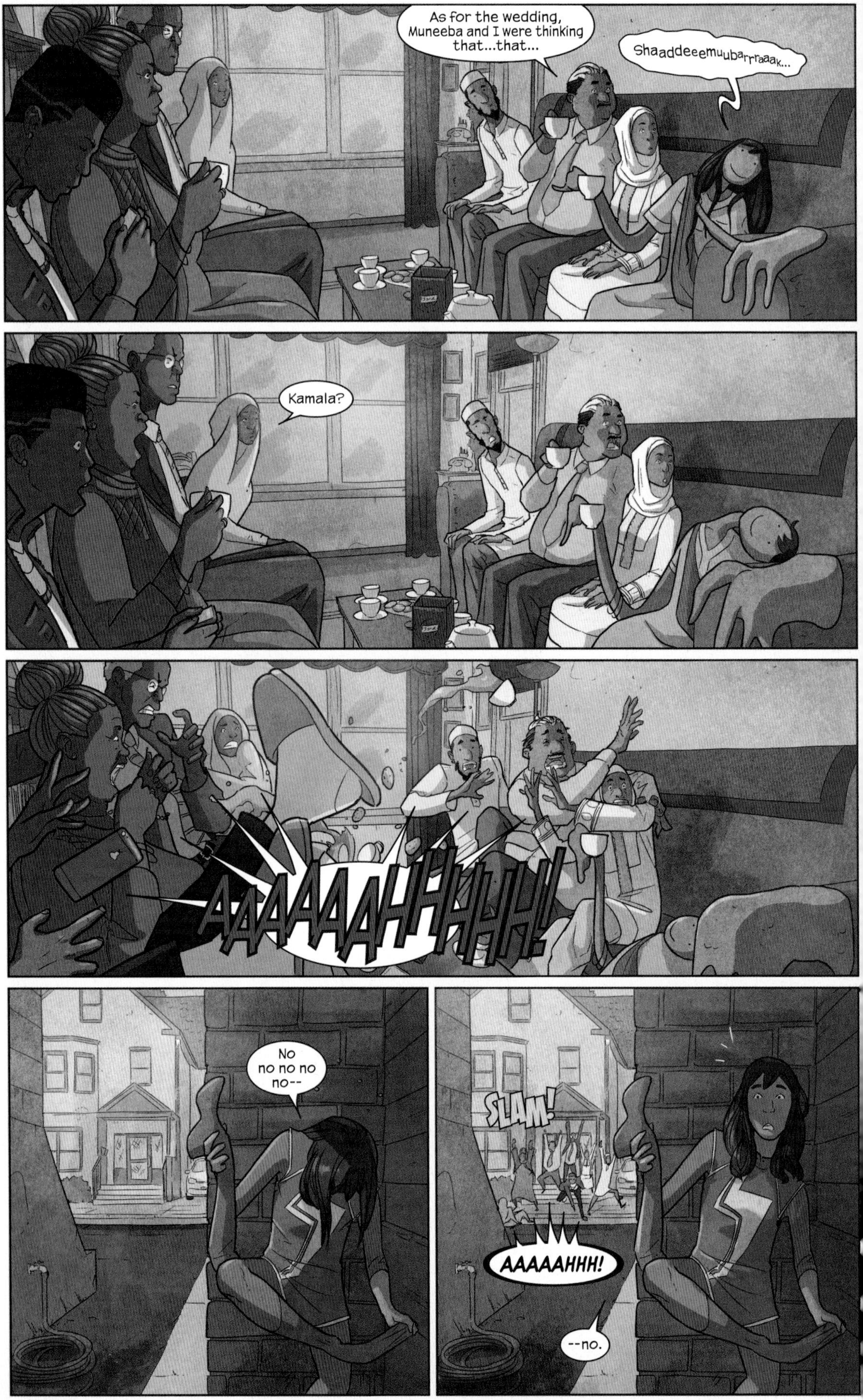
As for the wedding, Muneeba and I were thinking that...that...
Shaaddeeemuubarrraaak...
Kamala?
AAAAAAHHHHHH!
No no no no no--
SLAM!
AAAAAHHH!
--no.

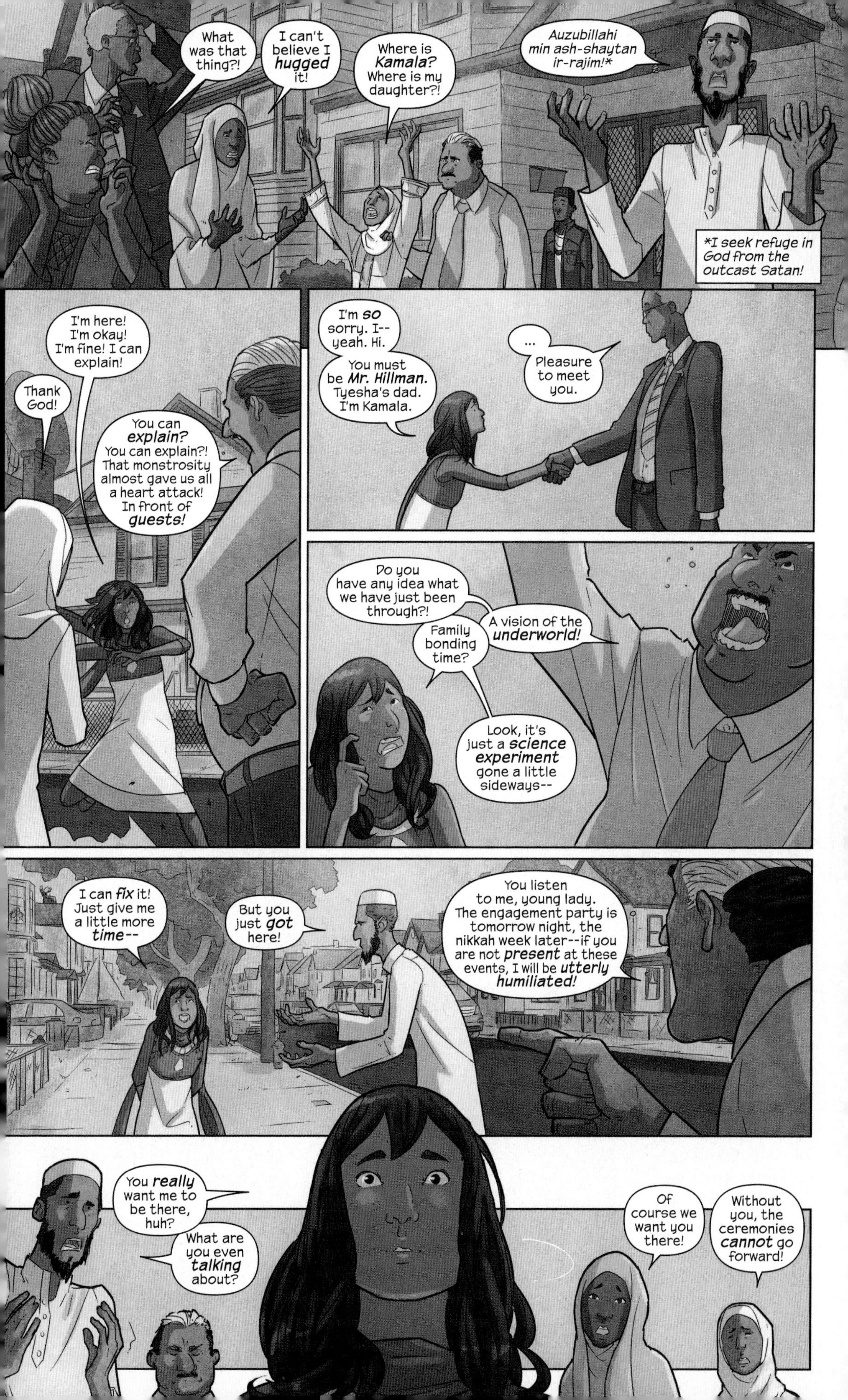

What was that thing?!
I can't believe I hugged it!
Where is Kamala? Where is my daughter?!
Auzubillahi min ash-shaytan ir-rajim!*
*I seek refuge in God from the outcast Satan!
I'm here! I'm okay! I'm fine! I can explain!
Thank God!
You can explain? You can explain?! That monstrosity almost gave us all a heart attack! In front of guests!
I'm so sorry. I-- yeah. Hi.
You must be Mr. Hillman. Tyesha's dad. I'm Kamala.
...
Pleasure to meet you.
Do you have any idea what we have just been through?!
A vision of the underworld!
Family bonding time?
Look, it's just a science experiment gone a little sideways--
I can fix it! Just give me a little more time--
But you just got here!
You listen to me, young lady. The engagement party is tomorrow night, the nikkah week later--if you are not present at these events, I will be utterly humiliated!
You really want me to be there, huh?
What are you even talking about?
Of course we want you there!
Without you, the ceremonies cannot go forward!

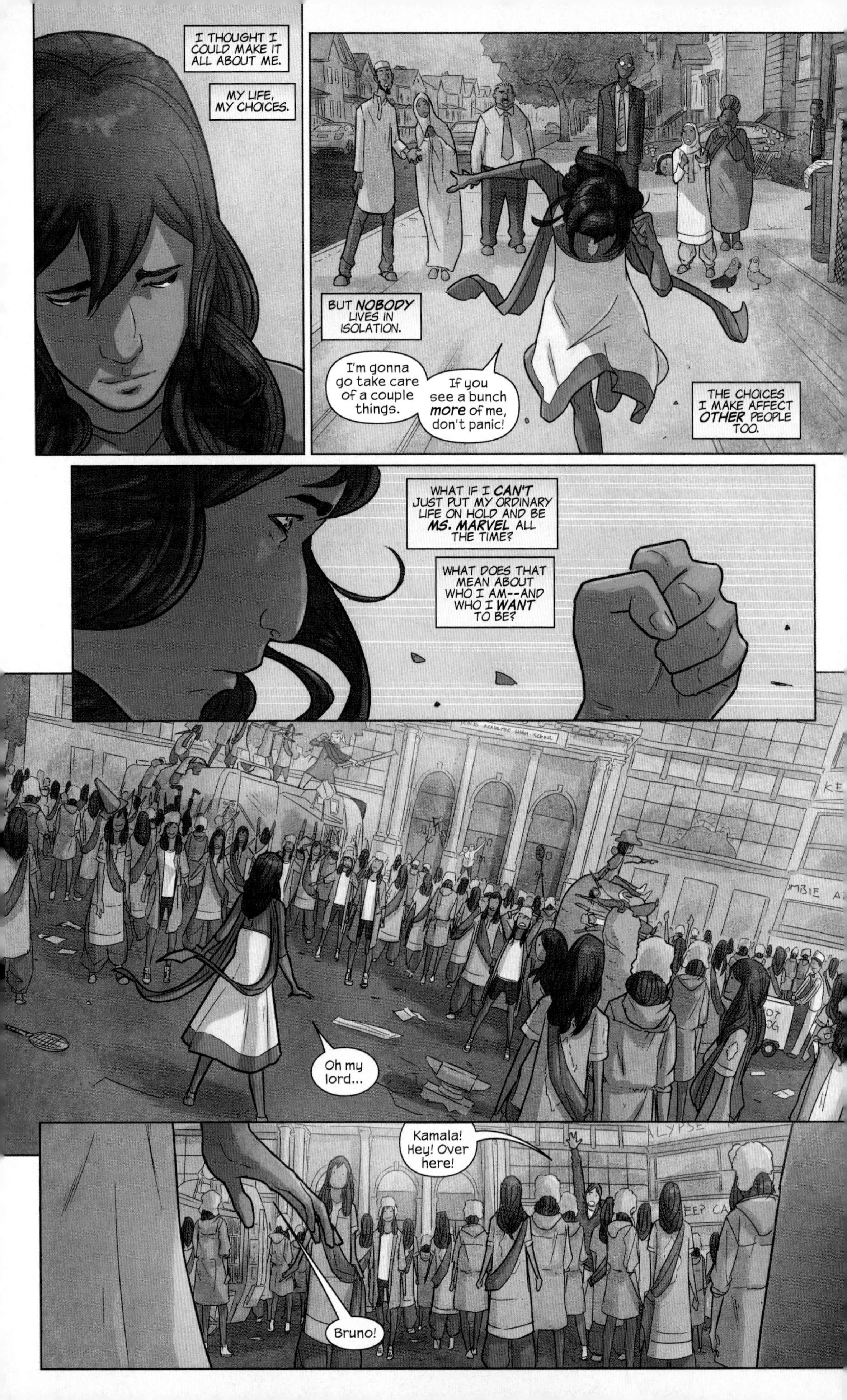

I THOUGHT I COULD MAKE IT ALL ABOUT ME.
MY LIFE, MY CHOICES.
BUT NOBODY LIVES IN ISOLATION.
I'm gonna go take care of a couple things.
If you see a bunch more of me, don't panic!
THE CHOICES I MAKE AFFECT OTHER PEOPLE TOO.
WHAT IF I CAN'T JUST PUT MY ORDINARY LIFE ON HOLD AND BE MS. MARVEL ALL THE TIME?
WHAT DOES THAT MEAN ABOUT WHO I AM--AND WHO I WANT TO BE?
Oh my lord...
Kamala! Hey! Over here!
Bruno!

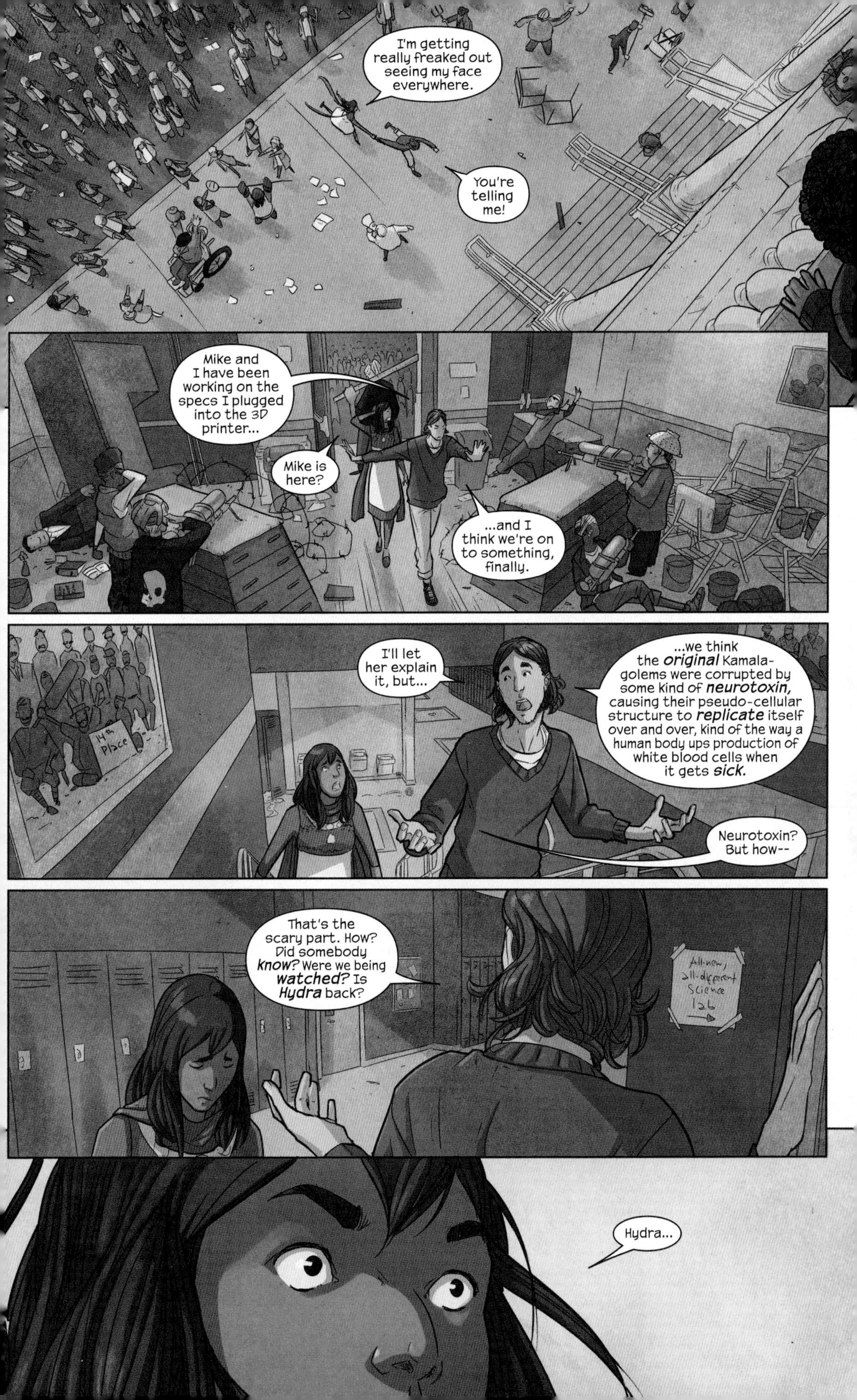

I'm getting really freaked out seeing my face everywhere.
You're telling me!
Mike and I have been working on the specs I plugged into the 3D printer...
Mike is here?
...and I think we're on to something, finally.
14th Place
I'll let her explain it, but...
...we think the original Kamala-golems were corrupted by some kind of neurotoxin, causing their pseudo-cellular structure to replicate itself over and over, kind of the way a human body ups production of white blood cells when it gets sick.
Neurotoxin? But how--
That's the scary part. How? Did somebody know? Were we being watched? Is Hydra back?
All-new, all-different Science lab
Hydra...

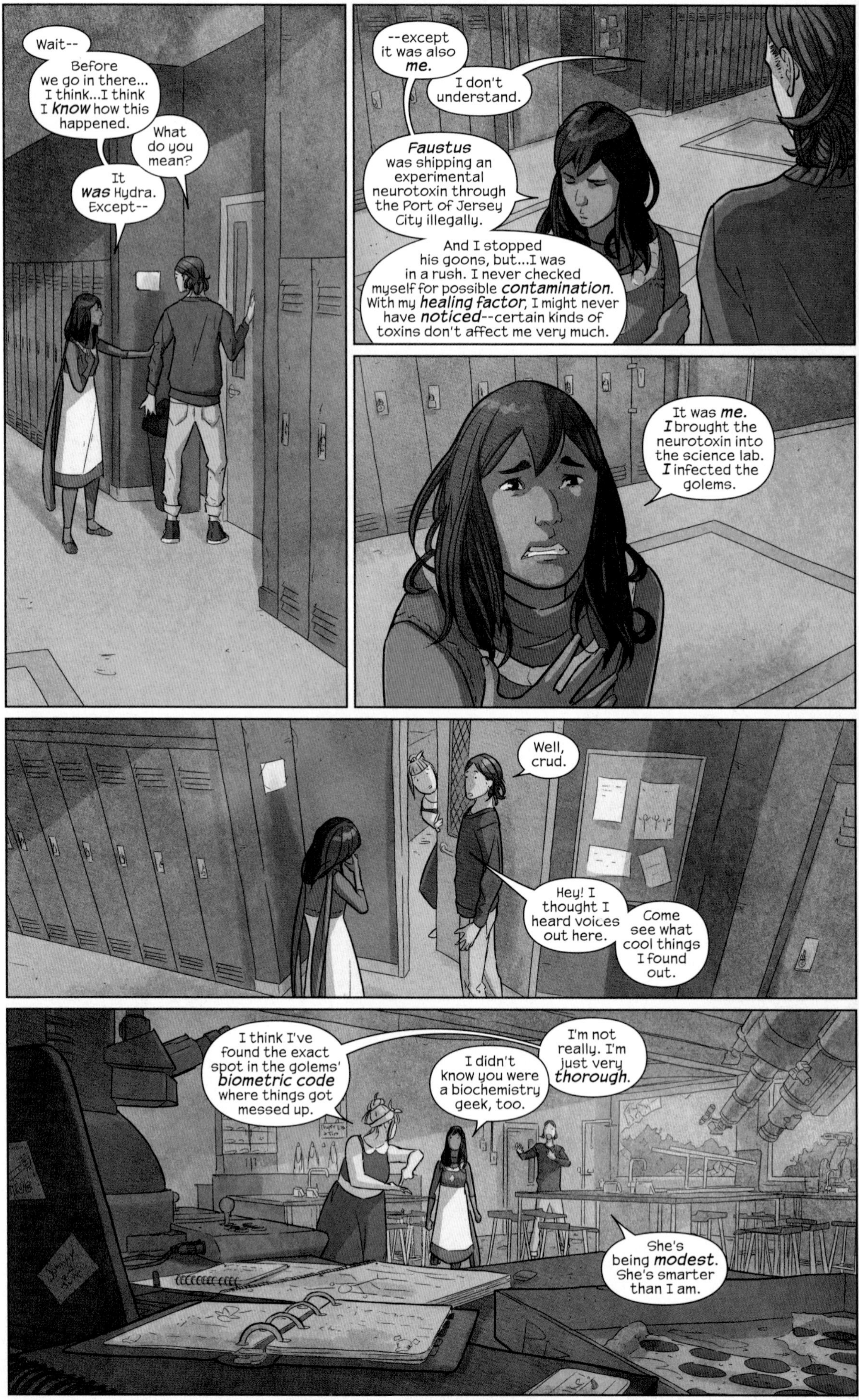
Wait--
Before we go in there... I think...I think I *know* how this happened.
What do you mean?
It *was* Hydra. Except--
--except it was also *me.*
I don't understand.
Faustus was shipping an experimental neurotoxin through the Port of Jersey City illegally.
And I stopped his goons, but...I was in a rush. I never checked myself for possible *contamination.* With my *healing factor,* I might never have *noticed*--certain kinds of toxins don't affect me very much.
It was *me. I* brought the neurotoxin into the science lab. *I* infected the golems.
Well, crud.
Hey! I thought I heard voices out here.
Come see what cool things I found out.
I think I've found the exact spot in the golems' *biometric code* where things got messed up.
I didn't know you were a biochemistry geek, too.
I'm not really. I'm just very *thorough.*
She's being *modest.* She's smarter than I am.

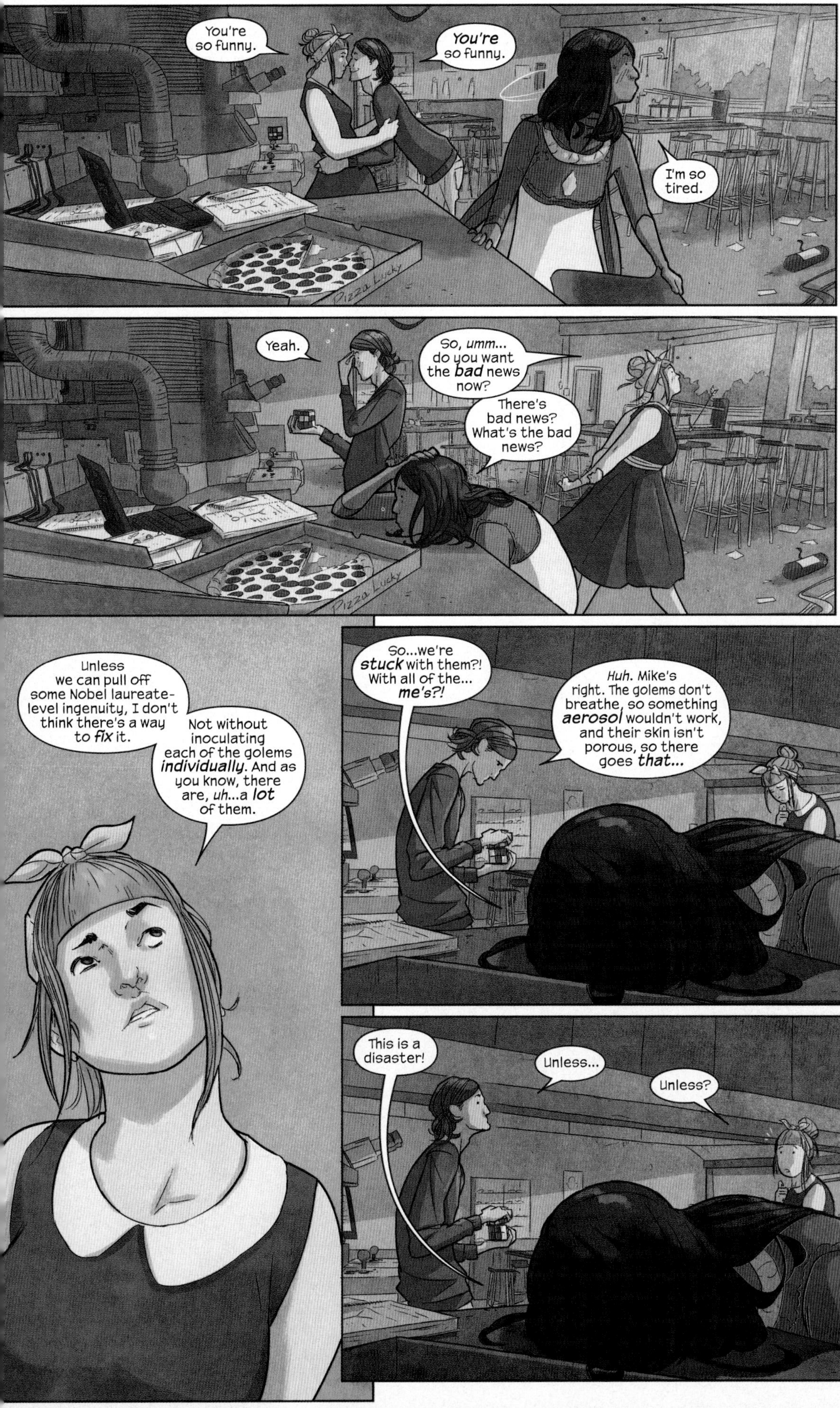

You're so funny.
You're so funny.
I'm so tired.
Yeah.
So, umm... do you want the bad news now?
There's bad news? What's the bad news?
Unless we can pull off some Nobel laureate-level ingenuity, I don't think there's a way to fix it.
Not without inoculating each of the golems individually. And as you know, there are, uh...a lot of them.
So...we're stuck with them?! With all of the... me's?!
Huh. Mike's right. The golems don't breathe, so something aerosol wouldn't work, and their skin isn't porous, so there goes that...
This is a disaster!
Unless...
Unless?
Pizza Lucky

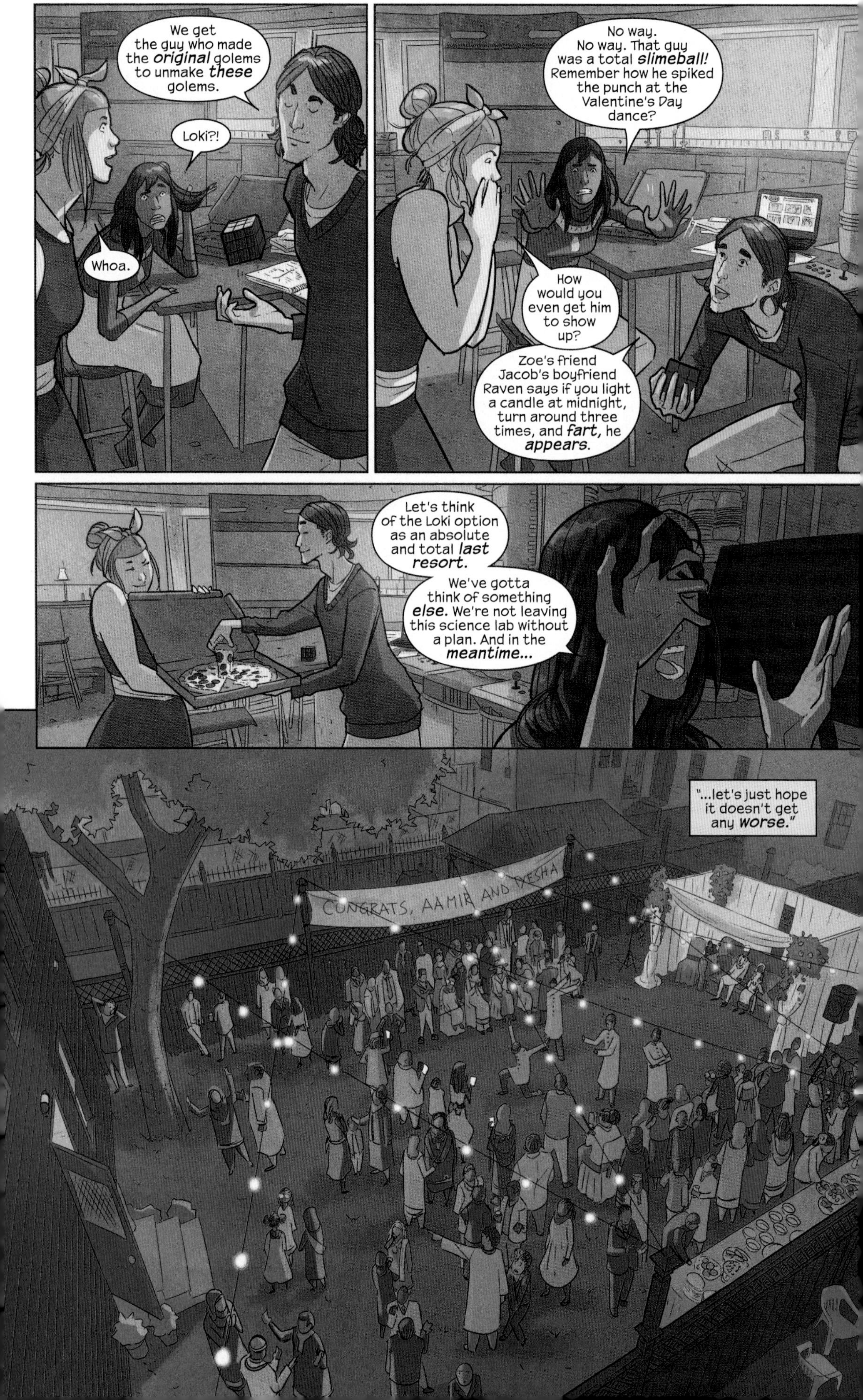

We get the guy who made the *original* golems to unmake *these* golems.
Loki?!
Whoa.
No way. No way. That guy was a total *slimeball!* Remember how he spiked the punch at the Valentine's Day dance?
How would you even get him to show up?
Zoe's friend Jacob's boyfriend Raven says if you light a candle at midnight, turn around three times, and *fart,* he *appears*.
Let's think of the Loki option as an absolute and total *last resort.*
We've gotta think of something *else.* We're not leaving this science lab without a plan. And in the *meantime...*
"...let's just hope it doesn't get any *worse.*"
CONGRATS, AAMIR AND TYESHA

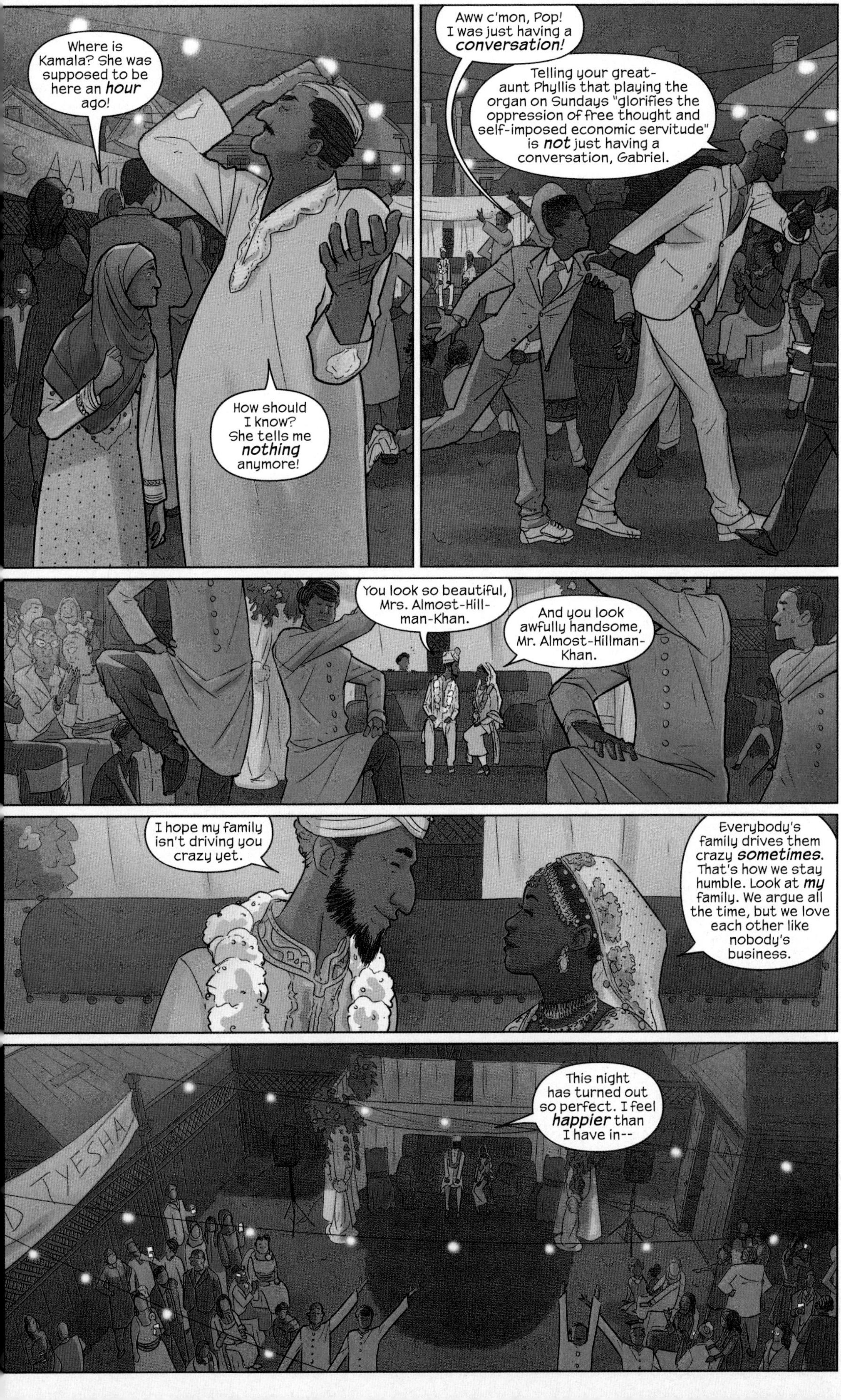

Where is Kamala? She was supposed to be here an *hour* ago!
How should I know? She tells me *nothing* anymore!
Aww c'mon, Pop! I was just having a *conversation*!
Telling your great-aunt Phyllis that playing the organ on Sundays "glorifies the oppression of free thought and self-imposed economic servitude" is *not* just having a conversation, Gabriel.
You look so beautiful, Mrs. Almost-Hillman-Khan.
And you look awfully handsome, Mr. Almost-Hillman-Khan.
I hope my family isn't driving you crazy yet.
Everybody's family drives them crazy *sometimes*. That's how we stay humble. Look at *my* family. We argue all the time, but we love each other like nobody's business.
TYESHA
This night has turned out so perfect. I feel *happier* than I have in--

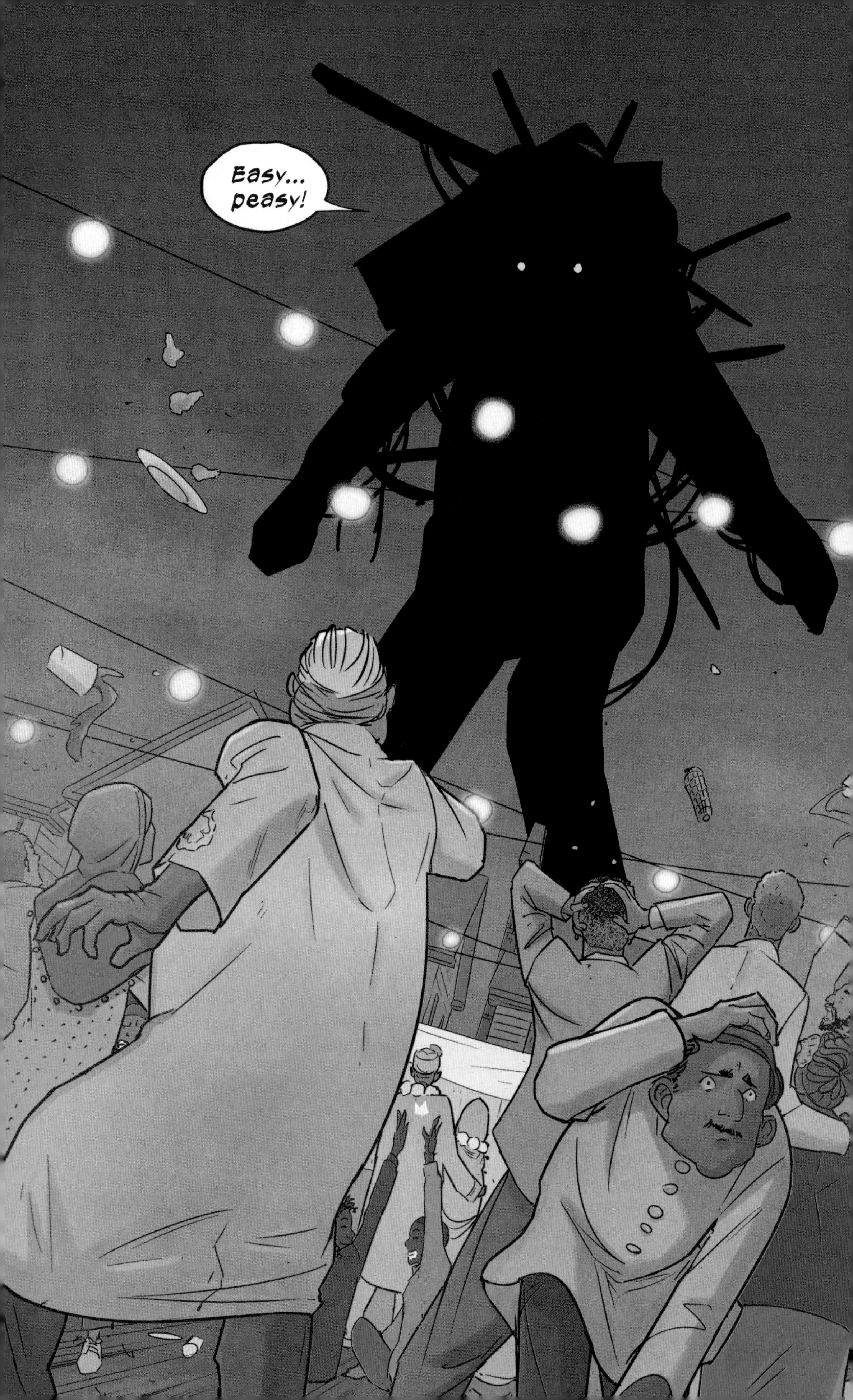
Easy... peasy!

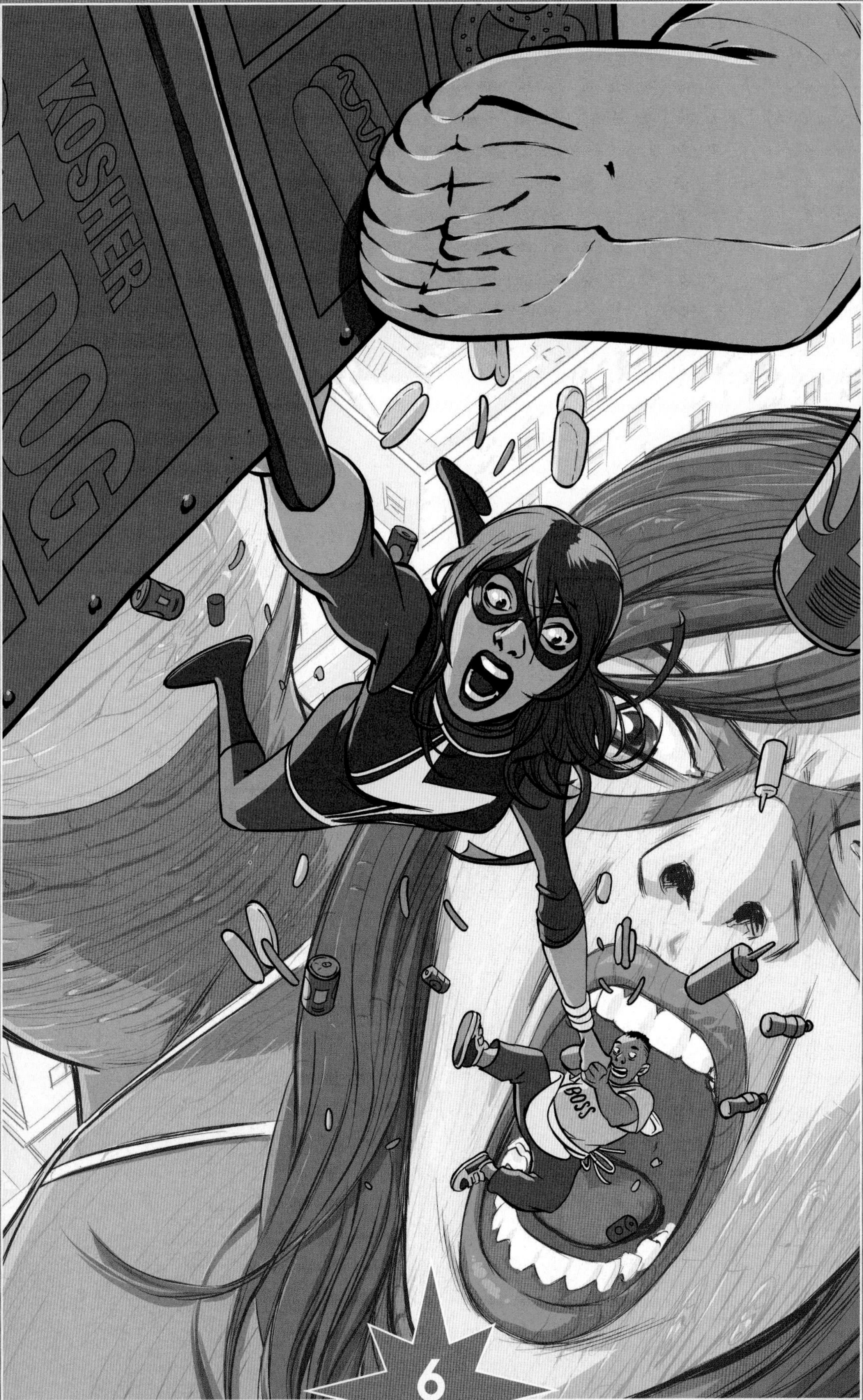
KOSHER
DOG
BOSS
6

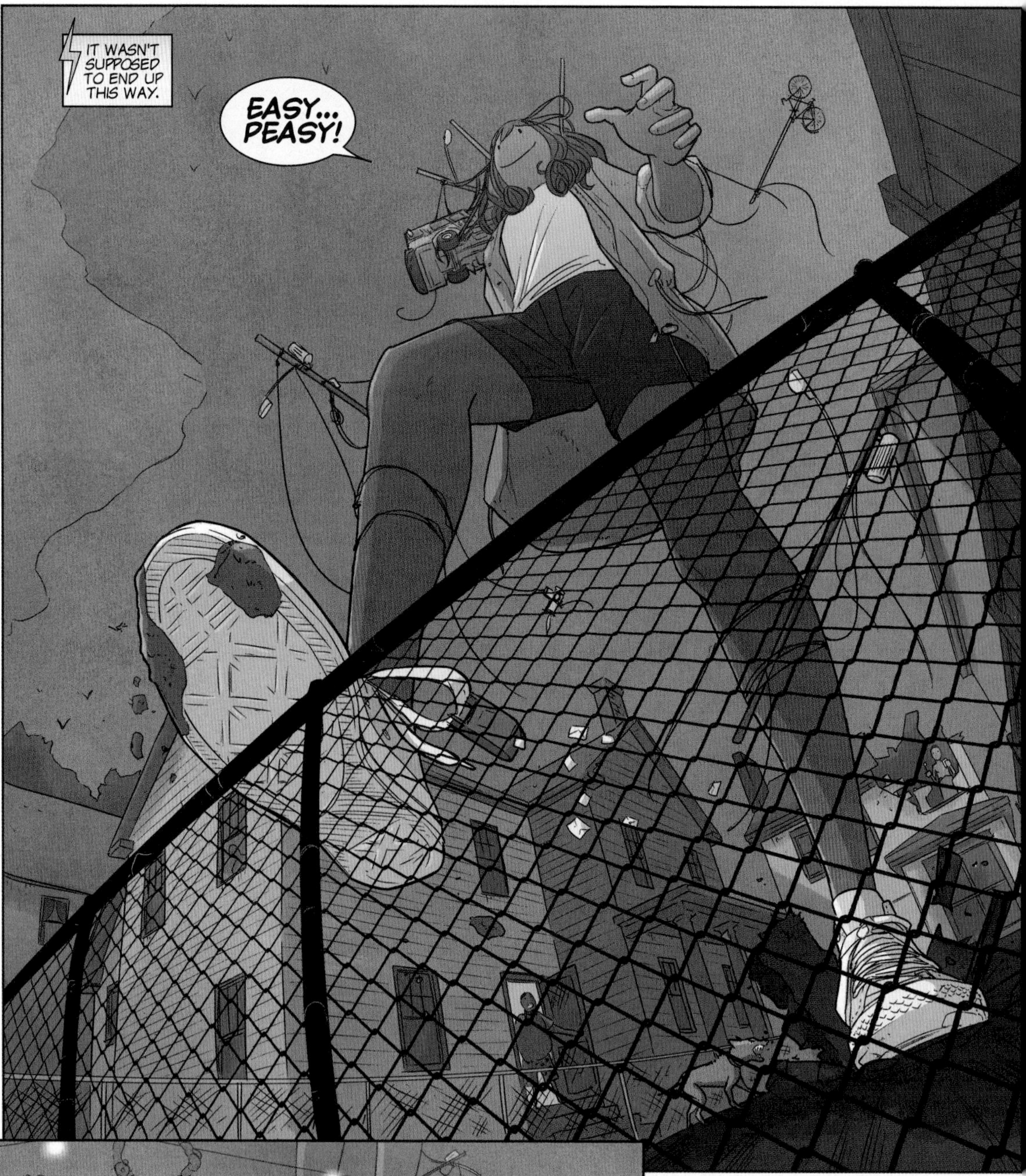
IT WASN'T SUPPOSED TO END UP THIS WAY.
EASY... PEASY!

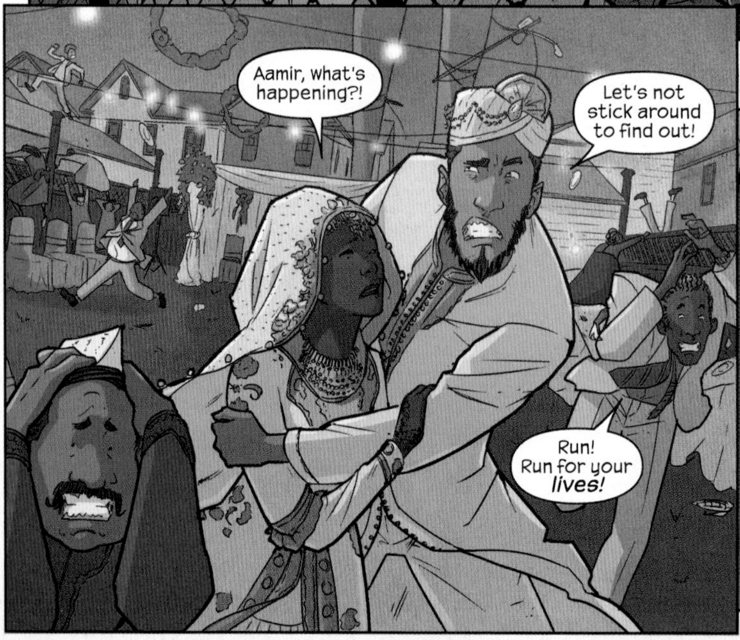
Aamir, what's happening?!
Let's not stick around to find out!
Run! Run for your *lives!*

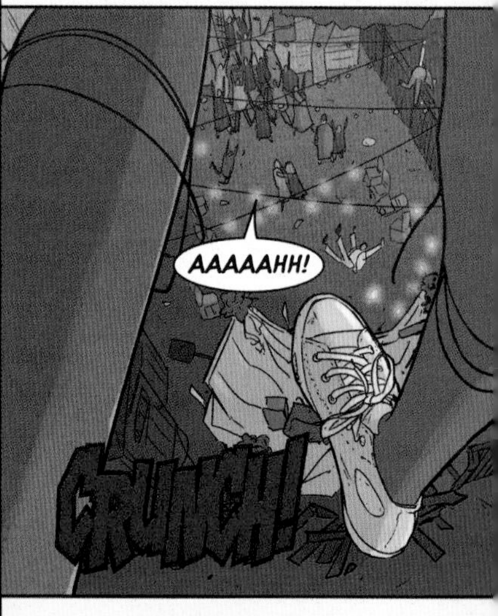
AAAAAHH!
CRUNCH!

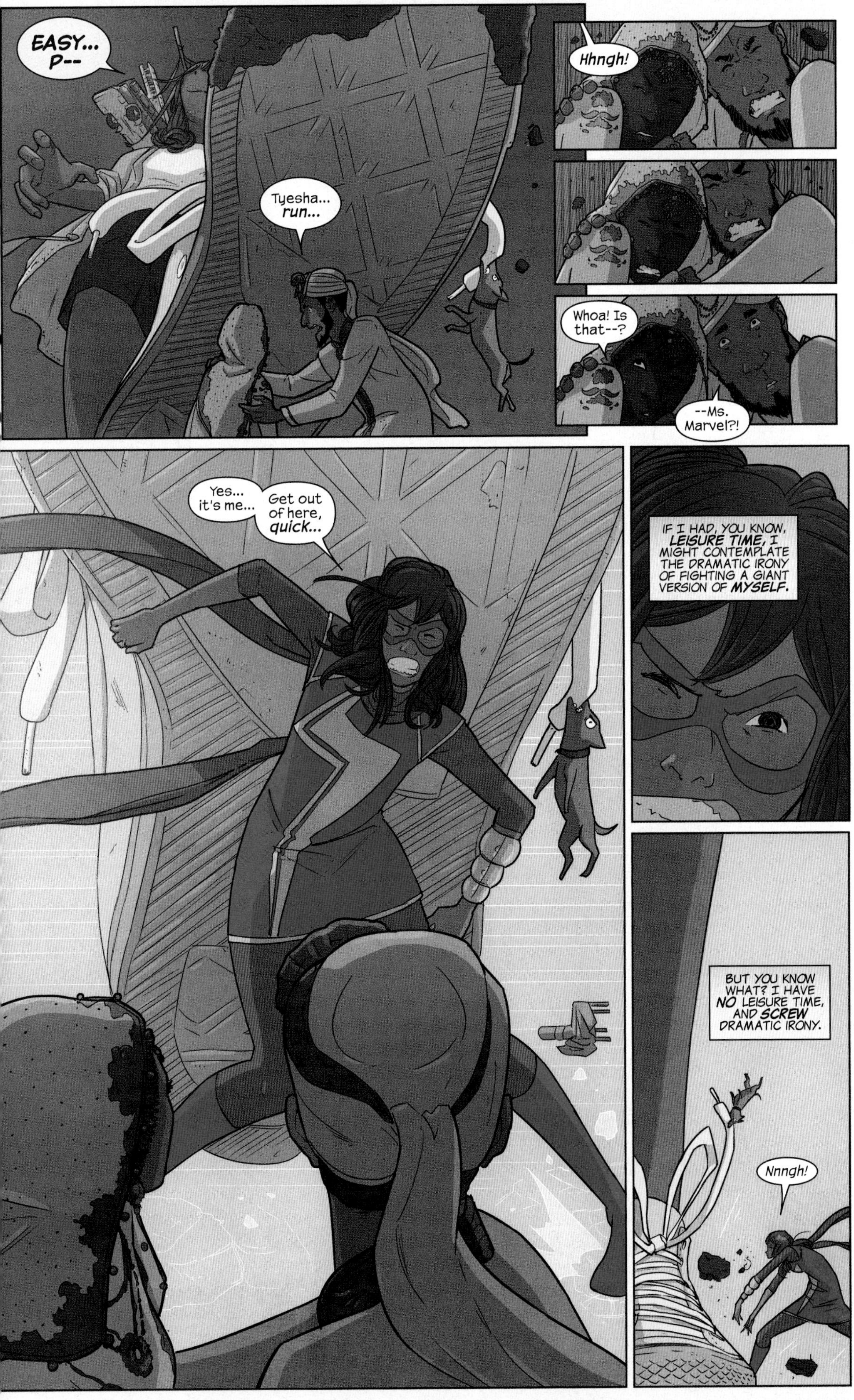
EASY... P--
Tyesha... run...
Hhngh!
Whoa! Is that--?
--Ms. Marvel?!
Yes... it's me...
Get out of here, quick...
IF I HAD, YOU KNOW, LEISURE TIME, I MIGHT CONTEMPLATE THE DRAMATIC IRONY OF FIGHTING A GIANT VERSION OF MYSELF.
BUT YOU KNOW WHAT? I HAVE NO LEISURE TIME, AND SCREW DRAMATIC IRONY.
Nnngh!

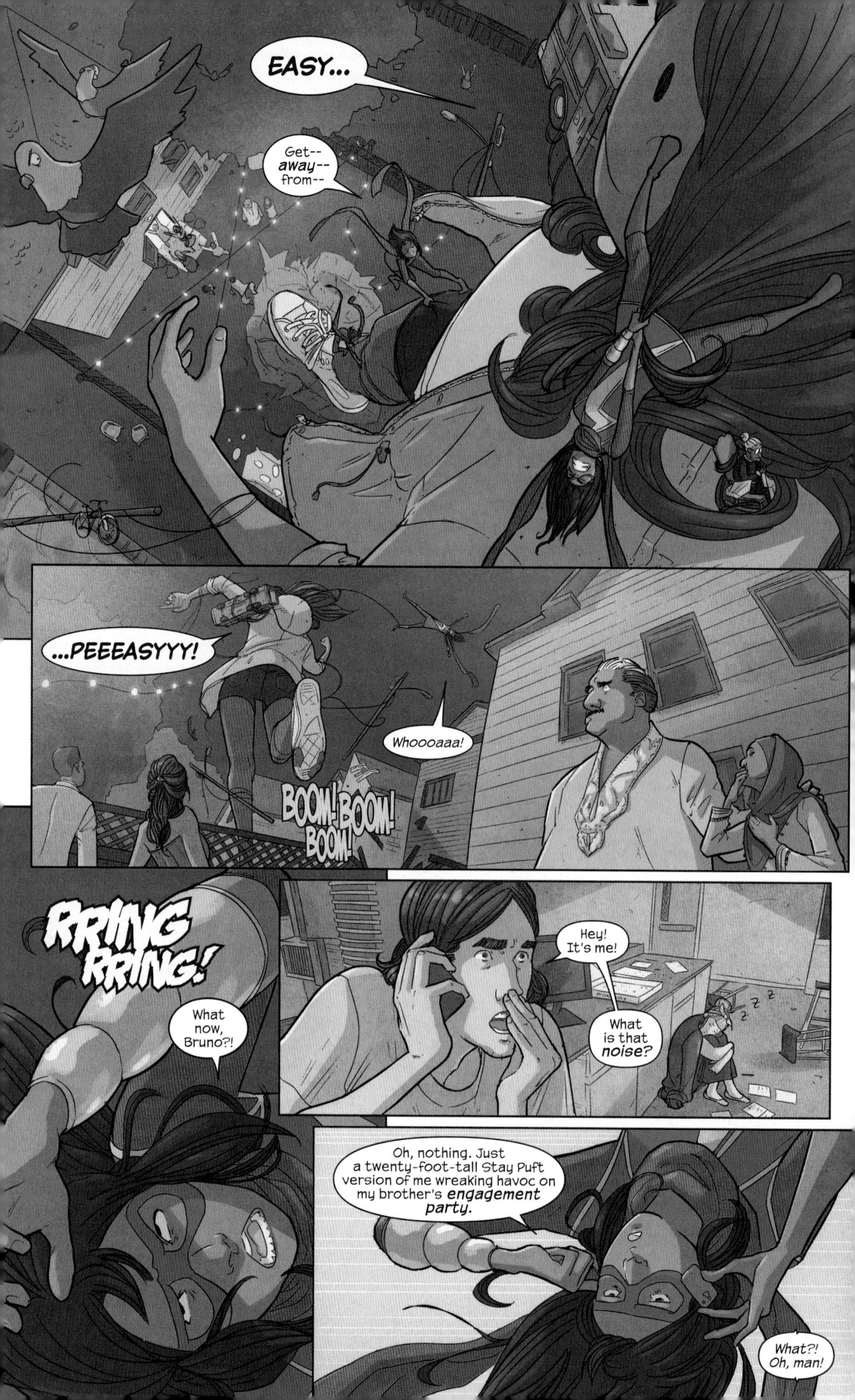
EASY...
Get-- away-- from--
...PEEEASYYY!
Whoooaaa!
BOOM! BOOM! BOOM!
RRING RRING!
What now, Bruno?!
Hey! It's me!
What is that noise?
Z Z Z
Oh, nothing. Just a twenty-foot-tall Stay Puft version of me wreaking havoc on my brother's engagement party.
What?! Oh, man!

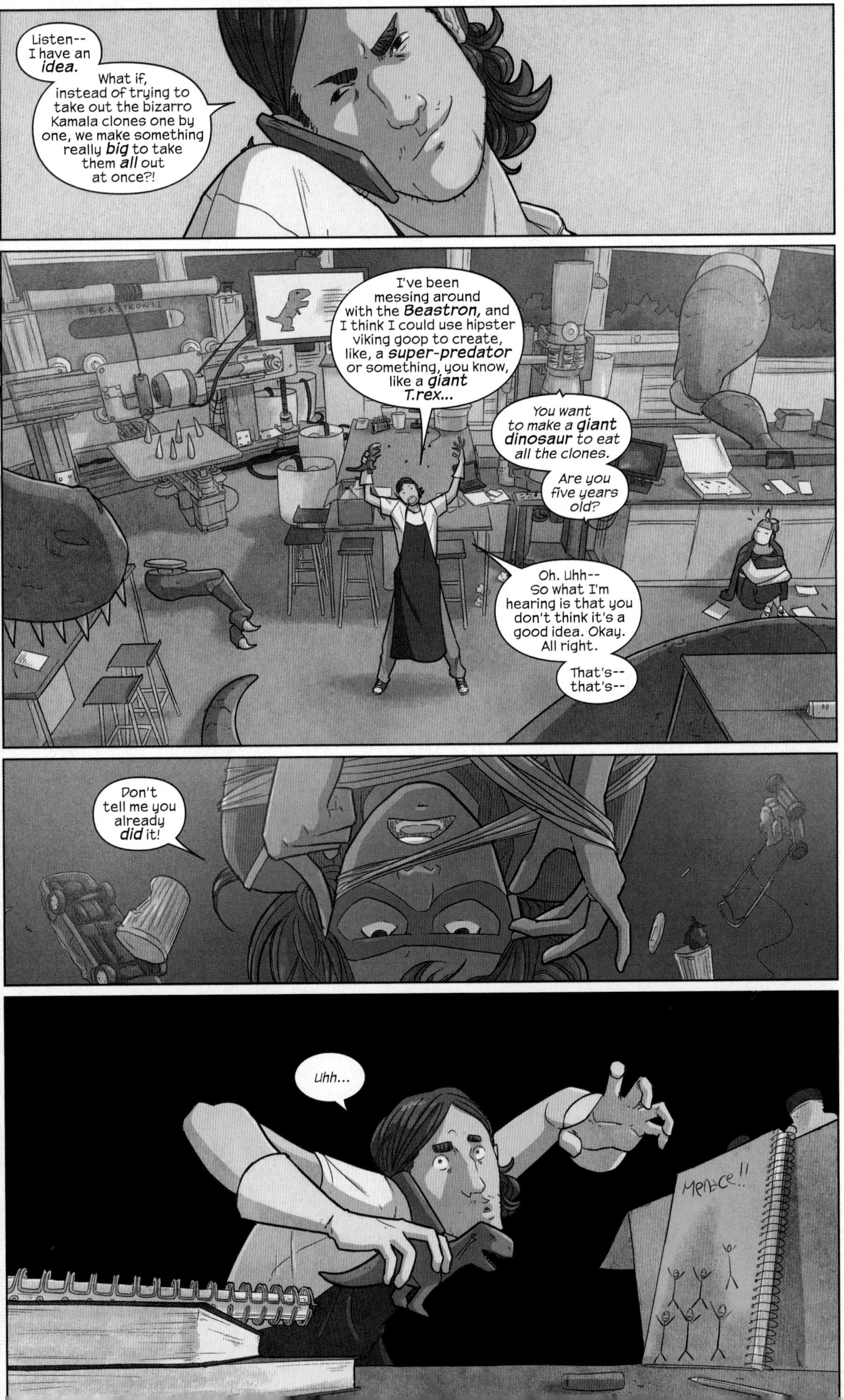

Listen-- I have an idea.
What if, instead of trying to take out the bizarro Kamala clones one by one, we make something really big to take them all out at once?!
I've been messing around with the Beastron, and I think I could use hipster viking goop to create, like, a super-predator or something, you know, like a giant T.rex...
You want to make a giant dinosaur to eat all the clones.
Are you five years old?
Oh. Uhh-- So what I'm hearing is that you don't think it's a good idea. Okay. All right.
That's-- that's--
Don't tell me you already did it!
Uhh...
Menace!!

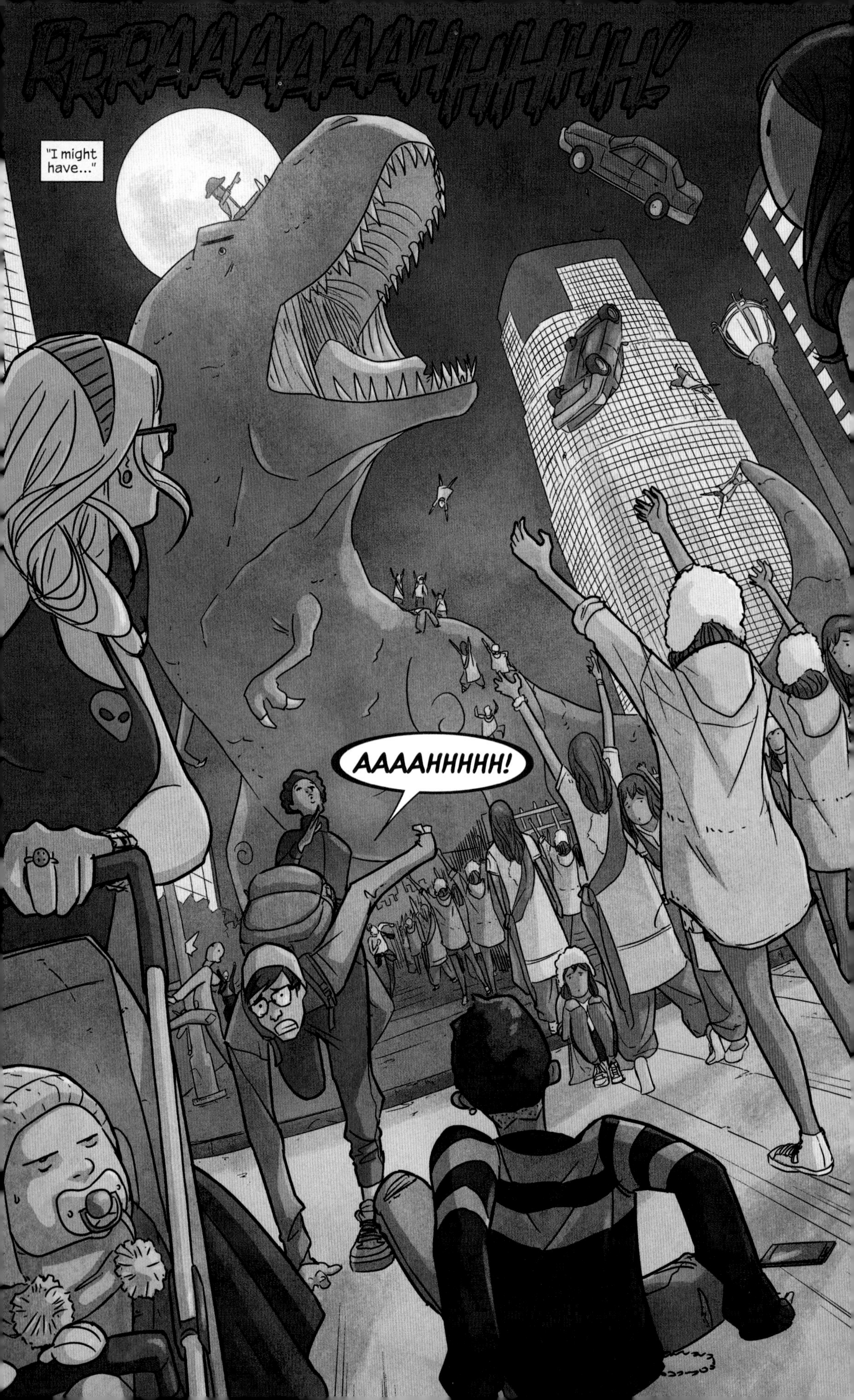
RRRAAAAAAAHHHHHH!
"I might have..."
AAAAHHHHH!

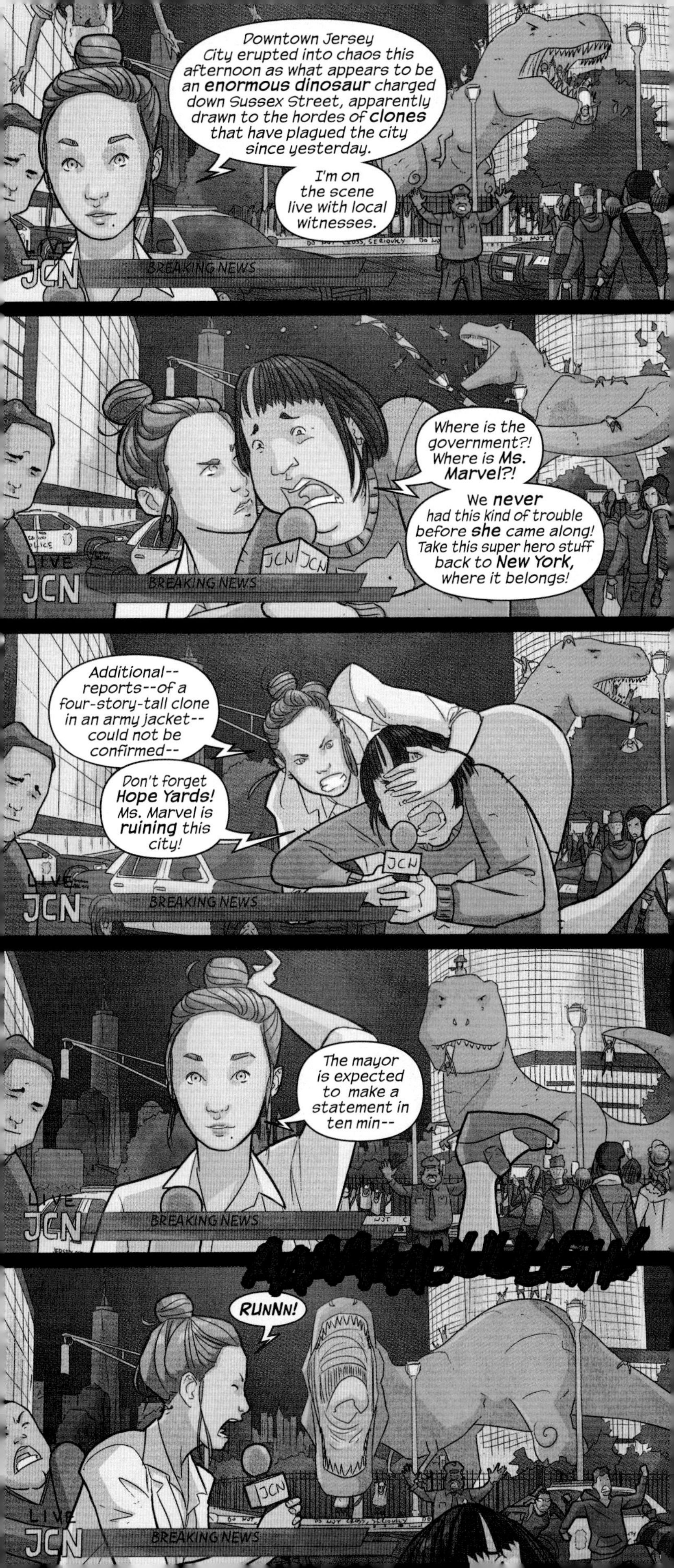
Downtown Jersey City erupted into chaos this afternoon as what appears to be an **enormous dinosaur** charged down Sussex Street, apparently drawn to the hordes of **clones** that have plagued the city since yesterday.
I'm on the scene live with local witnesses.
LIVE
JCN
BREAKING NEWS
Where is the government?! Where is **Ms. Marvel**?!
We **never** had this kind of trouble before **she** came along! Take this super hero stuff back to **New York**, where it belongs!
LIVE
JCN
BREAKING NEWS
Additional-- reports--of a four-story-tall clone in an army jacket-- could not be confirmed--
Don't forget **Hope Yards!** Ms. Marvel is **ruining** this city!
LIVE
JCN
BREAKING NEWS
The mayor is expected to make a statement in ten min--
LIVE
JCN
BREAKING NEWS
RUNNN!
LIVE
JCN
BREAKING NEWS

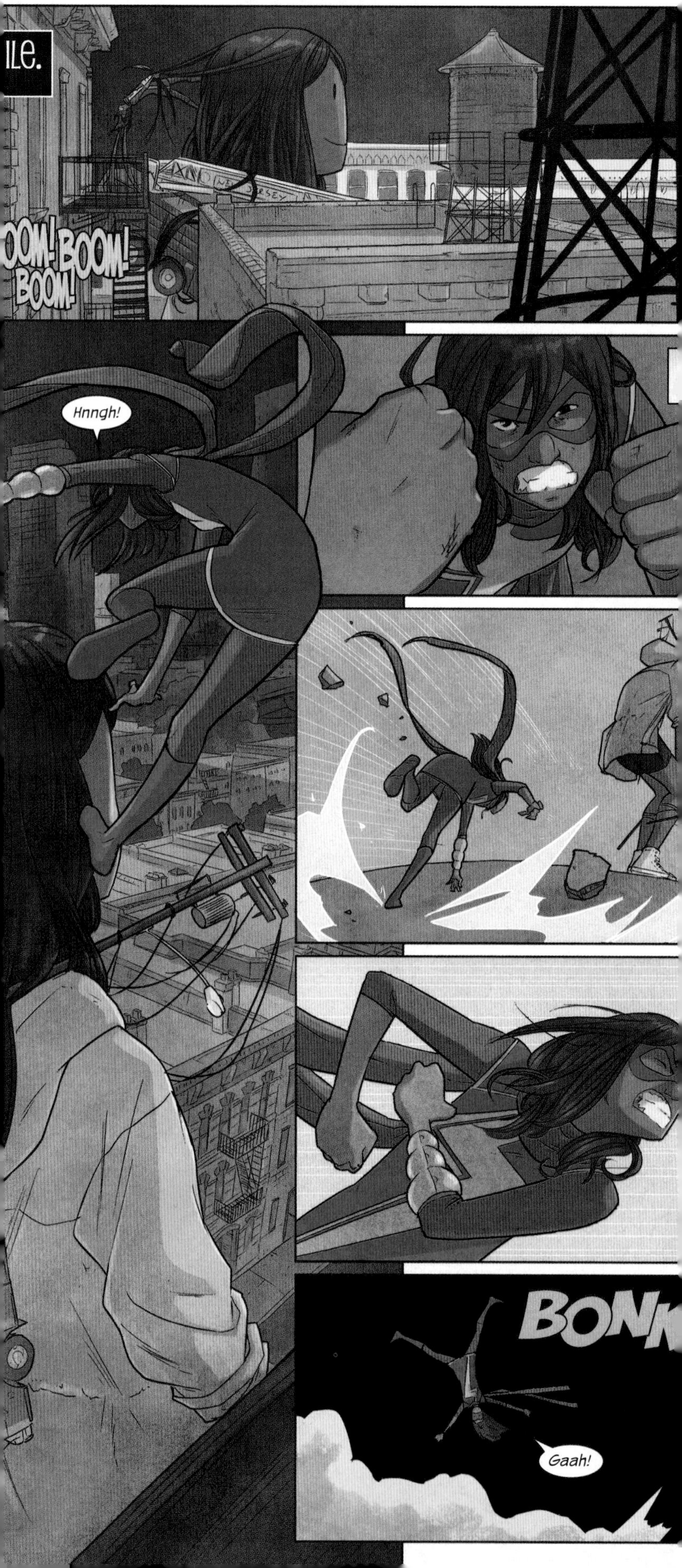

ILE.
OOM! BOOM!
BOOM!
Hnngh!
BONK
Gaah!

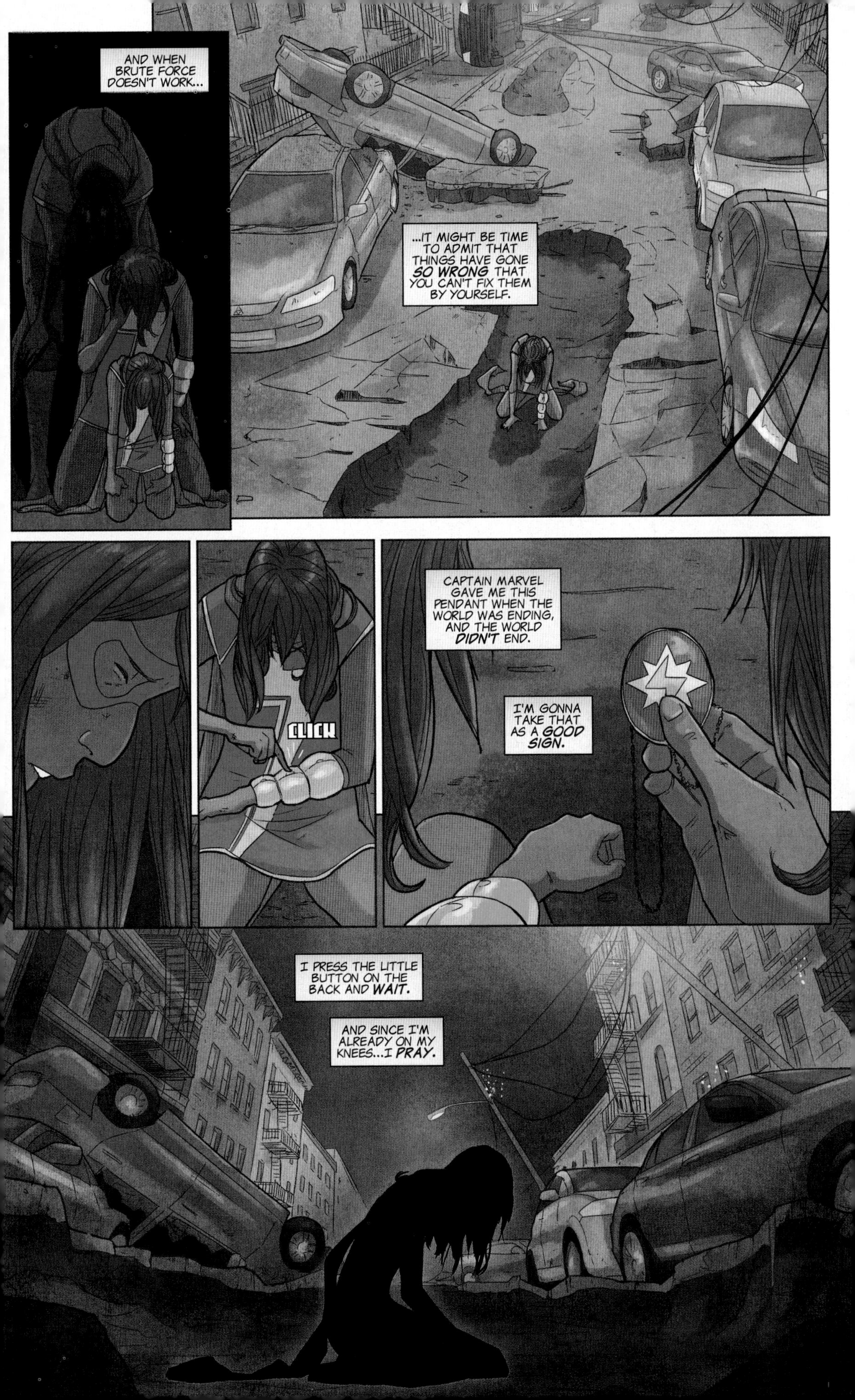
AND WHEN BRUTE FORCE DOESN'T WORK...
...IT MIGHT BE TIME TO ADMIT THAT THINGS HAVE GONE SO WRONG THAT YOU CAN'T FIX THEM BY YOURSELF.
CLICK
CAPTAIN MARVEL GAVE ME THIS PENDANT WHEN THE WORLD WAS ENDING, AND THE WORLD DIDN'T END.
I'M GONNA TAKE THAT AS A GOOD SIGN.
I PRESS THE LITTLE BUTTON ON THE BACK AND WAIT.
AND SINCE I'M ALREADY ON MY KNEES...I PRAY.

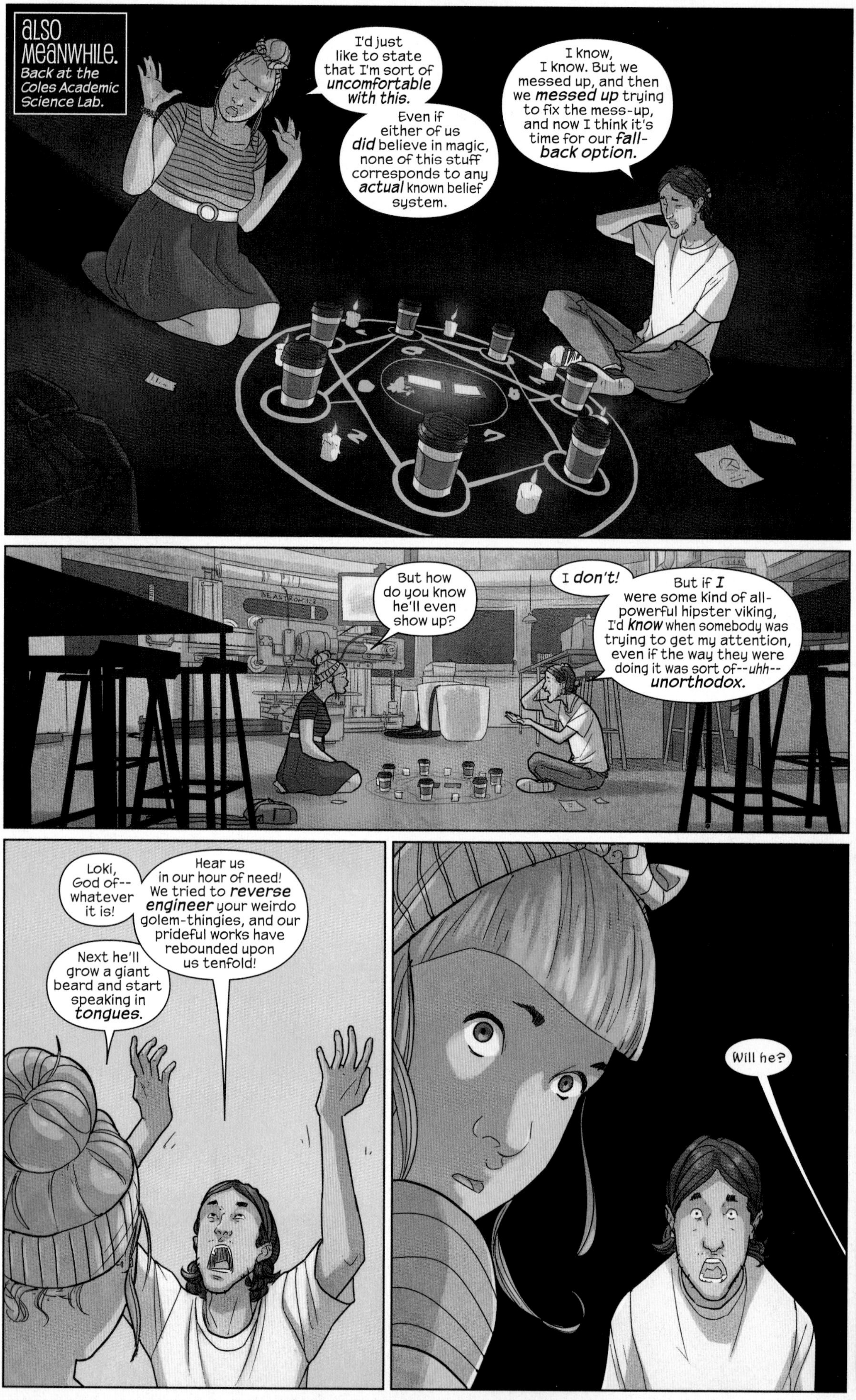
ALSO MEANWHILE. Back at the Coles Academic Science Lab.
I'd just like to state that I'm sort of uncomfortable with this.
Even if either of us did believe in magic, none of this stuff corresponds to any actual known belief system.
I know, I know. But we messed up, and then we messed up trying to fix the mess-up, and now I think it's time for our fall-back option.
But how do you know he'll even show up?
I don't!
But if I were some kind of all-powerful hipster viking, I'd know when somebody was trying to get my attention, even if the way they were doing it was sort of--uhh--unorthodox.
Loki, God of--whatever it is!
Hear us in our hour of need! We tried to reverse engineer your weirdo golem-thingies, and our prideful works have rebounded upon us tenfold!
Next he'll grow a giant beard and start speaking in tongues.
Will he?

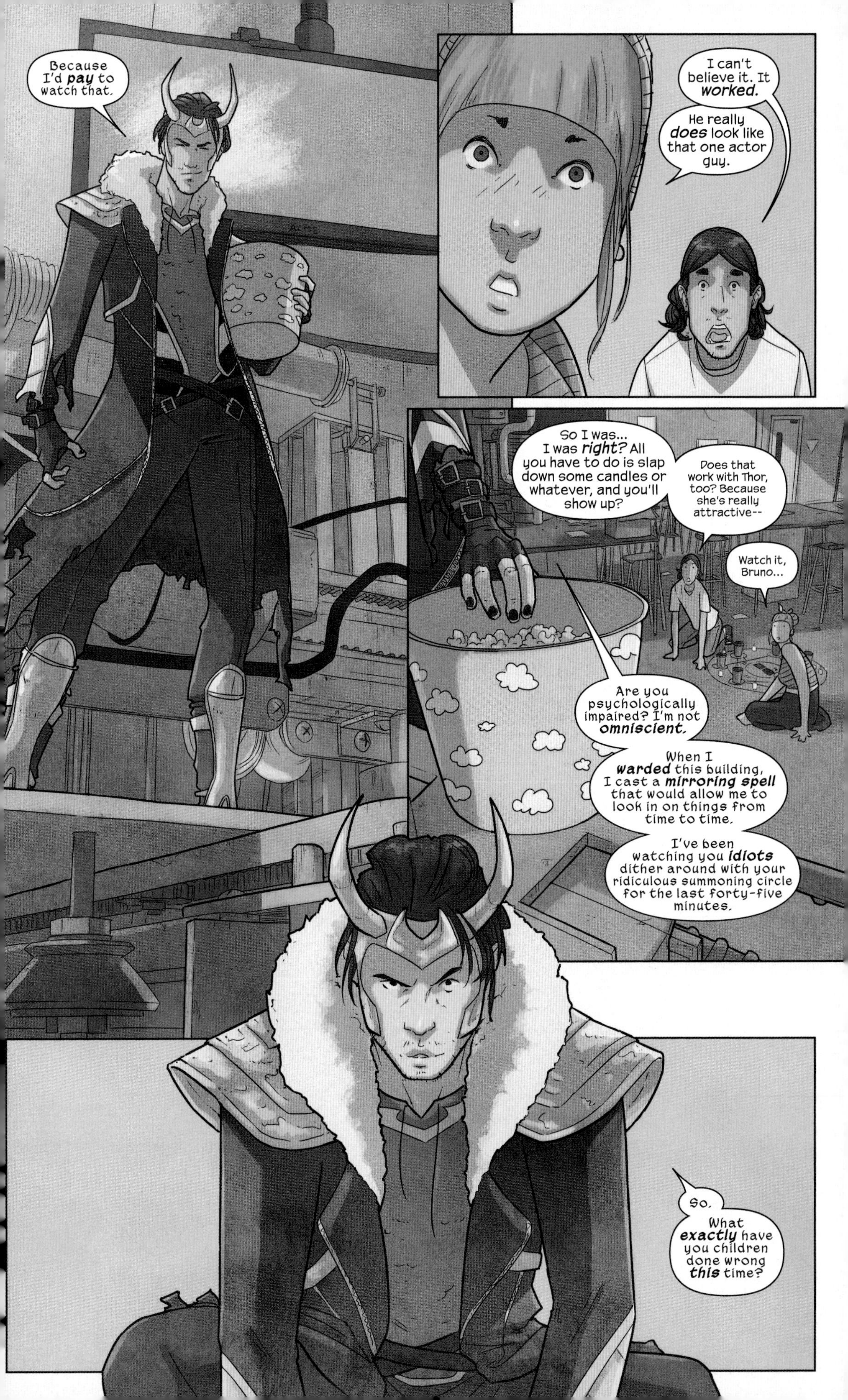
Because I'd **pay** to watch that.
I can't believe it. It **worked.**
He really **does** look like that one actor guy.
So I was... I was **right?** All you have to do is slap down some candles or whatever, and you'll show up?
Does that work with Thor, too? Because she's really attractive--
Watch it, Bruno...
Are you psychologically impaired? I'm not **omniscient.**
When I **warded** this building, I cast a **mirroring spell** that would allow me to look in on things from time to time.
I've been watching you **idiots** dither around with your ridiculous summoning circle for the last forty-five minutes.
So.
What **exactly** have you children done wrong **this** time?

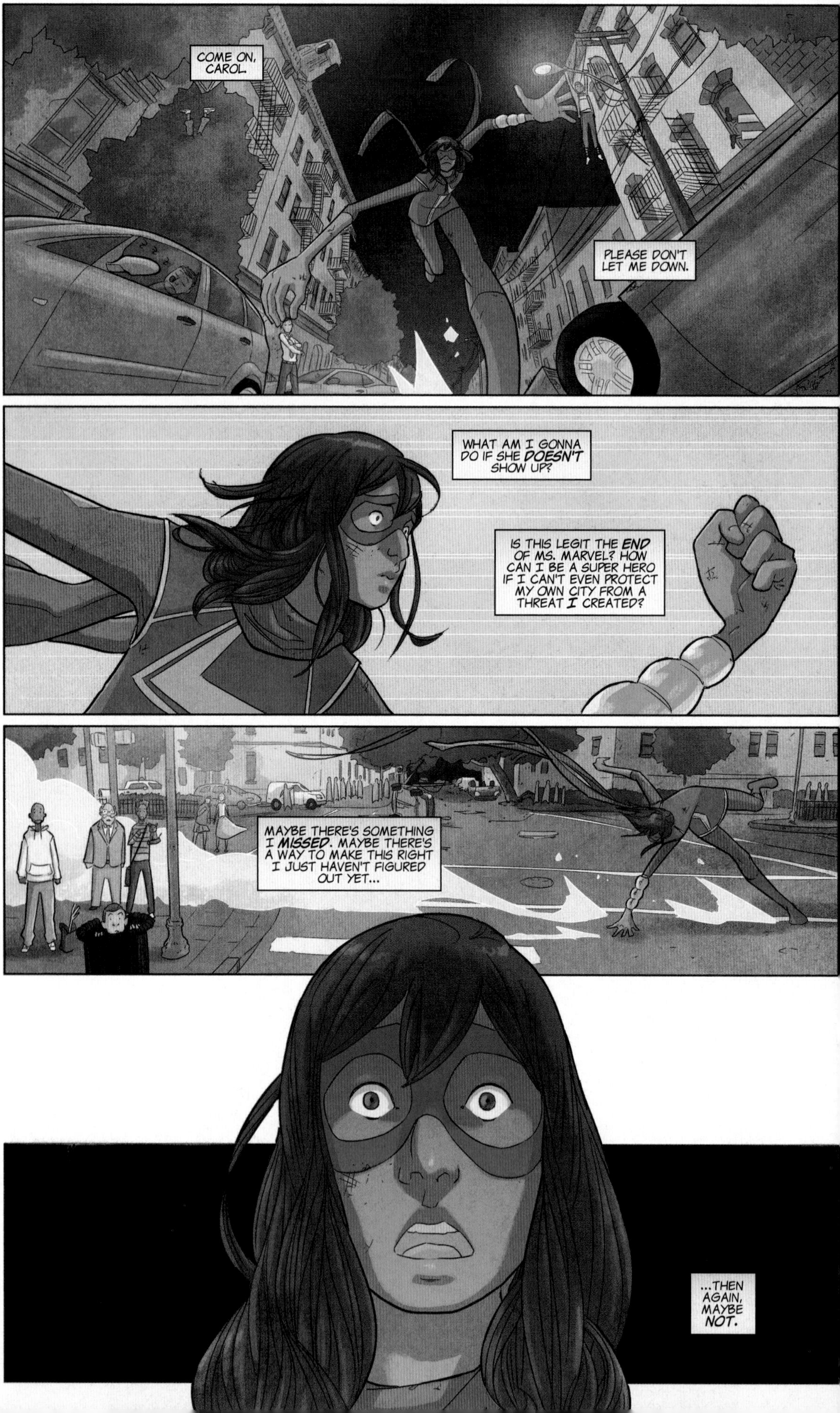
COME ON, CAROL.
PLEASE DON'T LET ME DOWN.
WHAT AM I GONNA DO IF SHE DOESN'T SHOW UP?
IS THIS LEGIT THE END OF MS. MARVEL? HOW CAN I BE A SUPER HERO IF I CAN'T EVEN PROTECT MY OWN CITY FROM A THREAT I CREATED?
MAYBE THERE'S SOMETHING I MISSED. MAYBE THERE'S A WAY TO MAKE THIS RIGHT I JUST HAVEN'T FIGURED OUT YET...
...THEN AGAIN, MAYBE NOT.

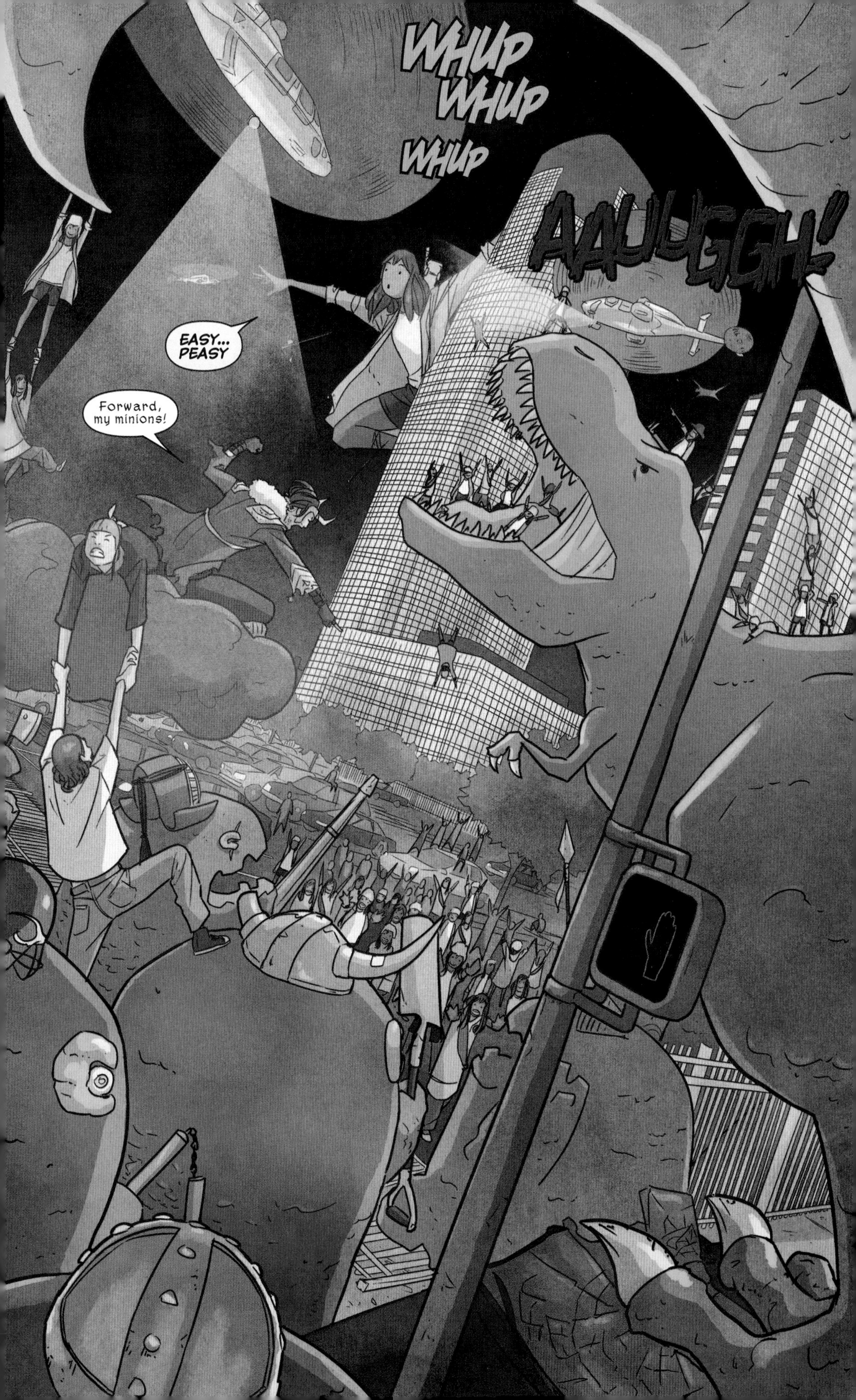
WHUP
WHUP
WHUP
AAUUGGH!
EASY... PEASY
Forward, my minions!

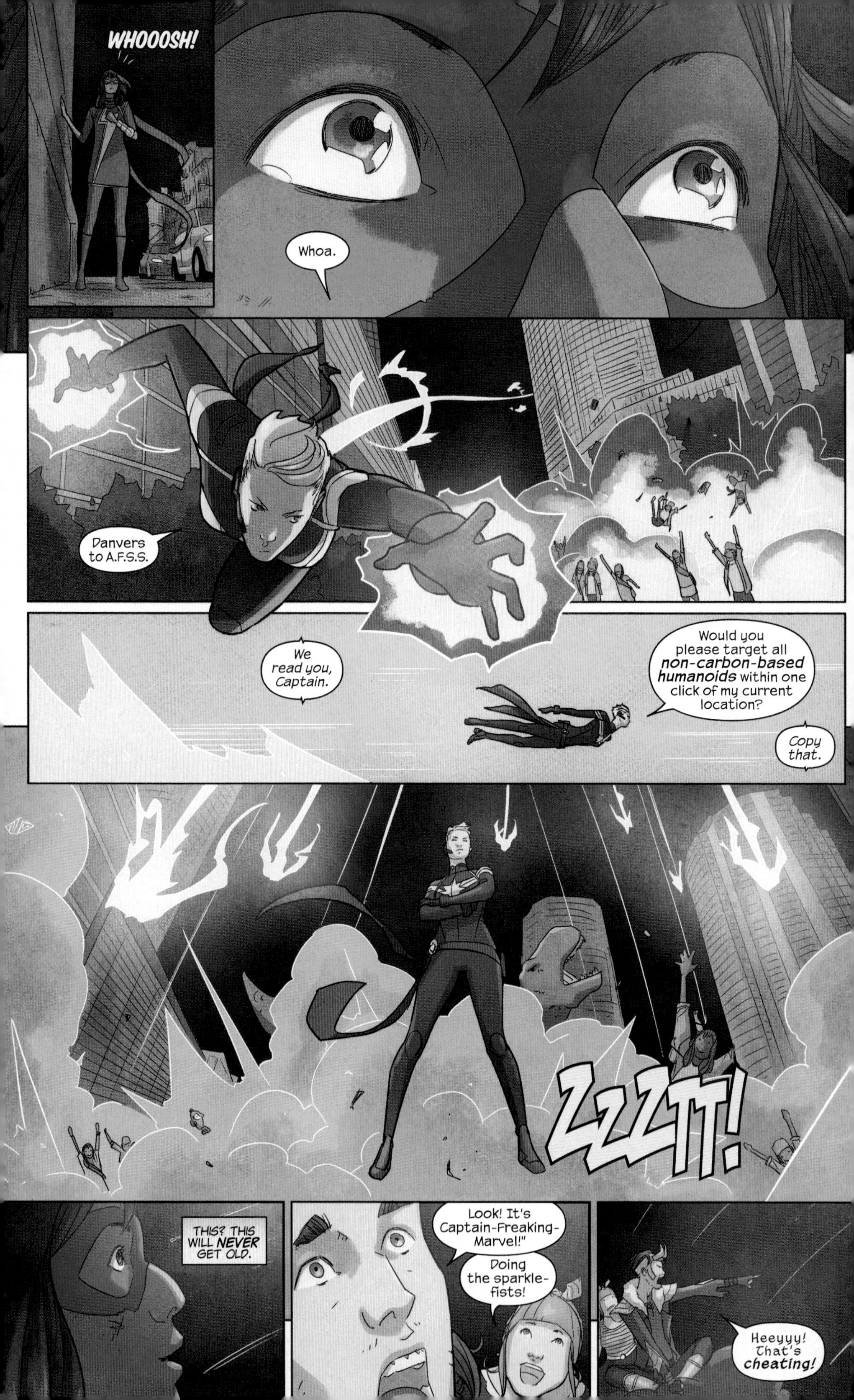
WHOOOSH!
Whoa.
Danvers to A.F.S.S.
We read you, Captain.
Would you please target all **non-carbon-based humanoids** within one click of my current location?
Copy that.
ZzZTT!
THIS? THIS WILL **NEVER** GET OLD.
Look! It's Captain-Freaking-Marvel!"
Doing the sparkle-fists!
Heeyyy! That's **cheating!**

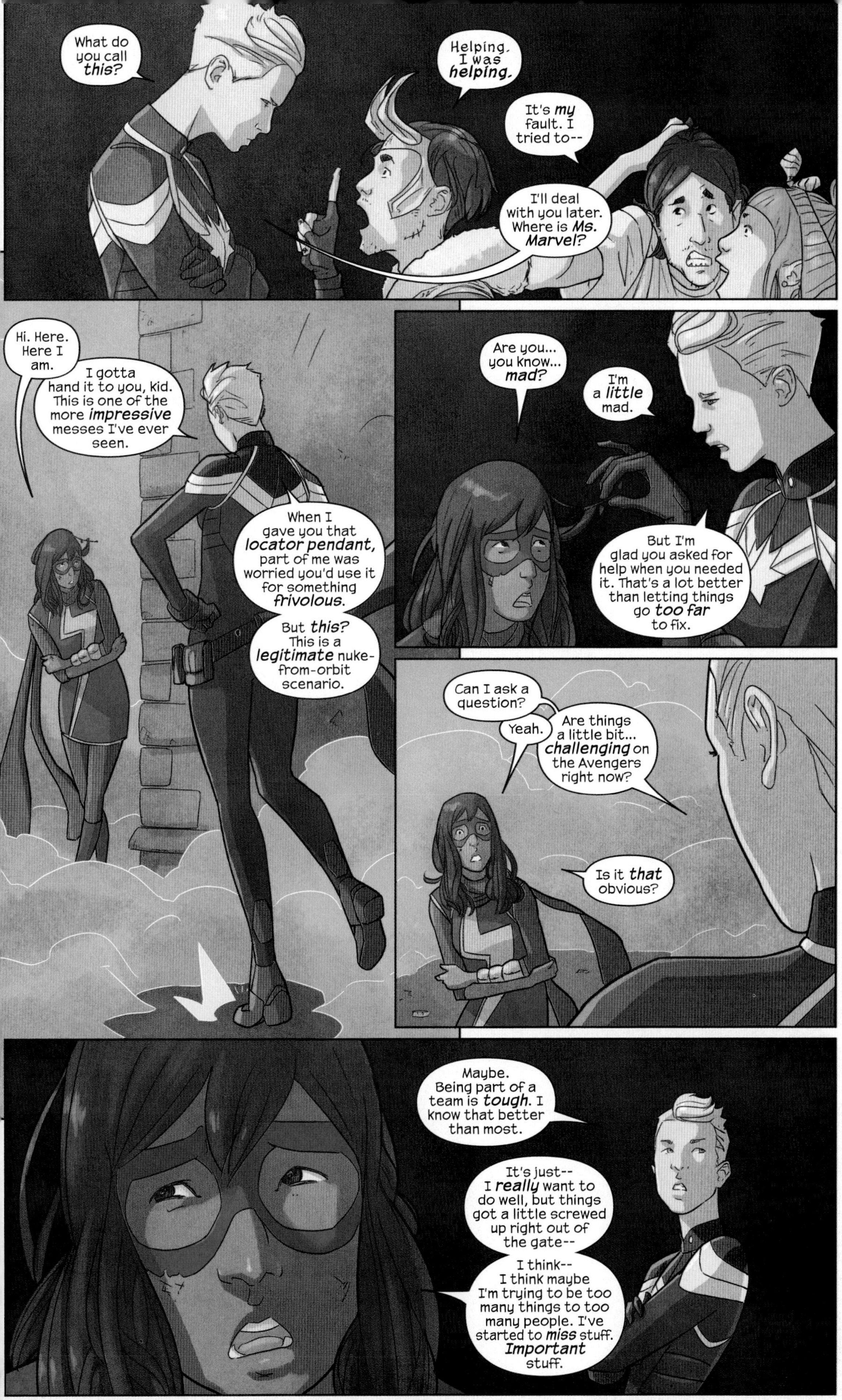

What do you call *this?*
Helping. I was *helping.*
It's *my* fault. I tried to--
I'll deal with you later. Where is *Ms. Marvel?*
Hi. Here. Here I am.
I gotta hand it to you, kid. This is one of the more *impressive* messes I've ever seen.
When I gave you that *locator pendant,* part of me was worried you'd use it for something *frivolous.*
But *this?* This is a *legitimate* nuke-from-orbit scenario.
Are you... you know... *mad?*
I'm a *little* mad.
But I'm glad you asked for help when you needed it. That's a lot better than letting things go *too far* to fix.
Can I ask a question?
Yeah.
Are things a little bit... *challenging* on the Avengers right now?
Is it *that* obvious?
Maybe. Being part of a team is *tough.* I know that better than most.
It's just-- I *really* want to do well, but things got a little screwed up right out of the gate--
I think-- I think maybe I'm trying to be too many things to too many people. I've started to *miss* stuff. *Important* stuff.

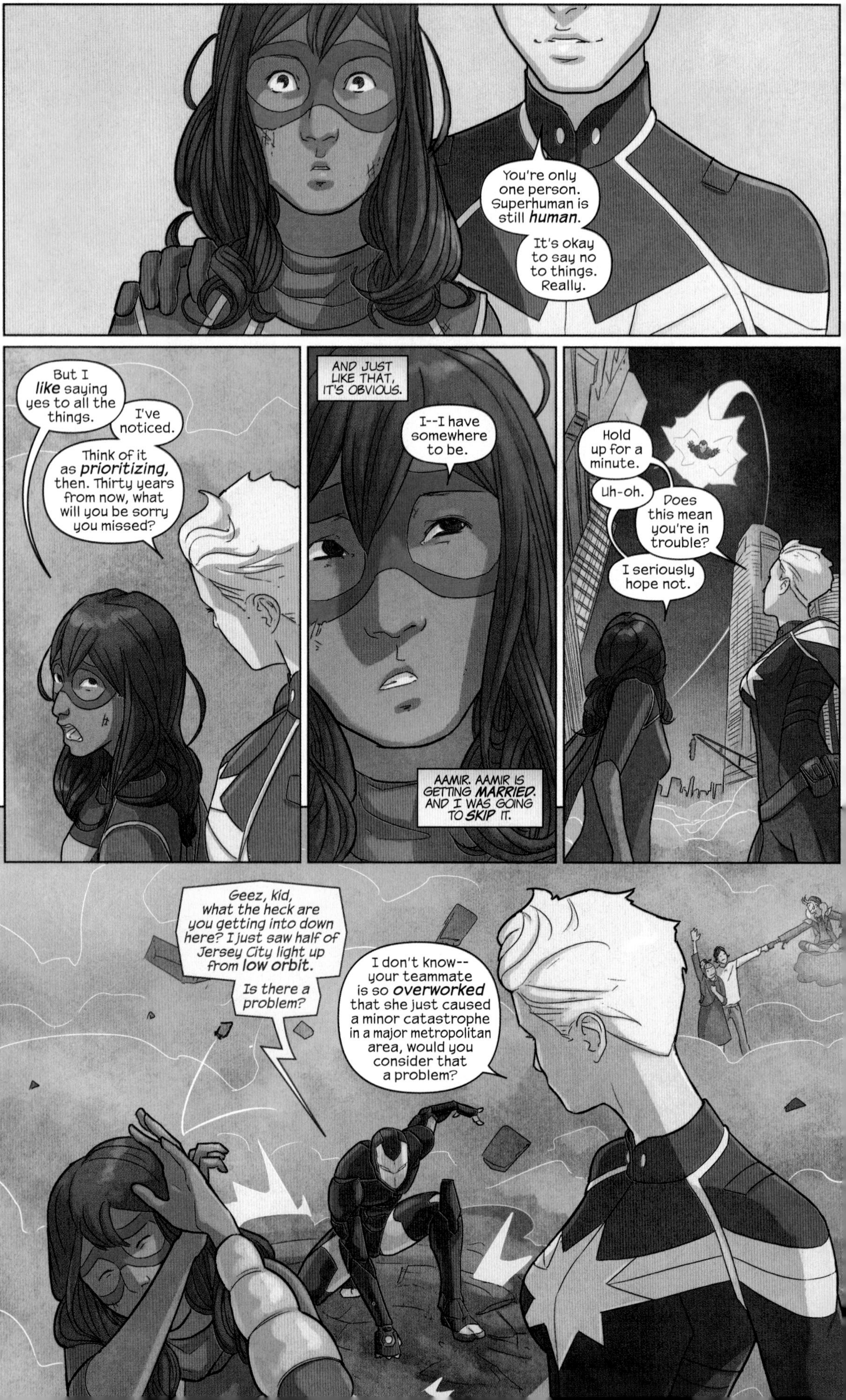
You're only one person. Superhuman is still human.
It's okay to say no to things. Really.
But I like saying yes to all the things.
I've noticed.
Think of it as prioritizing, then. Thirty years from now, what will you be sorry you missed?
AND JUST LIKE THAT, IT'S OBVIOUS.
I--I have somewhere to be.
AAMIR. AAMIR IS GETTING MARRIED. AND I WAS GOING TO SKIP IT.
Hold up for a minute.
Uh-oh.
Does this mean you're in trouble?
I seriously hope not.
Geez, kid, what the heck are you getting into down here? I just saw half of Jersey City light up from low orbit.
Is there a problem?
I don't know--your teammate is so overworked that she just caused a minor catastrophe in a major metropolitan area, would you consider that a problem?

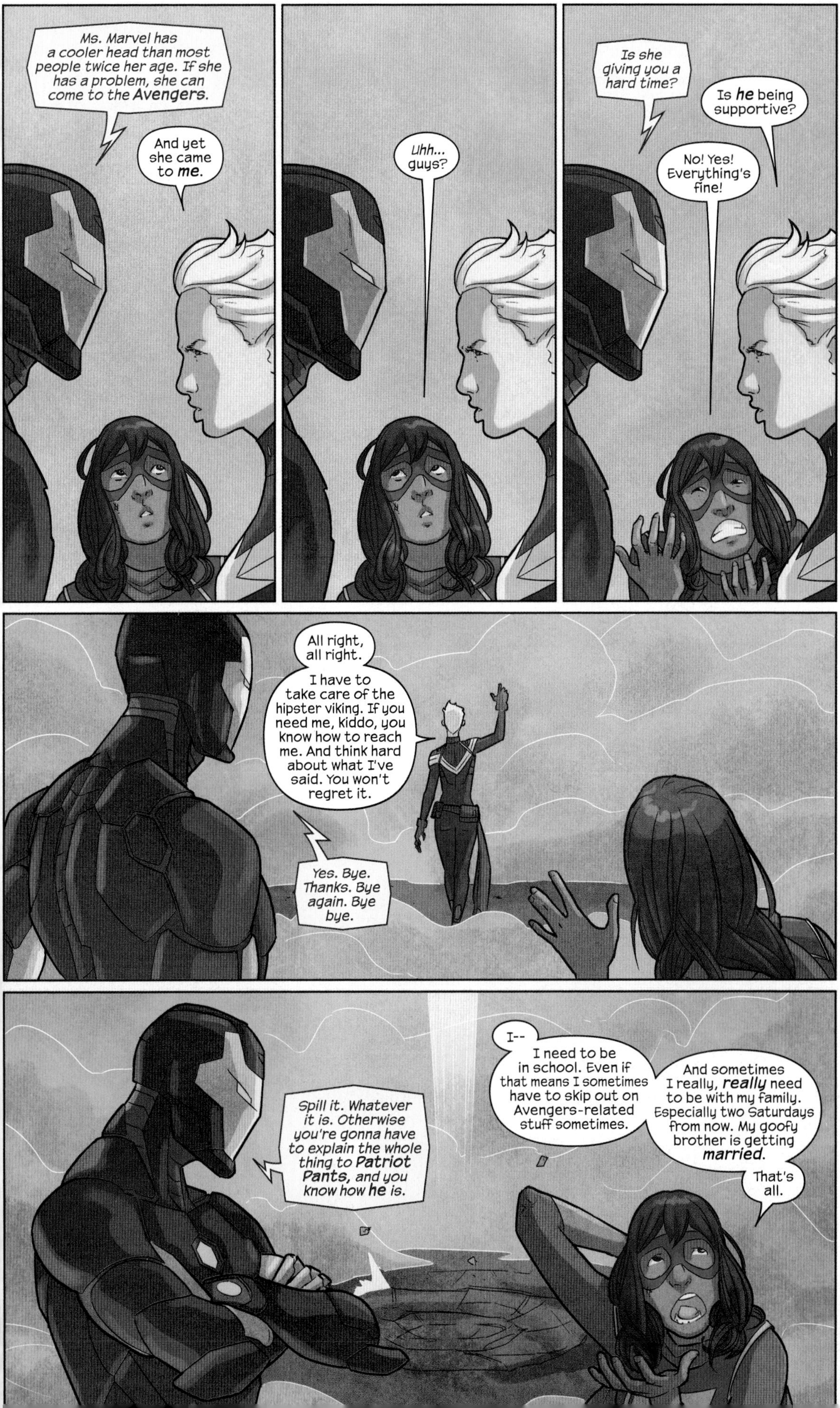
Ms. Marvel has a cooler head than most people twice her age. If she has a problem, she can come to the **Avengers**.
And yet she came to **me**.
Uhh... guys?
Is she giving you a hard time?
Is **he** being supportive?
No! Yes! Everything's fine!
All right, all right.
I have to take care of the hipster viking. If you need me, kiddo, you know how to reach me. And think hard about what I've said. You won't regret it.
Yes. Bye. Thanks. Bye again. Bye bye.
Spill it. Whatever it is. Otherwise you're gonna have to explain the whole thing to **Patriot Pants,** and you know how **he** is.
I--
I need to be in school. Even if that means I sometimes have to skip out on Avengers-related stuff sometimes.
And sometimes I really, ***really*** need to be with my family. Especially two Saturdays from now. My goofy brother is getting ***married***.
That's all.

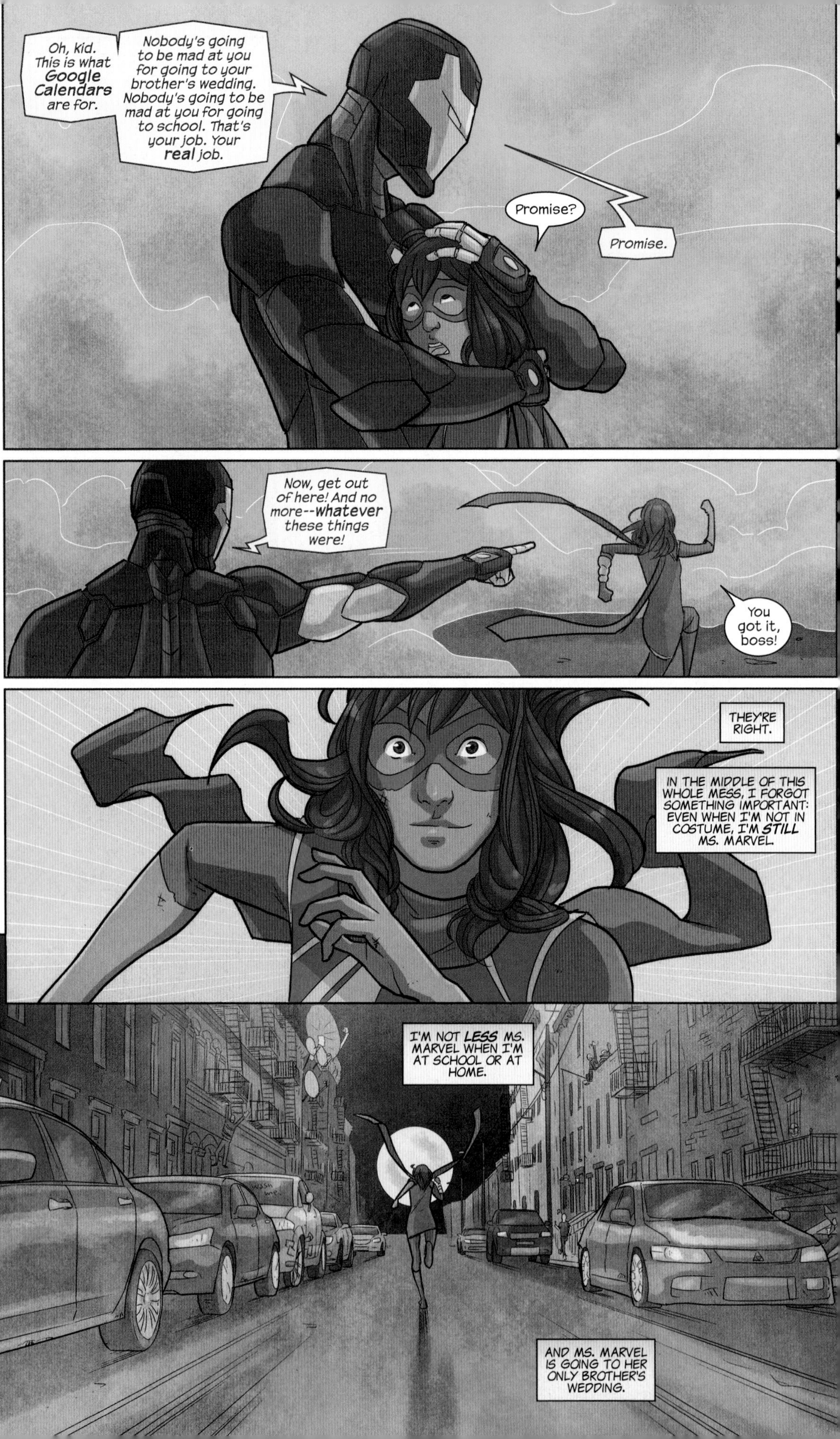

Oh, kid. This is what Google Calendars are for.
Nobody's going to be mad at you for going to your brother's wedding. Nobody's going to be mad at you for going to school. That's your job. Your real job.
Promise?
Promise.
Now, get out of here! And no more--whatever these things were!
You got it, boss!
THEY'RE RIGHT.
IN THE MIDDLE OF THIS WHOLE MESS, I FORGOT SOMETHING IMPORTANT: EVEN WHEN I'M NOT IN COSTUME, I'M STILL MS. MARVEL.
I'M NOT LESS MS. MARVEL WHEN I'M AT SCHOOL OR AT HOME.
AND MS. MARVEL IS GOING TO HER ONLY BROTHER'S WEDDING.

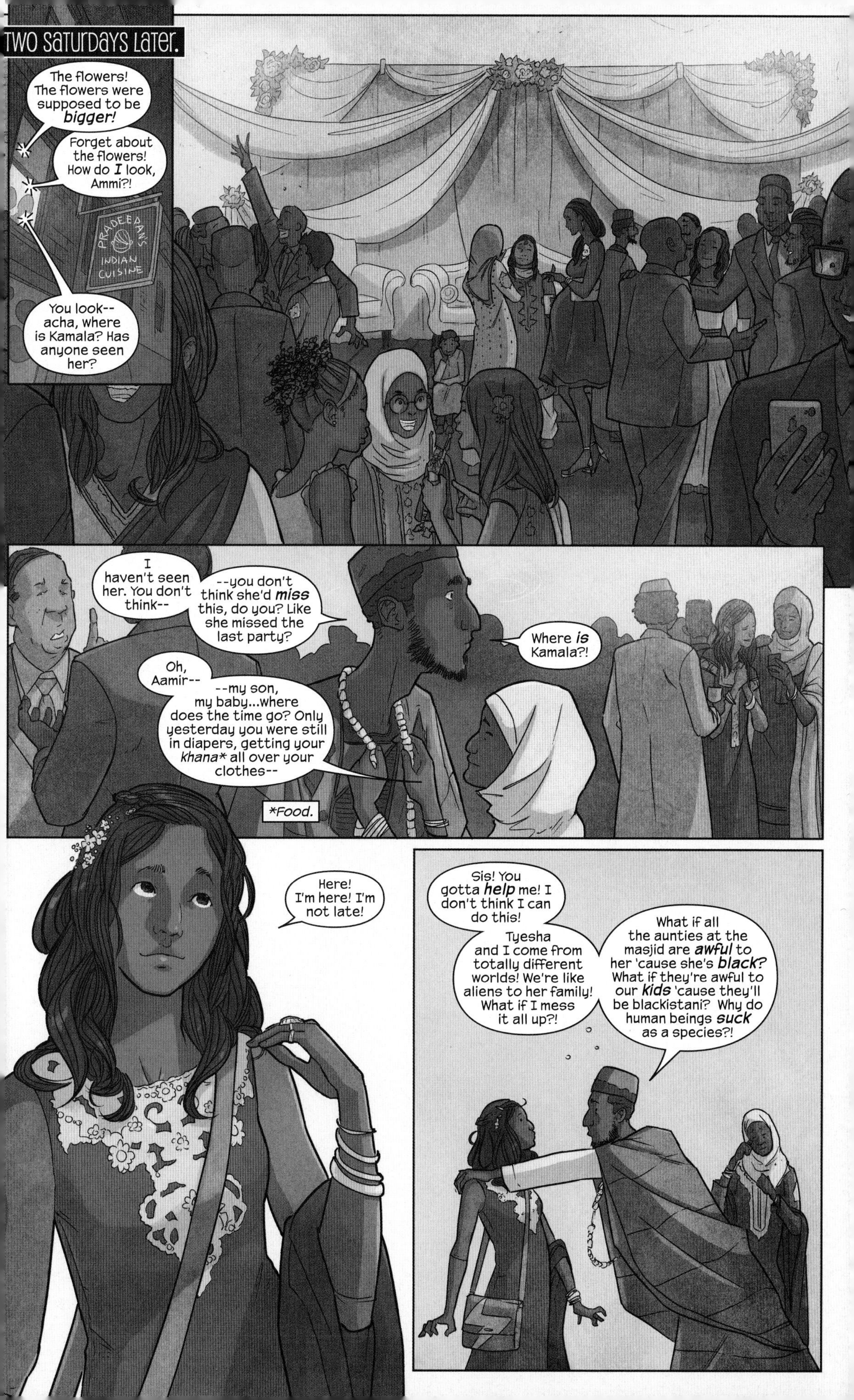
TWO SATURDAYS LATER.
The flowers! The flowers were supposed to be bigger!
Forget about the flowers! How do I look, Ammi?!
PRADEEPAN'S INDIAN CUISINE
You look-- acha, where is Kamala? Has anyone seen her?
I haven't seen her. You don't think--
--you don't think she'd miss this, do you? Like she missed the last party?
Where is Kamala?!
Oh, Aamir--
--my son, my baby...where does the time go? Only yesterday you were still in diapers, getting your khana* all over your clothes--
*Food.
Here! I'm here! I'm not late!
Sis! You gotta help me! I don't think I can do this!
Tyesha and I come from totally different worlds! We're like aliens to her family! What if I mess it all up?!
What if all the aunties at the masjid are awful to her 'cause she's black? What if they're awful to our kids 'cause they'll be blackistani? Why do human beings suck as a species?!

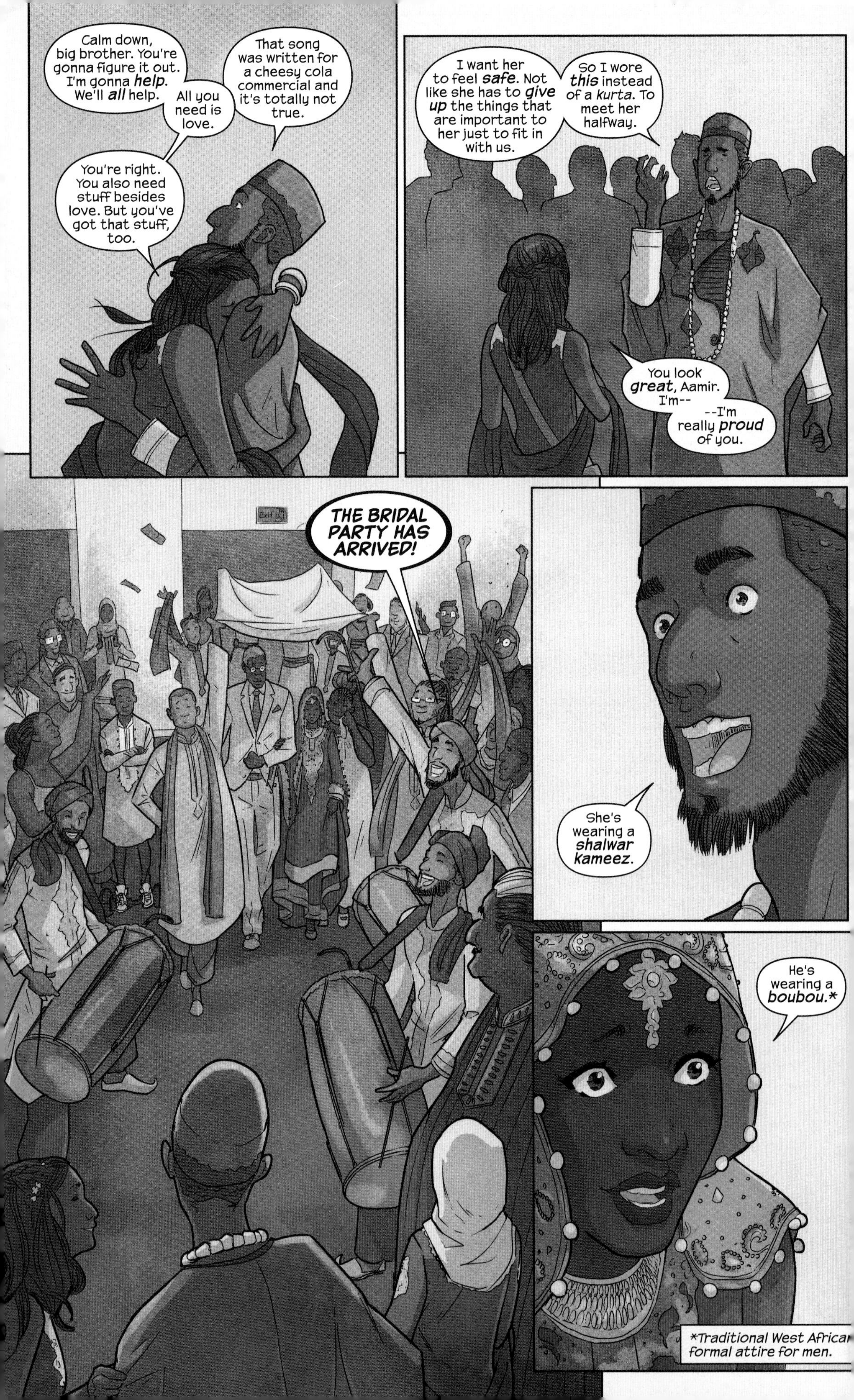

Calm down, big brother. You're gonna figure it out. I'm gonna *help*. We'll *all* help.
All you need is love.
That song was written for a cheesy cola commercial and it's totally not true.
You're right. You also need stuff besides love. But you've got that stuff, too.
I want her to feel *safe*. Not like she has to *give up* the things that are important to her just to fit in with us.
So I wore *this* instead of a *kurta*. To meet her halfway.
You look *great*, Aamir. I'm--
--I'm really *proud* of you.
Exit
THE BRIDAL PARTY HAS ARRIVED!
She's wearing a *shalwar kameez*.
He's wearing a *boubou.**
*Traditional West African formal attire for men.

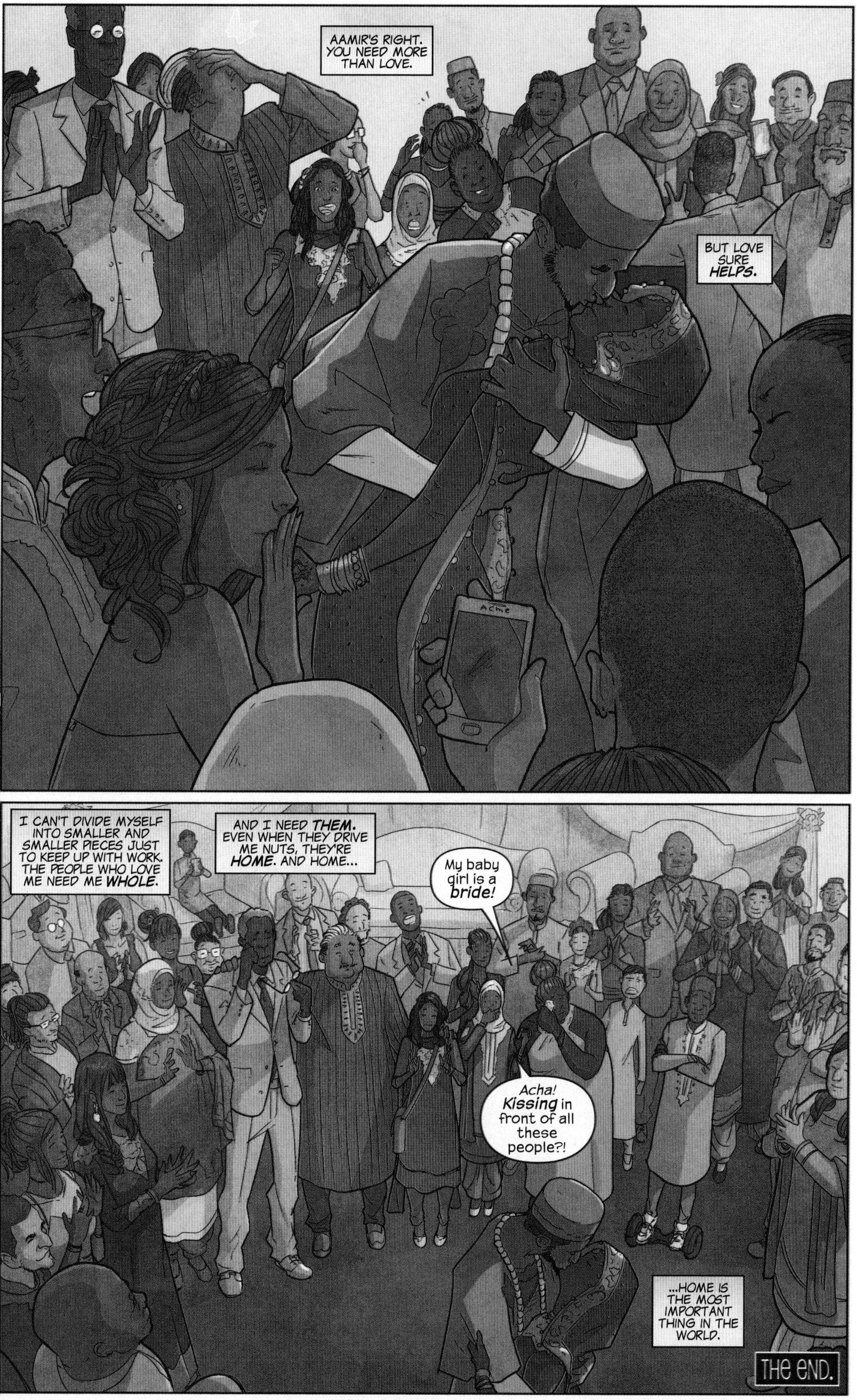
AAMIR'S RIGHT. YOU NEED MORE THAN LOVE.
BUT LOVE SURE HELPS.
I CAN'T DIVIDE MYSELF INTO SMALLER AND SMALLER PIECES JUST TO KEEP UP WITH WORK. THE PEOPLE WHO LOVE ME NEED ME WHOLE.
AND I NEED THEM. EVEN WHEN THEY DRIVE ME NUTS, THEY'RE HOME. AND HOME...
My baby girl is a bride!
Acha! Kissing in front of all these people?!
...HOME IS THE MOST IMPORTANT THING IN THE WORLD.
THE END.

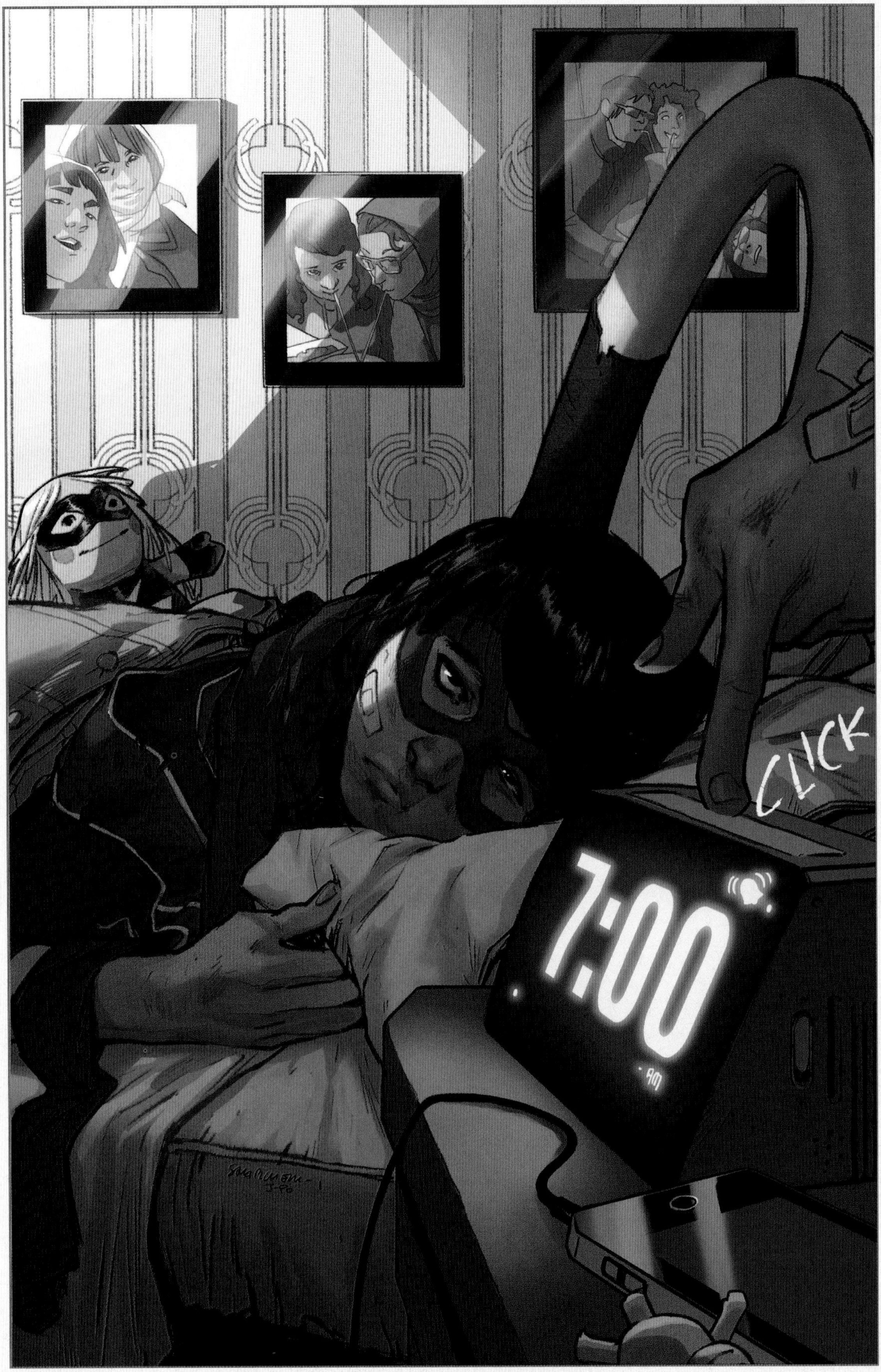
CLICK
7:00
AM

MS. MARVEL #1 VARIANT
BY SARA PICHELLI & JUSTIN PONSOR

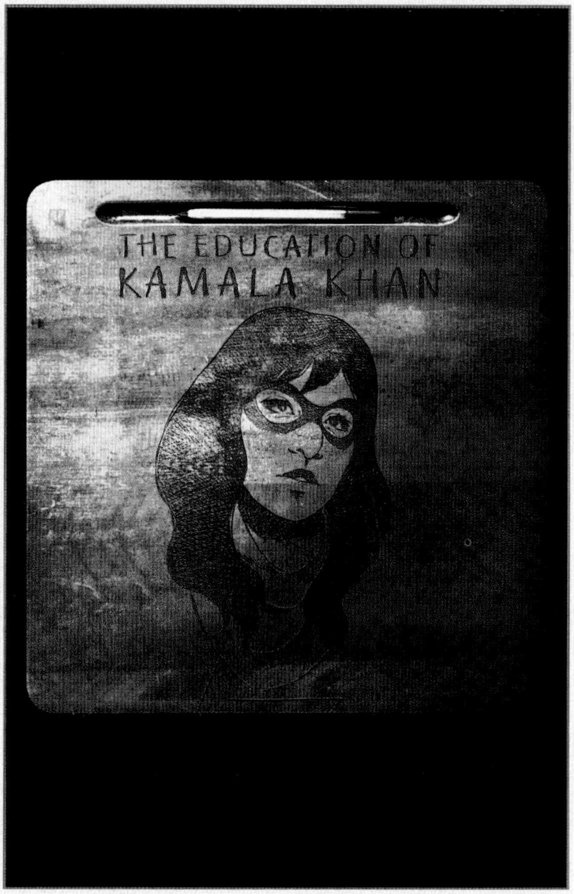
THE EDUCATION OF
KAMALA KHAN

MS. MARVEL #1 HIP-HOP VARIANT
BY JENNY FRISON

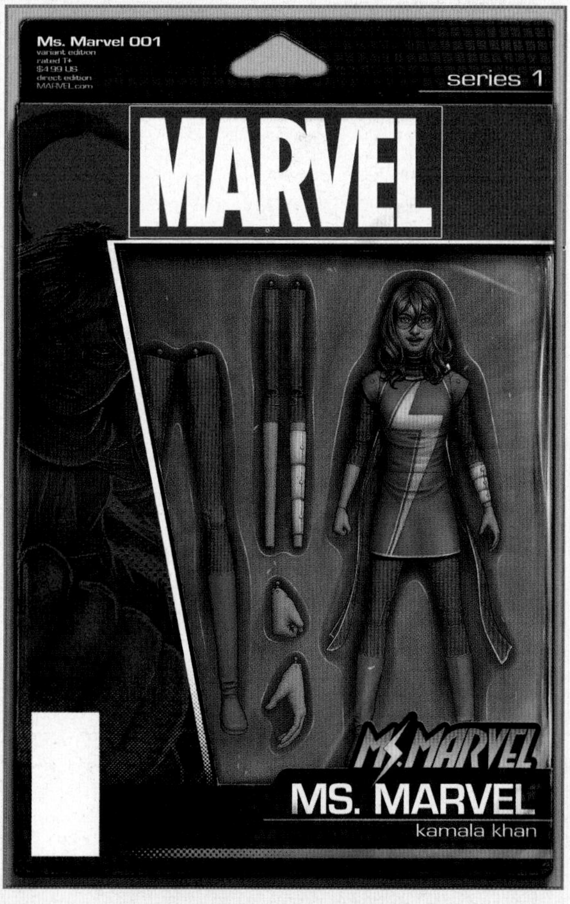
Ms. Marvel 001
variant edition
rated T+
$4.99 US
direct edition
MARVEL.com
series 1
MARVEL
MS.MARVEL
MS. MARVEL
kamala khan

MS. MARVEL #1 ACTION FIGURE VARIANT
BY JOHN TYLER CHRISTOPHER

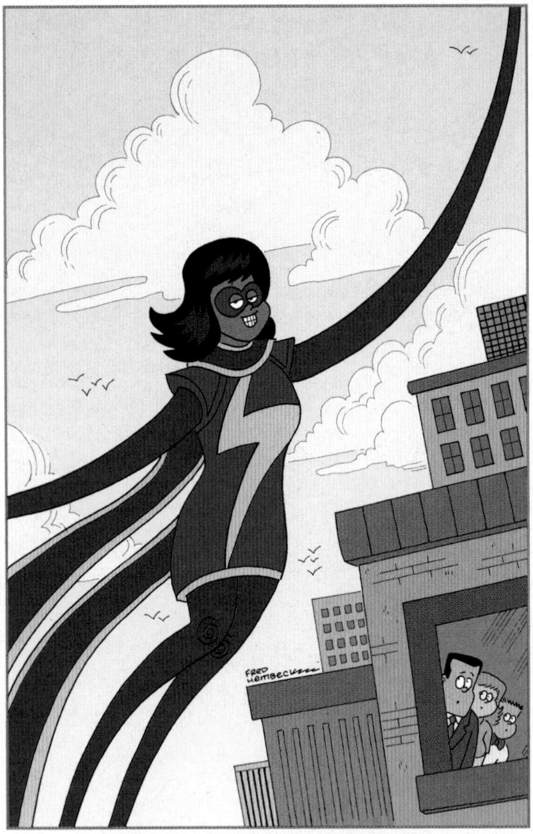

MS. MARVEL #2 VARIANT
BY FRED HEMBECK & RACHELLE ROSENBERG

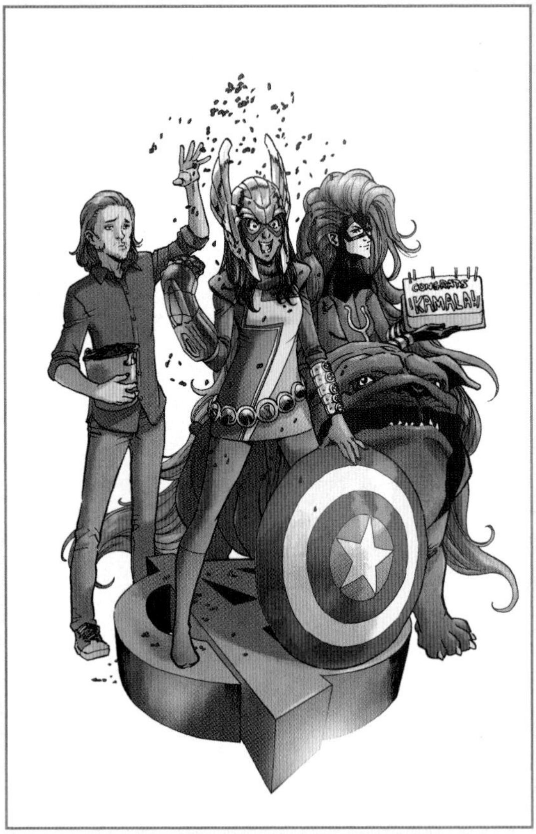
CONGRATS
¡KAMALA!

MS. MARVEL #2 VARIANT
BY TAKESHI MIYAZAWA & IAN HERRING

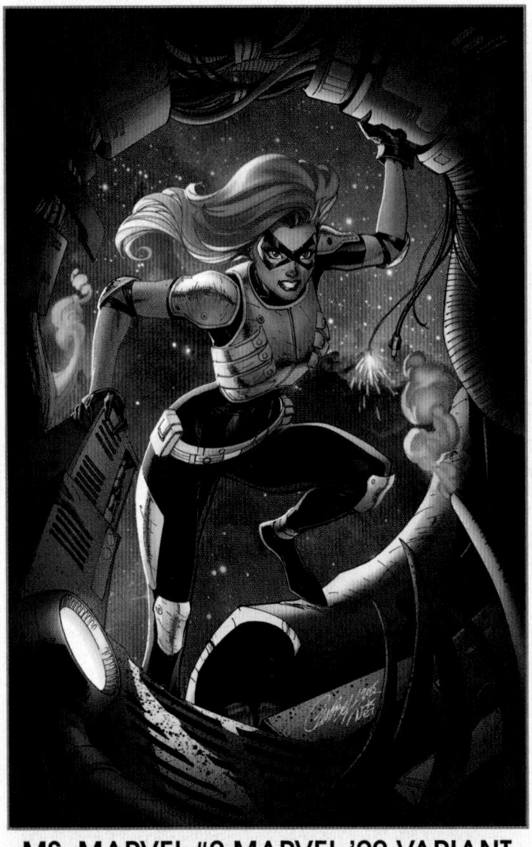

MS. MARVEL #2 MARVEL '92 VARIANT
BY J. SCOTT CAMPBELL & NEI RUFFINO

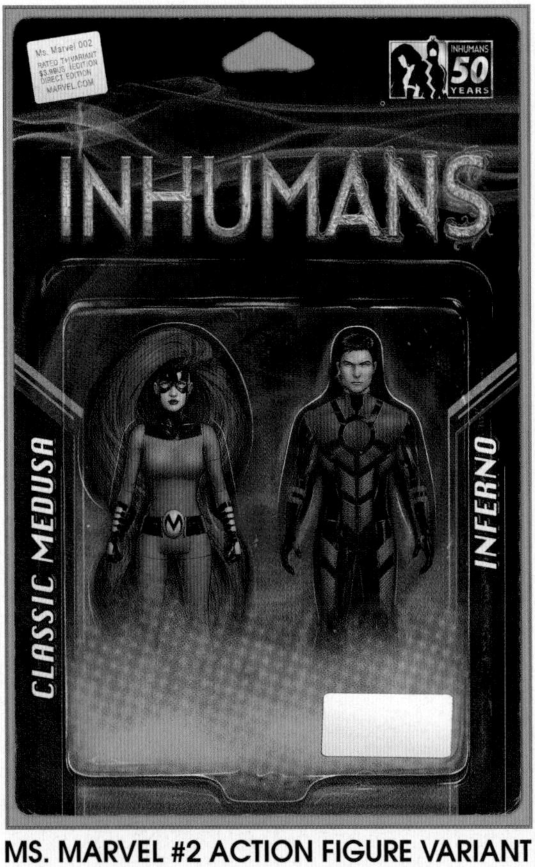
INHUMANS 50 YEARS
INHUMANS
CLASSIC MEDUSA
INFERNO

MS. MARVEL #2 ACTION FIGURE VARIANT
BY JOHN TYLER CHRISTOPHER

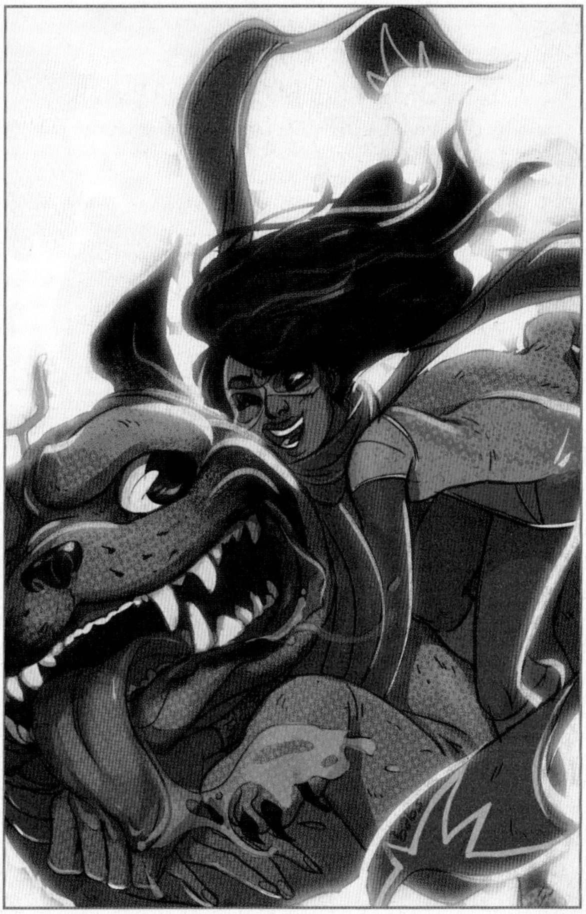

MS. MARVEL #3 VARIANT
BY BABS TARR

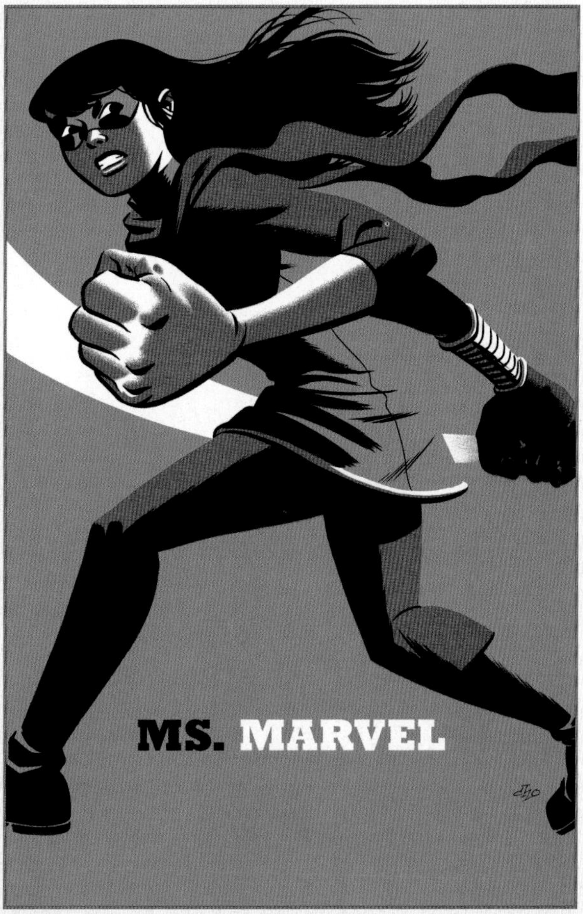
MS. MARVEL

MS. MARVEL #4 VARIANT
BY MICHAEL CHO

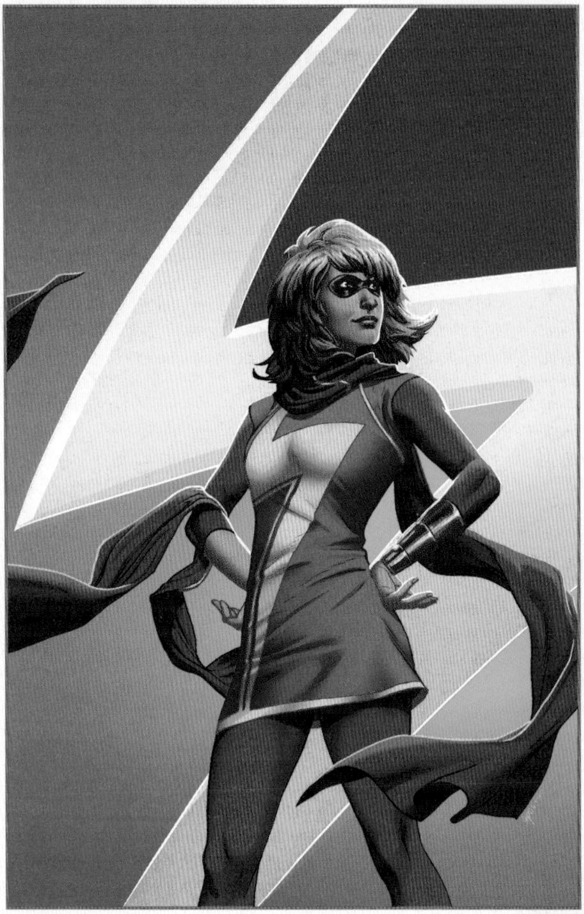

MS. MARVEL #5
WOMEN OF MARVEL VARIANT
BY EMA LUPACCHINO & GURU-EFX

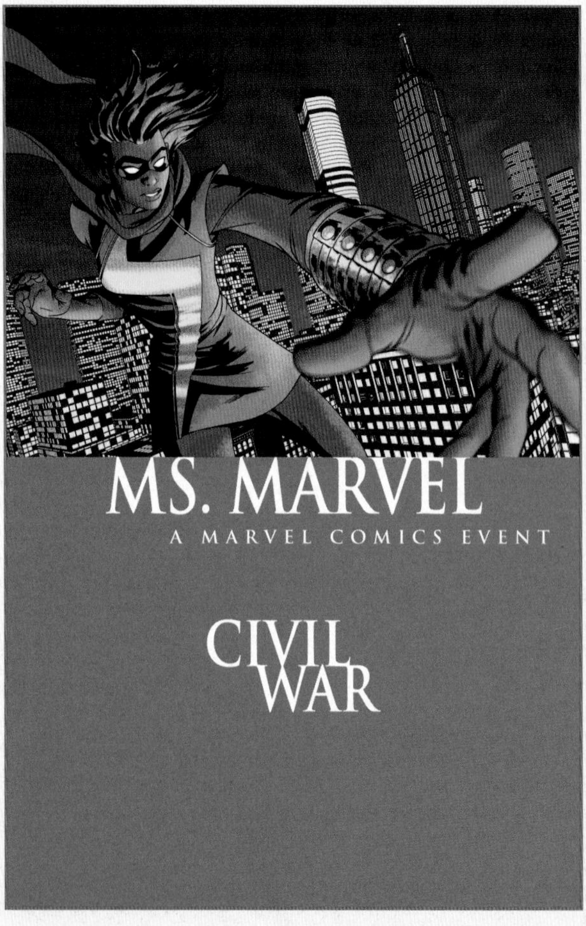
MS. MARVEL
A MARVEL COMICS EVENT
CIVIL WAR

MS. MARVEL #6 CIVIL WAR VARIANT
BY MIKE McKONE